Other Books and Series by Jeff Bowen

Applications for Enrollment of Chickasaw Newborn Act of 1905
Volumes I thru VII

Cherokee Intermarried White 1906 Volume I thru X

Applications for Enrollment of Creek Newborn Act of 1905
Volumes I thru XIV

Applications for Enrollment of Choctaw Newborn Act of 1905
Volume I, II, III, IV, V, VI, VII, VIII, IX, X, XI, XII, XIII, XIV & XV

Visit our website at **www.nativestudy.com** to learn more about these and other books and series by Jeff Bowen

APPLICATIONS FOR ENROLLMENT OF CHOCTAW NEWBORN ACT OF 1905

VOLUME XVI

TRANSCRIBED BY
JEFF BOWEN

NATIVE STUDY
Gallipolis, Ohio
USA

Other Books and Series by Jeff Bowen

1901-1907 Native American Census Seneca, Eastern Shawnee, Miami, Modoc, Ottawa, Peoria, Quapaw, and Wyandotte Indians (Under Seneca School, Indian Territory)

1932 Census of The Standing Rock Sioux Reservation with Births And Deaths 1924-1932

Census of The Blackfeet, Montana, 1897- 1901 Expanded Edition

Eastern Cherokee by Blood, 1906-1910, Volumes I thru XIII

Choctaw of Mississippi Indian Census 1929-1932 with Births and Deaths 1924-1931 Volume I
Choctaw of Mississippi Indian Census 1933, 1934 & 1937, Supplemental Rolls to 1934 & 1935 with Births and Deaths 1932-1938, and Marriages 1936-1938 Volume II

Eastern Cherokee Census Cherokee, North Carolina 1930-1939 Census 1930-1931 with Births And Deaths 1924-1931 Taken By Agent L. W. Page Volume I
Eastern Cherokee Census Cherokee, North Carolina 1930-1939 Census 1932-1933 with Births And Deaths 1930-1932 Taken By Agent R. L. Spalsbury Volume II
Eastern Cherokee Census Cherokee, North Carolina 1930-1939 Census 1934-1937 with Births and Deaths 1925-1938 and Marriages 1936 & 1938 Taken by Agents R. L. Spalsbury And Harold W. Foght Volume III

Seminole of Florida Indian Census, 1930-1940 with Birth and Death Records, 1930-1938

Texas Cherokees 1820-1839 A Document For Litigation 1921

Choctaw By Blood Enrollment Cards 1898-1914 Volumes I thru XVII

Starr Roll 1894 (Cherokee Payment Rolls) Districts: Canadian, Cooweescoowee, and Delaware Volume One
Starr Roll 1894 (Cherokee Payment Rolls) Districts: Flint, Going Snake, and Illinois Volume Two
Starr Roll 1894 (Cherokee Payment Rolls) Districts: Saline, Sequoyah, and Tahlequah; Including Orphan Roll Volume Three

Cherokee Intruder Cases Dockets of Hearings 1901-1909 Volumes I & II

Indian Wills, 1911-1921 Records of the Bureau of Indian Affairs Books One thru Seven;
Native American Wills & Probate Records 1911-1921

Other Books and Series by Jeff Bowen

Turtle Mountain Reservation Chippewa Indians 1932 Census with Births & Deaths, 1924-1932

Chickasaw By Blood Enrollment Cards 1898-1914 Volume I thru V

Cherokee Descendants East An Index to the Guion Miller Applications Volume I
Cherokee Descendants West An Index to the Guion Miller Applications Volume II (A-M)
Cherokee Descendants West An Index to the Guion Miller Applications Volume III (N-Z)

Applications for Enrollment of Seminole Newborn Freedmen, Act of 1905

Eastern Cherokee Census, Cherokee, North Carolina, 1915-1922, Taken by Agent James E. Henderson   *Volume I (1915-1916)*
Volume II (1917-1918)
Volume III (1919-1920)
Volume IV (1921-1922)

Complete Delaware Roll of 1898

Eastern Cherokee Census, Cherokee, North Carolina, 1923-1929, Taken by Agent James E. Henderson   *Volume I (1923-1924)*
Volume II (1925-1926)
Volume III (1927-1929)

Applications for Enrollment of Seminole Newborn Act of 1905 Volumes I & II

North Carolina Eastern Cherokee Indian Census 1898-1899, 1904, 1906, 1909-1912, 1914 Revised and Expanded Edition

1932 Hopi and Navajo Native American Census with Birth & Death Rolls (1925-1931) Volume 1 - Hopi
1932 Hopi and Navajo Native American Census with Birth & Death Rolls (1930-1932) Volume 2 - Navajo

Western Navajo Reservation Navajo, Hopi and Paiute 1933 Census with Birth & Death Rolls 1925-1933

Cherokee Citizenship Commission Dockets 1880-1884 and 1887-1889 Volumes I thru V

Copyright © 2013
by Jeff Bowen

ALL RIGHTS RESERVED
No part of this publication may be reproduced
or used in any form or manner whatsoever
without previous written permission from the
copyright holder or publisher.

Originally published:
Baltimore, Maryland
2013

Reprinted by:

Native Study LLC
Gallipolis, OH
www.nativestudy.com
2020

Library of Congress Control Number: 2020918113

ISBN: 978-1-64968-109-6

Made in the United States of America.

This series is dedicated to the descendants of the Choctaw newborn listed in these applications.

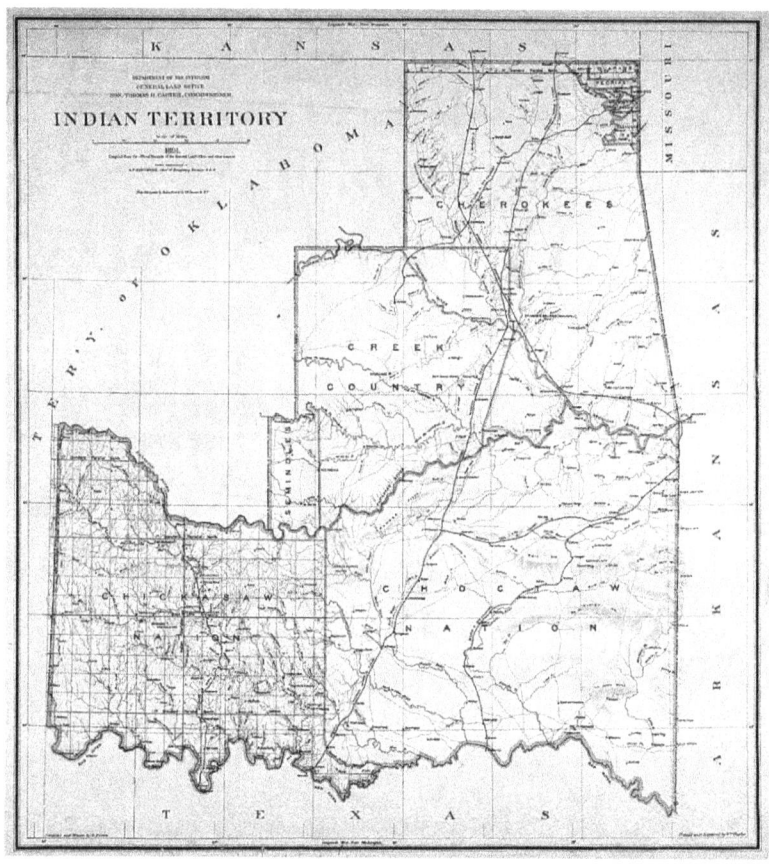

This map of Indian Territory shows how large the Choctaw and Chickasaw Nations' land base was that contained huge deposits of asphalt and coal. Just the size and territory involved was flooded with the "Grafters".

DEPARTMENT OF THE INTERIOR.

Commissioner to the Five Civilized Tribes.

NOTICE.

Opening of Land Office at Wewoka,
IN THE SEMINOLE NATION, INDIAN TERRITORY.

Notice is hereby given that on Monday, September 4, 1905, the Commissioner to the Five Civilized Tribes will establish a land office at Wewoka, in the Seminole Nation, Indian Territory, for the purpose of allowing citizens and freedmen of the Seminole Nation to select allotments of land for their minor children enrolled under the Act of Congress approved March 3, 1905 (33 Stat. L 1060), and for the further purpose of allowing citizens and freedmen of the Seminole Nation, whose allotments are incomplete, to select additional land in order to bring the value of their allotments up to the standard of $309.09, as nearly as may be practicable.

Each child whose enrollment in accordance with the Act of March 3, 1905, has been duly approved by the Secretary of the Interior, is entitled to receive an alllotment of forty acres without regard to the character or value of the land selected.

Selection of allotments for minor children must be made by their citizen or freedmen parents or by a duly appointed guardian, or curator, or by a duly appointed administrator.

TAMS BIXBY,
Commissioner.

Muskogee, Indian Territory,
July 29, 1905.

This particular notice for the Seminole and Creek Newborn makes mention of the Act of 1905. It is likely that a similar notice was posted in the Choctaw and Chickasaw Nations for the registration of newborn children.

DEPARTMENT OF THE INTERIOR,
Commission to the Five Civilized Tribes.

Rules and Regulations Governing the Selection of Allotments and the Designation of Homesteads in the Choctaw and Chickasaw Nations.

1. Selections of allotments and designations of homesteads for adult citizens and selections of allotments for adult freedmen must be made in person except as herein otherwise provided.
2. Applications to have land set apart and homesteads designated for duly identified Mississippi Choctaws must be made personally before the Commission to the Five Civilized Tribes. Fathers may apply for their minor children and if the father be dead the mother may apply. Husbands may apply for wives. Applications for orphans, insane persons and persons of unsound mind may be made by duly appointed guardian or curator, and for aged and infirm persons and prisoners by agents duly authorized thereunto by power of attorney, in the discretion of said Commission.
3. At the time of the selection of allotment each citizen and duly identified Mississippi Choctaw shall designate as a homestead out of said selection land equal in value to one hundred and sixty acres of the average allottable land of the Choctaw and Chickasaw Nations, as nearly as may be.
4. Each Choctaw and Chickasaw freedman, at the time of selection shall designate as his or her allotment of the lands of the Choctaw and Chickasaw Nations, land equal in value to forty acres of the average allottable land of the Choctaw and Chickasaw Nations.
5. Citizens, freedmen and identified Mississippi Choctaws who are married, whether they have attained their majority or not, will be regarded as of age for the purpose of making selections.
6. Selections may be made by citizen and freedmen parents for unmarried male children under twenty-one years of age and for unmarried female children under eighteen years of age, and a male citizen or freedman may make selection for his wife, if she is entitled to make selection, unless she shall, at the time or previously thereto, protest in writing.
7. Where the father of an unmarried minor citizen, freedman or identified Mississippi Choctaw is a non-citizen, the citizen, freedman or identified Mississippi Choctaw mother of such children must make selection in person in behalf of said children.
8. Selections of allotments and designations of homesteads for minor citizens and selections of allotments for minor freedmen may be made by the citizen father or mother or freedman father or mother, as the case may be, or by a guardian, curator, or an administrator having charge of their estate, in the order named.
9. Selections of allotments and designations of homesteads for citizen, and selections of allotment for freedmen, prisoners, convicts, aged and infirm persons and soldiers and sailors of the United States on duty outside of Indian Territory, may be made by duly appointed agents under power of attorney, and for incompetents by guardians, curators, or other suitable person akin to them.
10. Selections may be made and homesteads designated by duly identified Mississippi Choctaws, who have, within one year after the date of their identification as such, made satisfactory proof of bona fide settlement within the Choctaw-Chickasaw country, at any time within six months after the date of their said identification.
11. Persons authorized to make selections by power of attorney, as provided in rules 2 and 9 hereof, must be the husband or wife, or a relative not further removed than a cousin of the first degree of the person for whom such selection is made.
12. It shall be the duty of the Commission to the Five Civilized Tribes to see that selections of allotments and designations of homesteads for the classes of persons mentioned in rules 2, 6, 7, 8 and 9 hereof, are made for the best interests of such persons.
13. Selections of allotments for citizens, freedmen and identified Mississippi Choctaws who have died subsequent to September 25, 1902, and before making a selection of allotment, shall be made by a duly appointed administrator or executor. If, however, such administrator or executor be not duly and expeditiously appointed, or fails to act promptly when appointed, or for any other cause such selections be not so made within a reasonable and practicable time, the Commission to the Five Civilized Tribes shall designate the lands thus to be allotted.
14. In determining the value of a selection the appraised value of the land selected shall be increased by the appraised value of such pine timber on such land as has heretofore been estimated by the Commission to the Five Civilized Tribes.
15. Selections of allotments may be made only by citizens and freedmen whose enrollment has been approved by the Secretary of the Interior, and by persons duly identified by the Commission to the Five Civilized Tribes as Mississippi Choctaws, and by none others.
16. When a selection of land has been made by a citizen, freedman or identified Mississippi Choctaw, and the land so selected is claimed by a person whose rights as a citizen or freedman have not been finally determined, contest for the land so selected may be instituted by the person claiming the land, formal application for the land being first made as is required by the Rules of Practice in Choctaw and Chickasaw allotment contest cases.

THE COMMISSION TO THE FIVE CIVILIZED TRIBES.
TAMS BIXBY, Chairman.

Muskogee, Indian Territory, March 24, 1903.

The above statement published prior to 1905, was established for what was supposed to be a set of guidelines when it came to allotments. But with supplemental agreements and Congressional legislation, time frames as well as rules and regulations often changed and were not the same for every tribe.

INTRODUCTION

The *Applications for Enrollment of Choctaw Newborn Act of 1905*, National Archive film M-1301, Rolls 50-57, are found under the heading of Applications for Enrollment of the Commission to the Five Civilized Tribes. For this series, I have transcribed the application forms filled out by individuals applying for enrollment in the Five Civilized Tribes under the Dawes Commission. These applications contain considerably more information than stated on the census cards found in series M-1186. M-1301 possesses its own numerical sequence, separate from M-1186. To find each party's roll number you would have to reference M-1186.

The Choctaw as well as the Chickasaw allotments were likely some of the most sought after properties in Indian Territory. There was supposed to be a 25-year restriction on the sale or lease of any Indian lands so as to insure that the owners wouldn't be swindled, but that isn't what happened. This fact is borne out in the Dawes Commission General Allotment Act, of February 8, 1887, Section 5, which "Provides that after an Indian person is allotted land, the United States will hold the land 'in trust [1] for the sole use and benefit of the Indian' (or his heirs if the Indian landowner dies) for a period of 25 years. (Land held in trust by the United States government cannot be sold or in anyway alienated by the Indian landowner, since the United States government considers the underlying ownership of the land held by itself and not the tribe. After the period of trust ends, the Indian landowner is free to sell the land and is free from any encumbrance from the United States.)"[1] Instead, Native Americans were exploited by the devious. The Choctaw and Chickasaw Districts both had huge asphalt and coal deposits, so there was pressure from outsiders to acquire them from the minute they were discovered. After repeated attacks throughout the years and many legislative changes, President "Roosevelt finally signed the Five Tribes Bill at noon on April 26, 1906, the forces seeking to end all restrictions were disappointed. Section 19 removed restrictions from the sale of all inherited land but directed that no full-bloods could sell their land for twenty-five years. The Act also prohibited leases for more than one year without the approval of the Secretary of the Interior."[2]

Angie Debo described the opportunists that wanted these Native American allotments as, "Grafters". The parents of the newborns enumerated within this series would no sooner receive the approval for their child's allotment than there would be someone there with cash in hand holding a new deed or lease for the parents to sign their child's birthright away. Angie Debo said it best, "As the business incapacity of the allottees became apparent, a horde of despoilers fastened themselves upon their property." According to Debo, "The term 'grafter' was applied as a matter of course to dealers in Indian land, and was frankly accepted by them. The speculative fever also affected Government employees so that it was almost impossible to prevent them from making personal investments."[3]

---

[1] General Allotment Act, Act of Feb. 8, 1887 (24 Stat. 388, ch. 119, 25 USCA 331)
[2] The Dawes Commission and the Allotment of the Five Civilized Tribes, 1893-1914 by Kent Carter, pg. 173
[3] And Still the Waters Run, Angie Debo, p. 92.

INTRODUCTION

According to the Department of Interior in 1905, "It is estimated that there will be added to the final rolls of the citizens and freedmen of the Choctaw and Chickasaw nations the names of 2,000 persons, including 1,500 new-born children to be enrolled under the provisions of the act of Congress approved March 3, 1905."[4]

The quote below explains, in detail, the requirements for qualifying as a newborn Choctaw, "By the act of Congress approved March 3, 1905 (H.R. 17474), entitled 'An act making appropriations for the current and contingent expenses of the Indian Department and for fulfilling treaty stipulations with various Indian tribes for the fiscal year ending June 30, 1906, and for other purposes,' it was provided as follows:

> 'That the Commission to the Five Civilized Tribes is hereby authorized for sixty days after the date of the approval of this act to receive and consider applications for enrollment of infant children born prior to September twenty-fifth, nineteen hundred and two, and who were living on said date, to citizens by blood of the Choctaw and Chickasaw tribes of Indians whose enrollment has been approved by the Secretary of the Interior prior to the date of the approval of this act; and to enroll and make allotments to such children.'

> 'That the Commission to the Five Civilized Tribes is authorized for sixty days after the date of the approval of this act to receive and consider applications for enrollment of children born subsequent to September twenty-fifth, nineteen hundred and two, and prior to March fourth, nineteen hundred and five, and who were living on said latter date, to citizens by blood of the Choctaw and Chickasaw tribes of Indians whose enrollment has been approved by the Secretary of the Interior prior to the date of the approval of this act; and to enroll and make allotments to such children.'

"Notice is hereby given that the Commission to the Five Civilized Tribes will, up to and inclusive of midnight, May 2, 1905, receive applications for the enrollment of infant children born prior to September 25, 1902, and who were living on said date, to citizens by blood of the Choctaw and Chickasaw tribes of Indians whose enrollment has been approved by the Secretary of the Interior prior to March 3, 1905."[5]

Following is the scope of these transcriptions: Besides the applications themselves, researchers will find the identities of other individuals within these applications -- doctors, lawyers, mid-wives, and other relatives -- that may help with you genealogical research.

Jeff Bowen
Gallipolis, Ohio
NativeStudy.com

---

[4] Annual Reports of the Department of the Interior For the Fiscal Year Ended June 30, 1905, p. 609.
[5] Annual Reports of the Department of the Interior For the Fiscal Year Ended June 30, 1905, p. 593.

Applications for Enrollment of Choctaw Newborn
Act of 1905 Volume XVI

gChoc New Born 1155
Tandy LeFlore
(Born Oct. 17, 1904)
Bee LeFlore
Born July 2, 1903
Dead

Bee LeFlore - Dead
No. 2. Dismissed
June 15, 1905)

DEPARTMENT OF THE INTERIOR,
COMMISSION TO THE FIVE CIVILIZED TRIBES.

Record in the matter of the application for enrollment as a citizen by blood of the Choctaw Nation of

BEN LeFLORE   7-NB-1155.

NEW-BORN AFFIDAVIT.

Number............

...Choctaw Enrolling Commission...

IN THE MATTER OF THE APPLICATION FOR ENROLLMENT, as a citizen of the Choctaw   Nation, of   Ben Leflore

born on the   2nd day of ___July___ 190 3

Name of father   W L Leflore   a citizen of   Choctaw
Nation final enrollment No. 7849
Name of mother   Mandy Leflore   a citizen of   white
Nation final enrollment No. — —

                                       Postoffice   Starr I.T.

1

Applications for Enrollment of Choctaw Newborn
Act of 1905   Volume XVI

AFFIDAVIT OF MOTHER.

UNITED STATES OF AMERICA
INDIAN TERRITORY
   Central   DISTRICT

I   Mandy Leflore   , on oath state that I am 22   years of age and a citizen by   White   of the ———   Nation, and as such have been placed upon the final roll of the ———Nation, by the Honorable Secretary of the Interior my final enrollment number being ——— ; that I am the lawful wife of   W L Leflore , who is a citizen of the   Choctaw   Nation, and as such has been placed upon the final roll of said Nation by the Honorable Secretary of the Interior, his final enrollment number being   7849   and that a   Male   child was born to me on the   2nd   day of   July   190 3; that said child has been named   Ben Leflore   , and is now ~~living~~. Dead

Witnesseth.   Mandy Leflore
   Must be two   ⎫   Forbis LeFlore
   Witnesses who ⎬
   are Citizens. ⎭   Albert Tann

   Subscribed and sworn to before me this   27th   day of   Feb   190 5

                              Martin Switzer
                                      Notary Public.

My commission expires:
Feb 4th 1909

AFFIDAVIT OF ATTENDING PHYSICIAN OR MIDWIFE

UNITED STATES OF AMERICA
INDIAN TERRITORY
   Central   DISTRICT

I,   S.L. Perkins   a   Physician   on oath state that I attended on Mrs.   Mandy Leflore   wife of   William L Leflore   on the   2nd   day of   July   , 190 3, that there was born to her on said date a   Male   child, that said child is now ~~living~~, dead and is said to have been named   Bee Leflore

                              S.L. Perkins   M.D.
   Subscribed and sworn to before me this, the   27th   day of   February   190 5

WITNESSETH: Martin Switzer   Notary Public.
   Must be two witnesses ⎧ Forbis LeFlore
   who are citizens   ⎨
                         ⎩ Albert Tann

Applications for Enrollment of Choctaw Newborn
Act of 1905 Volume XVI

We hereby certify that we are well acquainted with S.L. Perkins a Physician and know him to be reputable and of good standing in the community.

Forbis LeFlore _____

Albert Tann _____

My Commission expires
Feb 4ᵗʰ 1909

W.F.
7-NB-1155.

DEPARTMENT OF THE INTERIOR,
COMMISSION TO THE FIVE CIVILIZED TRIBES.

In the matter of the application for the enrollment of Ben (or Bee) LeFlore as a citizen by blood of the Choctaw Nation.

--oOo--

It appears from the record herein that on April 25, 1905, there was received by the Commission application for the enrollment of Ben (or Bee) LeFlore as a citizen by blood of the Choctaw Nation.

It further appears from the record in this case and the records of the Commission that the applicant was born on July 2, 1903; that he is a son of William LeFlore, a recognized and enrolled citizen by blood of the Choctaw Nation whose name appears as number 7849 upon the final roll of citizens by blood of the Choctaw Nation approved by the Secretary of the Interior January 17, 1903, and Mandy LeFlore, a white woman; and that said applicant died prior to March 4, 1905.

The Act of Congress approved March 3, 1905 (Public No. 212) among other things provides:
"That the Commission to the Five Civilized Tribes is authorized for sixty days after the date of the approval of this act to receive and consider applications for enrollment of children born subsequent to September twenty-fifth, nineteen hundred and two, and prior to March fourth, nineteen hundred and five, and who were living on said latter date, to citizens by blood of the Choctaw and Chickasaw tribes of Indians whose enrollment has been approved by the Secretary of the Interior prior to the date of the approval of this act; and to enroll and make allotments to such children."

It is, therefore, hereby ordered that the application for the enrollment of Ben LeFlore as a citizen by blood of the Choctaw Nation be dismissed, in accordance with the order of the Commission of March 31, 1905.

COMMISSION TO THE FIVE CIVILIZED TRIBES.

Applications for Enrollment of Choctaw Newborn
Act of 1905   Volume XVI

Muskogee, Indian Territory.
JUN 15 1905

Tams Bixby Commissioner.

---

7 NB 1155

Muskogee, Indian Territory, June 15, 1905.

William LeFlore,
    Blaine, Indian Territory.

COPY

Dear Sir:

    Inclosed herewith you will find a copy of the order of this Commission, dated June 15, 1905, dismissing the application for the enrollment of your infant child, Ben LeFlore as a citizen by blood of the Choctaw Nation.

        Respectfully,
        SIGNED
        Tams Bixby

Registered.
Incl. 7-NB-1155.
        Chairman.

---

7 NB 1155

Muskogee, Indian Territory, June 15, 1905.

Mansfield, McMurray & Cornish,
    Attorneys for Choctaw and Chickasaw Nations,
        South McAlester, Indian Territory.

Gentlemen:

    Inclosed herewith you will find a copy of the order of this Commission, dated June 15, 1905, dismissing the application for the enrollment of Ben Leflore as a citizen by blood of the Choctaw Nation.

        Respectfully,
        SIGNED
        Tams Bixby
        Chairman.

Incl. 7-NB-1155.

Applications for Enrollment of Choctaw Newborn
Act of 1905 Volume XVI

BIRTH AFFIDAVIT.

DEPARTMENT OF THE INTERIOR.
COMMISSION TO THE FIVE CIVILIZED TRIBES.

IN RE APPLICATION FOR ENROLLMENT, as a citizen of the   Choctaw   Nation, of Tandy LeFlore , born on the 17" day of Oct , 1904

Name of Father: William LeFlore   a citizen of the Choctaw Nation.
Name of Mother: Manda LeFlore   a citizen of the White Choctaw Nation.

Postoffice   Blaine I.T.

AFFIDAVIT OF MOTHER.

UNITED STATES OF AMERICA, Indian Territory,
      Central   DISTRICT.

I, Manda LeFlore , on oath state that I am 22 years of age and a citizen by Intermarriage , of the   Choctaw   Nation; that I am the lawful wife of   William LeFlore , who is a citizen, by   Blood   of the   Choctaw   Nation; that a Male   child was born to me on 17" day of Oct , 1904, that said child has been named Tandy Leflore , and is now living.

Manda Leflore

Witnesses To Mark:
{

Subscribed and sworn to before me this 20" day of April , 1905.

M.W. Newman
Notary Public.

AFFIDAVIT OF ATTENDING PHYSICIAN OR MID-WIFE.

UNITED STATES OF AMERICA, Indian Territory,
      Central   DISTRICT.

I,   Salena Shores   , a   Midwife   , on oath state that I attended on Mrs. Manda LeFlore , wife of   William LeFlore   on the 17" day of Oct , 1904; that there was born to her on said date a   male   child; that said child is now living and is said to have been named Tandy Leflore

Salena Shores

Witnesses To Mark:
{

Applications for Enrollment of Choctaw Newborn
Act of 1905   Volume XVI

Subscribed and sworn to before me this 20" day of   April   , 1905.

M.W. Newman
Notary Public.

NEW-BORN AFFIDAVIT.

Number

...Choctaw Enrolling Commission...

IN THE MATTER OF THE APPLICATION FOR ENROLLMENT, as a citizen of the Choctaw   Nation, of   Tandy Leflore

born on the 17th   day of   Oct   190 4

Name of father   W L Leflore   a citizen of   Choctaw
Nation final enrollment No. 7849
Name of mother   Mandy Leflore   a citizen of   White
Nation final enrollment No. ——

Postoffice   Starr I.T.

AFFIDAVIT OF MOTHER.

UNITED STATES OF AMERICA
INDIAN TERRITORY
   Central   DISTRICT

I   Mandy Leflore   , on oath state that I am   22   years of age and a citizen by   white   of the   ———   Nation, and as such have been placed upon the final roll of the ———Nation, by the Honorable Secretary of the Interior my final enrollment number being ——— ; that I am the lawful wife of   W L Leflore   , who is a citizen of the   Choctaw   Nation, and as such has been placed upon the final roll of said Nation by the Honorable Secretary of the Interior, his final enrollment number being   7849   and that a   Male   child was born to me on the   17th   day of   October   190 4; that said child has been named   Tandy Leflore   , and is now living.

Witnesseth.   Mandy Leflore
  Must be two } Forbis LeFlore
  Witnesses who
  are Citizens.   Albert Tann

Applications for Enrollment of Choctaw Newborn
Act of 1905   Volume XVI

Subscribed and sworn to before me this 27th   day of   Feb   190 5

Martin Switzer
Notary Public.

My commission expires:
Feb 4th 1909

Affidavit of Attending Physician or Midwife

UNITED STATES OF AMERICA,
INDIAN TERRITORY,
Central   DISTRICT

I,   Callina[sic] Shores   a   Midwife on oath state that I attended on Mrs. ~~William~~ Mandy Leflore   wife of   William Leflore on the   17th   day of   Oct , 190 4, that there was born to her on said date a   Male   child, that said child is now living, and is said to have been named   Tandy Leflore

Cellena Shores
Subscribed and sworn to before me this the   27   day of   February   1905

Martin Switzer
Notary Public.

WITNESSETH:
Must be two witnesses who are citizens and know the child.   { OM Krebbs

My Commission expires
Feb 4th 1909.

We hereby certify that we are well acquainted with   Callina Shores a   Midwife   and know   her   to be reputable and of good standing in the community.

Must be two citizen witnesses.   { OM Krebbs

Applications for Enrollment of Choctaw Newborn
Act of 1905 Volume XVI

7-2693.

Muskogee, Indian Territory, April 26, 1905.

William Leflore,
    Blaine, Indian Territory.

Dear Sir:

    Receipt is hereby acknowledged of the affidavits of Manda Leflore and Salena Shores to the birth of Tandy Leflore, son of William and Manda Leflore, October 17, 1904, and the same have been filed with our records as an application for the enrollment of said child.

        Respectfully,

                Chairman.

7--NB--1155

Muskogee, Indian Territory, June 1, 1905.

William LeFlore,
    Blain[sic], Indian Territory.

Dear Sir:

    Referring to the application for the enrollment of your infant child, Tandy Leflore, born October 17, 1904, it is noted from the affidavits heretofore filed in this office that the applicant claims through you.

    In this event it will be necessary that you file in this office, either the original, or a certified copy of the license and certificate of your marriage to the applicant's mother, Manda LeFlore.

        Respectfully,

                Chairman.

Applications for Enrollment of Choctaw Newborn
Act of 1905 Volume XVI

C O P Y   7--NB--1155
           MARRIAGE --- CERTIFICATE.

This is to certify that William LeFlore and Amanda Stovers were lawfully married by me, this the fourth day of September, 1902.

(signed)   E. Z. Moore.

County Judge, Skullyville Co.
Choctaw Nation, I. T.

Witness: Mrs. E. A. Moore

UNITED STATES OF AMERICA,
    INDIAN TERRITORY,   sct:
WESTERN - - - - DISTRICT.

I,   Chas E Webster   , a Notary Public duly commissioned and acting within and for the Western District of the Indian Territory, do HEREBY CERTIFY, above and foregoing to be a full, true and correct copy of the original Marriage Certificate between William LeFlore and Amanda Stovers now on file with the Commission to the Five Civilized Tribes.

Given under my hand and seal this the 7th day of June, A. D. 1905.

Chas E Webster
Notary Public.

Choc New Born 1156
    John Henry Ratterree
    (Born Jan. 4, 1904)

BIRTH AFFIDAVIT.
DEPARTMENT OF THE INTERIOR.
COMMISSION TO THE FIVE CIVILIZED TRIBES.

IN RE APPLICATION FOR ENROLLMENT, as a citizen of the   Choctaw   Nation, of John Henry Ratterree   , born on the 4" day of January , 1904

Name of Father: William E Ratterree   a citizen of the   U.S.   ~~Nation~~.
Name of Mother: Rina J Ratterree ne *Rina J Durant* a citizen of the   Choctaw Nation.

9

Applications for Enrollment of Choctaw Newborn
Act of 1905   Volume XVI

Postoffice   Gilmore, I.T.

AFFIDAVIT OF MOTHER.

UNITED STATES OF AMERICA, Indian Territory, }
Central   DISTRICT.

I,   Rina J Ratterree, ne Rina J Durant   , on oath state that I am   20   years of age and a citizen by   Blood   , of the   Choctaw   Nation; that I am the lawful wife of   William E Ratterree   , who is a citizen, ~~by~~ ——— of the   U.S.   Nation; that a   Male   child was born to me on   4   day of   January   , 1904; that said child has been named   John Henry   , and was living March 4, 1905.

Rina J Ratterree

Witnesses To Mark:
{

Subscribed and sworn to before me this   7   day of   April   , 1905

My Commission Expires   Columbus L Woods
    Feb 2 1908   Notary Public.

AFFIDAVIT OF ATTENDING PHYSICIAN OR MID-WIFE.

UNITED STATES OF AMERICA, Indian Territory, }
Central   DISTRICT.

I,   Ben D Woodson   , a   Practicing Physician , on oath state that I attended on Mrs.   Rina J Ratterree ne Rina J Durant   , wife of   William E Ratterree   on the   4 day of   January   , 1904; that there was born to her on said date a   male   child; that said child was living March 4, 1905, and is said to have been named   John Henry

D Woodson M.D.

Witnesses To Mark:
{

Subscribed and sworn to before me this   4   day of   April   , 1905

My Commission Expires   Columbus L Woods
    Feb 2 1908   Notary Public.

Applications for Enrollment of Choctaw Newborn
Act of 1905   Volume XVI

7-5632.

Muskogee, Indian Territory, April 26, 1905.

William E. Ratterree,
    Gilmore, Indian Territory.

Dear Sir:

    Receipt is hereby acknowledged of the affidavits of Rina J. Ratterree and Ben D. Woodson, to the birth of John Henry Ratterree, child of William E. and Rina J. Ratterree, January 4, 1904, and the same have been filed with our records as an application for the enrollment of said child.

                    Respectfully,

                                              Chairman.

Choc New Born 1157
    Lemuel Henry Collins
    (Born Jan. 10, 1905)

BIRTH AFFIDAVIT.

DEPARTMENT OF THE INTERIOR.
COMMISSION TO THE FIVE CIVILIZED TRIBES.

    IN RE APPLICATION FOR ENROLLMENT, as a citizen of the   Choctaw   Nation, of Lemuel Henry Collins   , born on the 10th day of   January , 1905

Name of Father: Joseph Collins   a citizen of the   Choctaw   Nation.
Name of Mother: Mattie Collins   a citizen of the   Choctaw   Nation.

                    Postoffice   Shoals, Ind Ter

AFFIDAVIT OF MOTHER.

UNITED STATES OF AMERICA, Indian Territory, }
    Central   DISTRICT. }

    I, Mattie Collins   , on oath state that I am 19   years of age and a citizen by   blood   , of the   Choctaw   Nation; that I am the lawful wife of   Joseph Collins   , who is a citizen, by blood   of the   Choctaw   Nation; that a

Applications for Enrollment of Choctaw Newborn
Act of 1905   Volume XVI

male   child was born to me on   10th   day of   January   , 1905; that said child has been named   Lemuel Henry Collins   , and was living March 4, 1905.

                          Mattie Collins

Witnesses To Mark:

    Subscribed and sworn to before me this   17th day of   April   , 1905

                          Wirt Franklin
                          Notary Public.

AFFIDAVIT OF ATTENDING PHYSICIAN OR MID-WIFE.

UNITED STATES OF AMERICA, Indian Territory,
   Central   DISTRICT.

    I,   Perry E.A. Fling   , a physician   , on oath state that I attended on Mrs.   Mattie Collins   , wife of   Joseph Collins   on the 10th day of January , 1905; that there was born to her on said date a   male   child; that said child was living March 4, 1905, and is said to have been named   Lemuel Henry Collins

                        Perry E.A. Fling

Witnesses To Mark:

    Subscribed and sworn to before me this   17th day of   April   , 1905

                        Wirt Franklin
                        Notary Public.

NEW-BORN AFFIDAVIT.

            Number..................

Choctaw Enrolling Commission.

    IN THE MATTER OF THE APPLICATION FOR ENROLLMENT, as a citizen of the Choctaw   Nation, of   Lemuel Henry Collins

born on the   10   day of   Jany   190 5

Name of father   Joseph Collins   a citizen of   Choctaw
Nation final enrollment No   14858

Applications for Enrollment of Choctaw Newborn
Act of 1905 Volume XVI

Name of mother   Mattie Collins   a citizen of   Choctaw
Nation final enrollment No   4074

                 Postoffice   Grant I.T.

AFFIDAVIT OF MOTHER.

UNITED STATES OF AMERICA, ⎫
     INDIAN TERRITORY,   ⎬
   Central   DISTRICT   ⎭

      I   Mattie Collins   on oath state that I am   17   years of age and a citizen by   Blood   of the   Choctaw   Nation, and as such have been placed upon the final roll of the   Choctaw   Nation, by the Honorable Secretary of the Interior my final enrollment number being   4074   ; that I am the lawful wife of   Joseph Collins   , who is a citizen of the   Choctaw   Nation, and as such has been placed upon the final roll of said Nation by the Honorable Secretary of the Interior, his final enrollment number being   14858   and that a   Male   child was born to me on the   10   day of   January   190 5 ; that said child has been named   Lemuel Henry Collins   , and is now living.

                                                   Mattie Collins

WITNESSETH:
   Must be two   ⎫   Chas E Bearden
   Witnesses who ⎬
   are Citizens.   ⎭   L E Oakes

      Subscribed and sworn to before me this   21   day of   Jany   190 5

                                            J.P. Ward
                                                        Notary Public.
My commission expires   April 28/08

Affidavit of Attending Physician or Midwife

UNITED STATES OF AMERICA, ⎫
     INDIAN TERRITORY,   ⎬
   Central   DISTRICT   ⎭

      I,   Perry Fling   a   Physician on oath state that I attended on Mrs. Mattie Collins   wife of   Joseph Collins on the   10. day of   Jany   , 190 5, that there was born to her on said date a   Male   child, that said child is now living, and is said to have been named   Lemuel Henry Collins

                                               Perry Fling   M. D.

      Subscribed and sworn to before me this the   21   day of   Jany   1905

                                               J.P. Ward
                                                    Notary Public.

Applications for Enrollment of Choctaw Newborn
Act of 1905   Volume XVI

WITNESSETH:

Must be two witnesses who are citizens and know the child.
{ Chas E Bearden
  L E Oakes

We hereby certify that we are well acquainted with   Perry Fling
a   Physician   and know   him   to be reputable and of good standing in the community.

Must be two citizen witnesses.
{ Chas E Bearden
  L E Oakes

Choc New Born 1158
    Luther Lee Dowland
    (Born May 18, 1903)
    Myrtle Lee Dowland
    (Born May 18, 1903)

NEW-BORN AFFIDAVIT.

Number

Choctaw Enrolling Commission.

IN THE MATTER OF THE APPLICATION FOR ENROLLMENT, as a citizen of the Choctaw   Nation, of   Myrtle Lee Dowland

born on the   18   day of   May   1903

Name of father   Frank Dowland   a citizen of   Choctaw
Nation final enrollment No   692
Name of mother   Mattie Dowland   a citizen of   Choctaw
Nation final enrollment No   4067

Postoffice   Boswell I.T.

Applications for Enrollment of Choctaw Newborn
Act of 1905   Volume XVI

AFFIDAVIT OF MOTHER.

UNITED STATES OF AMERICA,
INDIAN TERRITORY,
Central   DISTRICT

I   Mattie Dowland   on oath state that I am   20   years of age and a citizen by   Blood   of the   Choctaw   Nation, and as such have been placed upon the final roll of the   Choctaw   Nation, by the Honorable Secretary of the Interior my final enrollment number being   4067   ; that I am the lawful wife of   Frank Dowland   , who is a citizen of the   Choctaw   Nation, and as such has been placed upon the final roll of said Nation by the Honorable Secretary of the Interior, his final enrollment number being   692   and that a   Female   child was born to me on the   18   day of   May   190 3 ; that said child has been named   Myrtle Lee Dowland   , and is now living.

Mattie Dowland

WITNESSETH:
Must be two Witnesses who are Citizens.   John T Brown
    John A King

Subscribed and sworn to before me this   28   day of   January   190 5

R.E. Tanner
Notary Public.

My commission expires   March 26" 1906

BIRTH AFFIDAVIT.

DEPARTMENT OF THE INTERIOR,
COMMISSION TO THE FIVE CIVILIZED TRIBES.

In Re Application for Enrollment, as a citizen of the   Choctaw   Nation, of   Luther Lee Dowland , born on the 18th   day of   May   , 1903

Name of Father: Frank Dowland   a citizen of the   Choctaw   Nation.
Name of Mother: Mattie Dowland   a citizen of the   Choctaw   Nation.

Post-office   Crowder I.T.

Applications for Enrollment of Choctaw Newborn
Act of 1905   Volume XVI

AFFIDAVIT OF MOTHER.

UNITED STATES OF AMERICA,
  INDIAN TERRITORY,
  Central   District.

I, Mattie Dowland , on oath state that I am 18 years of age and a citizen by blood , of the Choctaw Nation; that I am the lawful wife of Frank Dowland , who is a citizen, by marriage of the Choctaw Nation; that a male child was born to me on 18th day of May , 1903 , that said child has been named Luther Lee Dowland , and is now living.

Mattie Dowland

WITNESSES TO MARK:

Subscribed and sworn to before me this 10th day of July , 1905.

JR Armstrong
NOTARY PUBLIC.
Com Ex Mar 11 1907

AFFIDAVIT OF ATTENDING PHYSICIAN OR MID-WIFE.

UNITED STATES OF AMERICA,
  INDIAN TERRITORY,
  Central   District.

I, Paralee Crowder , a Mid-wife , on oath state that I attended on Mrs. Mattie Dowland , wife of Frank Dowland on the 18th day of May, 1903 ; that there was born to her on said date a   male   child; that said child is now living and is said to have been named   Luther Lee Dowland

her
Paralee X Crowder
[sic]

WITNESSES TO MARK:
  Jos R Armstrong
  C M McRae

Subscribed and sworn to before me this 10th day of July , 1905.

JR Armstrong
NOTARY PUBLIC.
Com Ex Mar 11 1907

Applications for Enrollment of Choctaw Newborn
Act of 1905   Volume XVI

It appearing from the within affidavits that Luther Lee Dowland, born May 18, 1903, for whose enrollment as a citizen by blood of the Choctaw Nation, application was made under the Act of Congress approved March 3, 1905, (33 Stats., 1071), died November 28, 1904, it is hereby ordered that the application of said Luther Lee Dowland as a citizen by blood of the Choctaw Nation be dismissed.

Tams Bixby Commissioner.
Muskogee, Indian Territory.

DEPARTMENT OF THE INTERIOR.
COMMISSION TO THE FIVE CIVILIZED TRIBES.

In the matter of the death of   Luther Lee Dowland   a citizen of the   Choctaw   Nation, who formerly resided at or near   Crowder   , Ind. Ter., and died on the   28th   day of   November   , 1904

AFFIDAVIT OF RELATIVE.

UNITED STATES OF AMERICA, Indian Territory,
Southern   DISTRICT.

I,   Mattie Dowland   , on oath state that I am   20   years of age and a citizen by blood   , of the   Choctaw   Nation; that my postoffice address is   Boswell City   , Ind. Ter.; that I am   the mother   of   Luther Lee Dowland   who was a citizen, by blood   , of the   Choctaw   Nation and that said   Luther Lee Dowland   died on the   28th   day of   November   , 1904

Mattie Dowland

Witnesses To Mark:
  Wm O Brown

Subscribed and sworn to before me this   21st   day of   September   , 1905.

H.C. Miller
Notary Public.

Applications for Enrollment of Choctaw Newborn
Act of 1905 Volume XVI

BIRTH AFFIDAVIT.

DEPARTMENT OF THE INTERIOR.
COMMISSION TO THE FIVE CIVILIZED TRIBES.

IN RE APPLICATION FOR ENROLLMENT, as a citizen of the Choctaw Nation, of Myrtle Lee Dowland, born on the 18 day of May, 1903

Name of Father: Frank Dowland   a citizen of the Choctaw Nation.
Name of Mother: Mattie Dowland   a citizen of the Choctaw Nation.

Postoffice   Boswell Ind. Tery.

AFFIDAVIT OF MOTHER.

UNITED STATES OF AMERICA, Indian Territory,
Central   DISTRICT.

I, Mattie Dowland, on oath state that I am 20 years of age and a citizen by Blood, of the Choctaw Nation; that I am the lawful wife of Frank Dowland, who is a citizen, by Intermarriage of the Choctaw Nation; that a Female child was born to me on 18 day of May, 1903, that said child has been named Myrtle Lee Dowland, and is now living.

               Mattie Dowland

Witnesses To Mark:
{

Subscribed and sworn to before me this 10 day of April, 1905.

               R.E. Tanner
                   Notary Public.

AFFIDAVIT OF ATTENDING PHYSICIAN OR MID-WIFE.

UNITED STATES OF AMERICA, Indian Territory,
Central   DISTRICT.

I, Paralee Crowder, a midwife, on oath state that I attended on Mrs. Mattie Dowland, wife of Frank Dowland on the 18 day of May, 1903; that there was born to her on said date a female child; that said child is now living and is said to have been named Myrtle Lee Dowland

               Paralee Crowder

Witnesses To Mark:
{

Applications for Enrollment of Choctaw Newborn
Act of 1905   Volume XVI

Subscribed and sworn to before me this 10 day of April , 1905.

R.E. Tanner
Notary Public.

BIRTH AFFIDAVIT.

DEPARTMENT OF THE INTERIOR,
COMMISSION TO THE FIVE CIVILIZED TRIBES.

In Re Application for Enrollment, as a citizen of the Choctaw Nation, of Myrtle Lee Dowland , born on the 18th day of May , 1903

Name of Father: Frank Dowland   a citizen of the Choctaw Nation.
Name of Mother: Mattie Dowland   a citizen of the Choctaw Nation.

Post-office   Crowder I.T.

AFFIDAVIT OF MOTHER.

UNITED STATES OF AMERICA,
INDIAN TERRITORY,
Central   District.

I, Mattie Dowland , on oath state that I am 18 years of age and a citizen by blood , of the Choctaw Nation; that I am the lawful wife of Frank Dowland , who is a citizen, by marriage of the Choctaw Nation; that a female child was born to me on 18th day of May , 1903 , that said child has been named Myrtle Lee Dowland , and is now living.

Mattie Dowland

WITNESSES TO MARK:

Subscribed and sworn to before me this 10th day of July , 1905.

JR Armstrong
NOTARY PUBLIC.
Com Ex Mar 11 1907

Applications for Enrollment of Choctaw Newborn
Act of 1905   Volume XVI

AFFIDAVIT OF ATTENDING PHYSICIAN OR MID-WIFE.

UNITED STATES OF AMERICA, }
   INDIAN TERRITORY,
  Central   District.

    I,   Paralee Crowder   , a Mid-wife , on oath state that I attended on Mrs. ~~Frank~~ Mattie Dowland , wife of Frank Dowland on the 18th day of May, 1903 ; that there was born to her on said date a female child; that said child is now living and is said to have been named Myrtle Lee Dowland

                                         her
                              Paralee X Crowder

WITNESSES TO MARK: [sic]
  { Jos R Armstrong
    C M McRae

    Subscribed and sworn to before me this 10th day of July , 1905.

                                JR Armstrong
                                      NOTARY PUBLIC.
          Com Ex Mar 11 1907

Affidavit of Attending Physician or Midwife

UNITED STATES OF AMERICA, }
   INDIAN TERRITORY,
  Central   DISTRICT

    I,   Paralee Crowder   a   Midwife
on oath state that I attended on Mrs. Mattie Dowland   wife of Frank Dowland on the 18 day of May , 190 3, that there was born to her on said date a Female child, that said child is now living, and is said to have been named Myrtle Lee Dowland

                                        her
                            Paralee x Crowder   M. D.
                                     mark
    Subscribed and sworn to before me this the   28   day of   January   1905

                              R.E. Tanner
                                    Notary Public.

WITNESSETH:
  Must be two witnesses { John T Brown
  who are citizens and
  know the child.   J.A. King

Applications for Enrollment of Choctaw Newborn
Act of 1905   Volume XVI

We hereby certify that we are well acquainted with   Paralee Crowder
a   Midwife   and know   her   to be reputable and of good standing in the community.

Must be two citizen ⎰ John T Brown
witnesses.   ⎱ John A. King

7-NB-1158

Muskogee, Indian Territory, July 26, 1905.

Frank Dowland,
    Crowder, Indian Territory.

Dear Sir:

    Your attention is called to a communication addressed to you by the Commission to the Five Civilized Tribes, under date of June 1, 1905, requesting additional evidence in the matter of the enrollment of said child. of the enrollment [sic] your infant child Luther Lee Dowland, born May 18, 1903.

    In said letter you were requested to furnish affidavits that said child was living March 4, 1905, or in the event of his death, prior to that date, to furnish evidence as to date of death. No reply to this letter has been received.

    You are requested to give this matter your immediate attention as no further action can be taken relative to the enrollment of your said child until the evidence requested has been supplied.

        Respectfully,

                Commissioner.

7-NB-1158.

Muskogee, Indian Territory, September 27, 1905.

Frank Dowland,
    c/o George T. Crowder,
        Boswell, Indian Territory.

Dear Sir:

    In the matter of the application for the enrollment of your minor son Luther Lee Dowland, born May 18, 1903, as a citizen by blood of the Choctaw Nation you are

Applications for Enrollment of Choctaw Newborn
Act of 1905   Volume XVI

advised that the proof of birth of said child shows only that he was living on July 10, 1903.

    There is inclosed herewith blank for proof of birth and if said child was living March 4, 1905, you are requested to have the same properly filled out, executed and returned to this office. If said child died prior to March 4, 1905, you are requested to have the inclosed blank for proof of death filled out, properly executed and returned to this office.

                       Respectfully,

DC   Commissioner.
BC
    Env.

7-NB-1158

                                         Muskogee, Indian Territory, September 29, 1905.

George W. Crowder,
    Boswell, Indian Territory.

Dear Sir:

    Receipt is hereby acknowledged of your letter of the 23rd instant with which you transmitted your affidavit relative to the birth and death of your minor grandson, Luther Lee Dowland. You request to be advised as to whether or not this is sufficient evidence from which to determine the right of said child to enrollment.

    Said affidavit, in connection with the proof already on file, would be sufficient to determine the rights of said child were it not that said affidavit is defective inasmuch as the notary public, J. R. Armstrong, before whom the same was sworn to, neglected to affix his notarial seal to the same.

    The affidavit is therefore returned to you herewith and you are requested to have said notary public affix his seal to the same and return it to this office in the inclosed envelope.

                        Respectfully,

CTD-1   Commissioner.
    Env.

Applications for Enrollment of Choctaw Newborn
Act of 1905   Volume XVI

Muskogee, Indian Territory, November 28, 1905.

George W. Crowder,
    Boswell, Indian Territory.

Dear Sir:

    Receipt is hereby acknowledged of your affidavit relative to the birth and death of Luther Lee Dowland which has been corrected by having the seal of the notary attached thereto and the same has been filed with the record in this case as evidence of the death of the above named child.

Respectfully,

Acting Commissioner.

7-NB-1158.

COPY

Muskogee, Indian Territory, January 22, 1906.

Frank Dowland,
    Crowder, Indian Territory.

Dear Sir:

    You are hereby advised that on January 22, 1906, the Commissioner to the Five Civilized Tribes dismissed the application for the enrollment of your child, Luther Lee Dowland, as a citizen by blood of the Choctaw Nation, for the reason that he died prior to March 4, 1905.

Respectfully,
SIGNED

Tams Bixby
Commissioner.

Choc New Born 1159
    Rufus Claude Ireton
    (Born Feb. 9, 1903)
    Frederick Henry Ireton
    (Born Oct. 28, 1904)

Applications for Enrollment of Choctaw Newborn
Act of 1905 Volume XVI

BIRTH AFFIDAVIT.

DEPARTMENT OF THE INTERIOR.
COMMISSION TO THE FIVE CIVILIZED TRIBES.

IN RE APPLICATION FOR ENROLLMENT, as a citizen of the Choctaw Nation, of Rufus Claude Ireton, born on the 9th day of February, 1903

Name of Father: David R Ireton   a citizen of the Choctaw Nation.
Name of Mother: Minnie Ann Ireton   a citizen of the Choctaw Nation.

Postoffice   Ireton, Indian Territory.

AFFIDAVIT OF MOTHER.

UNITED STATES OF AMERICA, Indian Territory,
Southern   DISTRICT.

I, Minnie Ann Ireton, on oath state that I am 23 years of age and a citizen by Intermarriage, of the Choctaw Nation; that I am the lawful wife of David R Ireton, who is a citizen, by Blood of the Choctaw Nation; that a Male child was born to me on 9th day of February, 1903, that said child has been named Rufus Claude Ireton, and is now living.

                               Minnie Ann Ireton

Witnesses To Mark:
{

Subscribed and sworn to before me this 11th day of March, 1905.

My Commission expires
April 1st 1908   F.W. Trask
                                Notary Public.

AFFIDAVIT OF ATTENDING PHYSICIAN OR MID-WIFE.

UNITED STATES OF AMERICA, Indian Territory,
Southern   DISTRICT.

I, J B McBride, a Practicing Physician, on oath state that I attended on Mrs. Minnie Ann Ireton, wife of David R Ireton on the 9th day of February, 1903; that there was born to her on said date a male child; that said child is now living and is said to have been named Rufus Claude Ireton

                               M B McBride, M.D.

Witnesses To Mark:
{

Applications for Enrollment of Choctaw Newborn
Act of 1905   Volume XVI

Subscribed and sworn to before me this 14 day of March , 1905.

My Commission expires
March 29-1908

(Name Illegible)
Notary Public.

BIRTH AFFIDAVIT.

DEPARTMENT OF THE INTERIOR.
COMMISSION TO THE FIVE CIVILIZED TRIBES.

IN RE APPLICATION FOR ENROLLMENT, as a citizen of the   Choctaw   Nation, of Rufus Claude Ireton   , born on the 9th   day of   February , 1903

Name of Father: David R Ireton   a citizen of the   Choctaw   Nation.
Name of Mother: Minnie Ann Ireton   a citizen of the   Choctaw   Nation.

Postoffice   Ireton, I.T.

AFFIDAVIT OF MOTHER.

UNITED STATES OF AMERICA, Indian Territory,
   Southern   DISTRICT.

I,   Minnie R Ireton   , on oath state that I am   23   years of age and a citizen by   marriage   , of the   Choctaw   Nation; that I am the lawful wife of   David R Ireton   , who is a citizen, by blood   of the   Choctaw   Nation; that a male   child was born to me on   9th   day of   February   , 1903; that said child has been named   Rufus Claude Ireton   , and was living March 4, 1905.

Minnie Ann Ireton

Witnesses To Mark:

{

Subscribed and sworn to before me this 5th   day of   April   , 1905

JE Williams
Notary Public.

Applications for Enrollment of Choctaw Newborn
Act of 1905   Volume XVI

AFFIDAVIT OF ATTENDING PHYSICIAN OR MID-WIFE.

UNITED STATES OF AMERICA, Indian Territory,
Southern DISTRICT.

I, Anna Adair , a mid-wife , on oath state that I attended on Mrs. Minnie Ann Ireton , wife of David R Ireton on the 9th day of February , 1903; that there was born to her on said date a male child; that said child was living March 4, 1905, and is said to have been named Rufus Claude Ireton

Anna Adair

Witnesses To Mark:

Subscribed and sworn to before me this 15th day of April , 1905

J.D. Armstrong
Notary Public.
My commission expires Feb 25-1909

BIRTH AFFIDAVIT.

DEPARTMENT OF THE INTERIOR.
COMMISSION TO THE FIVE CIVILIZED TRIBES.

IN RE APPLICATION FOR ENROLLMENT, as a citizen of the Choctaw Nation, of Frederick Henry Ireton , born on the 28th day of October , 1904

Name of Father: David R Ireton   a citizen of the Choctaw Nation.
                                   Intermarried
Name of Mother: Minnie Ann Ireton   a citizen of the Choctaw Nation.

Postoffice   Ireton, Indian Territory

AFFIDAVIT OF MOTHER.

UNITED STATES OF AMERICA, Indian Territory,
Southern DISTRICT.

I, Minnie Ann Ireton , on oath state that I am 23 years of age and a citizen by Intermarriage , of the Choctaw Nation; that I am the lawful wife of David R Ireton , who is a citizen, by Blood of the Choctaw Nation; that a Male child was born to me on 28th day of October , 1904, that said child has been named Fredrick Henry Ireton , and is now living.

Minnie Ann Ireton

Applications for Enrollment of Choctaw Newborn
Act of 1905   Volume XVI

Witnesses To Mark:

{

Subscribed and sworn to before me this 11 day of March, 1905.
My Commission expires April 1st 1908

                                  F.W. Trask
                                  Notary Public.

AFFIDAVIT OF ATTENDING PHYSICIAN OR MID-WIFE.

UNITED STATES OF AMERICA, Indian Territory,   }
   Southern   DISTRICT.   }

I,   J B McBride   , a Practicing Physician , on oath state that I attended on Mrs.   Minnie Ann Ireton   , wife of   David R Ireton   on the   28th day of October   , 1904; that there was born to her on said date a   male   child; that said child is now living and is said to have been named   Frederick Henry Ireton

                              M B McBride, M.D.
Witnesses To Mark:

{

Subscribed and sworn to before me this 14 day of March, 1905.

   My Commission expires
     March 29.1908   (Name Illegible)
                                  Notary Public.

BIRTH AFFIDAVIT.
DEPARTMENT OF THE INTERIOR.
COMMISSION TO THE FIVE CIVILIZED TRIBES.

IN RE APPLICATION FOR ENROLLMENT, as a citizen of the   Choctaw   Nation, of Frederick Henry Ireton   , born on the 28th day of   October   , 1904

Name of Father: David R Ireton   a citizen of the   Choctaw   Nation.
Name of Mother: Minnie Ann Ireton   a citizen of the   Choctaw   Nation.

                        Postoffice   Ireton, I.T.

Applications for Enrollment of Choctaw Newborn
Act of 1905 Volume XVI

AFFIDAVIT OF MOTHER.

UNITED STATES OF AMERICA, Indian Territory, }
Southern   DISTRICT.

I, Minnie R Ireton, on oath state that I am 23 years of age and a citizen by marriage, of the Choctaw Nation; that I am the lawful wife of David R Ireton, who is a citizen, by blood of the Choctaw Nation; that a male child was born to me on 28th day of October, 1904; that said child has been named Frederick Henry Ireton, and was living March 4, 1905.

                                      Minnie Ann Ireton

Witnesses To Mark:
{

Subscribed and sworn to before me this 5th day of April, 1905

                                      JE Williams
                                          Notary Public.

AFFIDAVIT OF ATTENDING PHYSICIAN OR MID-WIFE.

UNITED STATES OF AMERICA, Indian Territory, }
Southern   DISTRICT.

I, Lone Burns, a Mid-wife, on oath state that I attended on Mrs. Minnie Ann Ireton, wife of David R Ireton on the 28th day of October, 1904; that there was born to her on said date a male child; that said child was living March 4, 1905, and is said to have been named Frederick Henry Ireton

                                      Lona Burns

Witnesses To Mark:
{

Subscribed and sworn to before me this 15th day of April, 1905

                                      J.D. Armstrong
                                        Notary Public.
                                        My commission expires Feb 25-1909

Applications for Enrollment of Choctaw Newborn
Act of 1905 Volume XVI

7-428

Muskogee, Indian Territory, April 24, 1905.

David R. Ireton,
    Ireton, Indian Territory.

Dear Sir:

Receipt is hereby acknowledged of the affidavits of Minnie Ann Ireton and Anna Adair to the birth of Rufus Claude Ireton, also the affidavits of Minnie Ann Ireton and Lona Burns, to the birth of Frederick Henry Ireton, children of David R. and Minnie Ann Ireton, February 9, 1903 and October 28, 1904, respectively, and the same have been filed with our records as an application for the enrollment of said children.

Respectfully,

Chairman.

7-NB-1159

Muskogee, Indian Territory, August 2, 1905.

David R. Ireton,
    Ireton, Indian Territory.

Dear Sir:

Receipt is hereby acknowledged of your letter of July 24, 1905, asking if your children Frederick Henry and Rufus Claude Ireton have been approved.

In reply to your letter you are advised that on July 22, 1905, the Secretary of the Interior approved the enrollment of your children Rufus Claude and Frederick Henry Ireton as citizens by blood of the Choctaw Nation.

Respectfully,

Commissioner.

Applications for Enrollment of Choctaw Newborn
Act of 1905   Volume XVI

Choc New Born 1160
   Charleyne Grant
   Born Oct. 13, 1904

BIRTH AFFIDAVIT.

DEPARTMENT OF THE INTERIOR.
COMMISSION TO THE FIVE CIVILIZED TRIBES.

IN RE APPLICATION FOR ENROLLMENT, as a citizen of the   Chocktaw[sic]   Nation, of   Charleyne Grant   , born on the   13th day of   October   , 1904

Name of Father: Charley M. Grant   a citizen of the   Chocktaw   Nation.
Name of Mother: Alice Grant   a citizen of the   Chocktaw   Nation.

Postoffice   Wynnewood, I.T.

AFFIDAVIT OF MOTHER.

UNITED STATES OF AMERICA, Indian Territory,
   Southern   DISTRICT.

I,   Alice Grant   , on oath state that I am   32   years of age and a citizen by intermarriage   , of the   Chocktaw   Nation; that I am the lawful wife of   Charley M. Grant   , who is a citizen, by blood   of the   Chocktaw   Nation; that a   Female   child was born to me on   13th day of   October   , 1904; that said child has been named   Charleyne Grant   , and was living March 4, 1905.

Alice Grant

Witnesses To Mark:
   Mrs J.N. Ivey
   (Name Illegible)

Subscribed and sworn to before me this   18th day of   April   , 1905

J L Stephens
   Notary Public.
   (Illegible)

Applications for Enrollment of Choctaw Newborn
Act of 1905   Volume XVI

AFFIDAVIT OF ATTENDING PHYSICIAN OR MID-WIFE.

UNITED STATES OF AMERICA, Indian Territory,
Southern   DISTRICT.

I,   G.W. Roberts   , a Physician   , on oath state that I attended on Mrs.   Alice Grant   , wife of   Charley M Grant   on the 13th day of October, 1904; that there was born to her on said date a   Female   child; that said child was living March 4, 1905, and is said to have been named   Charleyne Grant

Geo W Roberts M.D.

Witnesses To Mark:
{   Frank C. Robinson

Subscribed and sworn to before me this   April[sic]   day of   April   , 1905

Frank C. Robinson
Notary Public.

BIRTH AFFIDAVIT.

DEPARTMENT OF THE INTERIOR.
COMMISSION TO THE FIVE CIVILIZED TRIBES.

IN RE APPLICATION FOR ENROLLMENT, as a citizen of the   Choctaw   Nation, of   Charleyne Grant   , born on the   13th day of October   , 1904

Name of Father: Charley M. Grant   a citizen of the   Choctaw   Nation.
Name of Mother: Alice Grant   a citizen of the   Choctaw   Nation.

Postoffice   Wynnewood, Ind. Ter.

AFFIDAVIT OF ATTENDING PHYSICIAN OR MID-WIFE.

UNITED STATES OF AMERICA, Indian Territory,
Southern   DISTRICT.

I,   Geo W. Roberts   , a physician   , on oath state that I attended on Mrs.   Alice Grant   , wife of   Charley M Grant   on the 13th day of October, 1904; that there was born to her on said date a   female   child; that said child was living March 4, 1905, and is said to have been named   Charleyne Grant

Geo W Roberts M.D.

Witnesses To Mark:
{   Frank C. Robinson

Applications for Enrollment of Choctaw Newborn
Act of 1905 Volume XVI

Subscribed and sworn to before me this 7th day of June , 1905

                        Frank C. Robinson
                        Notary Public.

7-NB-1160.

Muskogee, Indian Territory, June 3, 1905.

Charley M. Grant,
    Wynnewood, Indian Territory.

Dear Sir:

    There is en closed herewith for execution affidavit of the attending physician, in the matter of the enrollment of your infant child, Charleyne Grant.

    The physician's affidavit heretofore filed in this office fails to show the date of execution. It will, therefore, be necessary that this affidavit be re-executed.

                Respectfully,

                            Commissioner in Charge.

VR 3-3.

7-NB 1160

Muskogee, Indian Territory, June 13, 1905.

Charley M. Grant,
    Wynnewood, Indian Territory.

Dear Sir:

    Receipt is hereby acknowledged of the affidavit of Geo. W. Roberts M. D. to the birth of Charleyne Grant, daughter of Charley M. and Alice Grant, October 13, 1904, and the same has been filed in the matter of the enrollment of said child.

                Respectfully,

                            Chairman.

Applications for Enrollment of Choctaw Newborn
Act of 1905 Volume XVI

Choc New Born 1161
    Elizabeth Scott
    (Born Dec. 16, 1902)

BIRTH AFFIDAVIT.

DEPARTMENT OF THE INTERIOR.
COMMISSION TO THE FIVE CIVILIZED TRIBES.

IN RE APPLICATION FOR ENROLLMENT, as a citizen of the Chocktaw[sic] Nation, of Elizebeth[sic] Scott, born on the 16 day of Dec, 1902

Name of Father: Chaplain Scott   a citizen of the Chocktaw Nation.
Name of Mother: Pheby Ethel Scott   a citizen of the Chocktaw Nation.

                Postoffice   Lebanon Ind Ter

AFFIDAVIT OF MOTHER.

UNITED STATES OF AMERICA, Indian Territory, }
   Sutherlstrict[sic]   DISTRICT. }

    I, Pheby Ethel Scott, on oath state that I am 21 years of age and a citizen by Blood, of the Chocktaw Nation; that I am the lawful wife of Chaplain, who is a citizen, by Intermarriage of the Chocktaw Nation; that a Female child was born to me on 16 day of December, 1902; that said child has been named Elizebeth Scott, and was living March 4, 1905.

                                  Pheby Ethel Scott

Witnesses To Mark:
  { J C Russell
    TL. Beeman

    Subscribed and sworn to before me this 16 day of April, 1905

(Seal)
My commission expires May 7 1907

                                    Jesse Turner
                                    Notary Public.

Applications for Enrollment of Choctaw Newborn
Act of 1905   Volume XVI

AFFIDAVIT OF ATTENDING PHYSICIAN OR MID-WIFE.

UNITED STATES OF AMERICA, Indian Territory, }
Southern   DISTRICT.

    I,   Rebeca Robbins   , a   mid wife   , on oath state that I attended on Mrs.   Pheby Ethel Scott   , wife of   Chaplain Scott   on the 16 day of   Dec , 1902; that there was born to her on said date a   Female   child; that said child was living March 4, 1905, and is said to have been named Elizebeth Scott

                                       her
                             Rebeca x Robbins
Witnesses To Mark: mark
  { LJ Robbins
    H L Loftis

    Subscribed and sworn to before me this 19   day of   April   , 1905

                          Jesse Turner
                                Notary Public.

BIRTH AFFIDAVIT.
DEPARTMENT OF THE INTERIOR.
COMMISSION TO THE FIVE CIVILIZED TRIBES.

    IN RE APPLICATION FOR ENROLLMENT, as a citizen of the   Choctaw   Nation, of Elizabeth Scott   , born on the   16 day of December , 1902

Name of Father: Chapling Scott   a citizen of the   Choctaw   Nation.
Name of Mother: Phebe Ethel Scott   a citizen of the   Choctaw   Nation.

                    Postoffice   Lebanon Ind Ter

AFFIDAVIT OF MOTHER.

UNITED STATES OF AMERICA, Indian Territory, }
Southern   DISTRICT.

    I,   Phebe Ethel Scott   , on oath state that I am   21   years of age and a citizen by   Blood   , of the   Choctaw   Nation; that I am the lawful wife of Chapling Scott   , who is a citizen, by Inter Marriage   of the   Choctaw   Nation; that a   Female   child was born to me on 16th   day of   December , 1902; that said child has been named   Elizabeth Scott   , and was living March 4, 1905.
                                     her
                           Phebe Ethel x Scott
                                  mark

Applications for Enrollment of Choctaw Newborn
Act of 1905   Volume XVI

Witnesses To Mark:
- J C Russell
- TL. Beeman

  Subscribed and sworn to before me this 19 day of April , 1905

         Jesse Turner
         Notary Public.

AFFIDAVIT OF ATTENDING PHYSICIAN OR MID-WIFE.

UNITED STATES OF AMERICA, Indian Territory,
 Southern   DISTRICT.

  I, Rebeca Robbins , a mid wife , on oath state that I attended on Mrs. Phebe Ethel Scott , wife of Chapling Scott on the 16 day of December , 1902; that there was born to her on said date a Female child; that said child was living March 4, 1905, and is said to have been named Elizabeth Scott

          her
        Rebeca x Robbins
Witnesses To Mark: mark
- Jack Robbins
- Tim Laufter

  Subscribed and sworn to before me this 19 day of April , 1905

         Jesse Turner
         Notary Public.

---

            7 NB 1161

     Muskogee, Indian Territory, May 5, 1905.
George A. Henshaw,
  Attorney at Law.
    Madill, Indian Territory.

Dear Sir:

  Receipt is hereby acknowledged of your letter of April 26, 1905, enclosing affidavits of Phebe Ethel Scott and Rebeca Robbins to the birth of Elizabeth Scott, daughter of Chapling and Phebe Ethel Scott, December 16, 1902, and the same have been filed with our records as an application for the enrollment of said child.

      Respectfully,
          Commissioner in Charge.

Applications for Enrollment of Choctaw Newborn
Act of 1905   Volume XVI

Choc New Born 1162
   Sinsie McKinney
   (Born Feb. 12, 1905)

BIRTH AFFIDAVIT.

DEPARTMENT OF THE INTERIOR.
COMMISSION TO THE FIVE CIVILIZED TRIBES.

IN RE APPLICATION FOR ENROLLMENT, as a citizen of the   Choctaw   Nation, of Sinsie McKinney   , born on the 12th day of February , 1905

Name of Father: Jackson McKinney   a citizen of the Choctaw   Nation.
Name of Mother: Cistin McKinney   a citizen of the Choctaw   Nation.

Postoffice

AFFIDAVIT OF MOTHER.

UNITED STATES OF AMERICA, Indian Territory,
   Central   DISTRICT.

I, Cistin McKinney   , on oath state that I am 27   years of age and a citizen by   blood   , of the   Choctaw   Nation; that I am the lawful wife of   Jackson McKinney   , who is a citizen, by blood   of the   Choctaw   Nation; that a female   child was born to me on 12th day of February   , 1905; that said child has been named   Sinsie McKinney   , and was living March 4, 1905.

                                                        her
                                              Cistin x McKinney
Witnesses To Mark: mark
   { Wright Anderson
     Simeon Going

Subscribed and sworn to before me this 12th day of June   , 1905

                              W.P. Wilson
                                   Notary Public.
         My commission expires Dec 1st 1905

Applications for Enrollment of Choctaw Newborn
Act of 1905   Volume XVI

AFFIDAVIT OF ATTENDING PHYSICIAN OR MID-WIFE.

UNITED STATES OF AMERICA, Indian Territory,
Central   DISTRICT.

I, Ardaline Tonehka , a midwife , on oath state that I attended on Mrs. Cistin McKinney , wife of Jackson McKinney on the 12th day of February , 1905; that there was born to her on said date a female child; that said child was living March 4, 1905, and is said to have been named Sinsie McKinney

                                                  her
Witnesses To Mark: Ardaline x Tonehka
                                    mark
{ Wright Anderson
  Simeon Going

Subscribed and sworn to before me this 12th day of June , 1905

                                       W.P. Wilson
                                            Notary Public.
My commission expires Dec 1st 1905

Birth Affidavit.

DEPARTMENT OF THE INTERIOR,
COMMISSION TO THE FIVE CIVILIZED TRIBES.

IN RE APPLICATION FOR ENROLLMENT, as a citizen of the Choctaw Nation, of Sinsie McKinney , born on the 12 day of February 1905

Name of Father: Jackson McKinney   a citizen of the Choctaw Nation.
Name of Mother: Cistin McKinney   a citizen of the Choctaw Nation.

                         Post Office   Lukfata, I.T.

AFFIDAVIT OF MOTHER.

UNITED STATES OF AMERICA,
INDIAN TERRITORY, | ss.
Central   DISTRICT.

I, Cistin McKinney , on oath state that I am 27 years of age and a citizen by blood of the Choctaw Nation Blood , of the Choctaw Nation; that I am lawful wife of Jackson McKinney , who is a citizen, by Blood of the Choctaw Nation; that a Female child was born to me on 12 day of February 1905 that said child has been named Sinsie McKinney , and was living March 4, 1905.

Applications for Enrollment of Choctaw Newborn
Act of 1905   Volume XVI

          Cistin McKinney

WITNESSES TO MARK:
 Lenas Wesley
 Simeon Going

Subscribed and sworn to before me this   17   day of   April   1905.

         W.P. Wilson
            Notary Public.

AFFIDAVIT OF ATTENDING PHYSICIAN OR MIDWIFE.

UNITED STATES OF AMERICA,
INDIAN TERRITORY, | ss.
 Central   DISTRICT.

  I,   Ardaline Tonehka   , a   midwife   , on oath state that I attended on Mrs.   Cistin McKinney   , wife of   Jackson McKinney   on the   12   day of   February   1905 that there was born to her on said date a   Female   child; that said child was living March 4, 1905, and is said to have been named   Sinsie McKinney

         Ardaline Tonehka

WITNESSES TO MARK:
 Lenas Wesley
 Simeon Going

Subscribed and sworn to before me this   17th   day of   April   1905.

         W.P. Wilson
            Notary Public.

            7-NB-1162/

      Muskogee, Indian Territory, June 3, 1905.

Jackson McKinney,
 Lukfata, Indian Territory.

Dear Sir:

  There is enclosed you herewith for execution application for the enrollment of your infant child, Sinsie McKinney, born February 12, 1905.
  In the application heretofore filed in this office it appears that W. P. Wilson, the Notary Public before whom the affidavits were executed, signed the name of Cistin

Applications for Enrollment of Choctaw Newborn
Act of 1905 Volume XVI

McKinney, the mother, Ardalin Tonihka, the midwife, and Lenas Wesley, one of the attesting witnesses. It will, therefore, be necessary that this application be re-executed.

In having these affidavits executed care should be exercised to see that all names are written in full, as they appear in the body of the affidavit. Persons who are able to write must sign the affidavits in their own hand, but in the event that either of the persons signing the affidavit are unable to write, signatures by mark must be attested by two witnesses who are able to write. Each affidavit must be executed before a Notary Public and the notarial seal and signature of the officer must be attached to each separate affidavit.

Respectfully,

Commissioner in Charge.

VR 3-2.

Choc New Born 1163
    Sallie Puryear Morgan
    (Born May 5, 1904)

BIRTH AFFIDAVIT.

DEPARTMENT OF THE INTERIOR.
COMMISSION TO THE FIVE CIVILIZED TRIBES.

IN RE APPLICATION FOR ENROLLMENT, as a citizen of the Choctaw Nation, of Sallie Puryear Morgan, born on the 5th day of May, 1904

Name of Father: Dick Morgan   a citizen of the Choctaw Nation.
Name of Mother: Lorena M Morgan   a citizen of the Choctaw Nation.

Postoffice   Durant I.T

AFFIDAVIT OF MOTHER.

UNITED STATES OF AMERICA, Indian Territory,
    Central   DISTRICT.

I, Lorena M Morgan, on oath state that I am thirty-three years of age and a citizen by blood, of the Choctaw Nation; that I am the lawful wife of Dick Morgan, who is a citizen, by marriage of the Choctaw Nation; that a female child was born to me on 5th day of May A.D., 1904; that said child has been named Sallie Puryear Morgan, and was living March 4, 1905.

Applications for Enrollment of Choctaw Newborn
Act of 1905   Volume XVI

Lorena M Morgan

Witnesses To Mark:
{

Subscribed and sworn to before me this 19 day of Apl , 1905

(Name Illegible)
Notary Public.

AFFIDAVIT OF ATTENDING PHYSICIAN OR MID-WIFE.

UNITED STATES OF AMERICA, Indian Territory,
Central   DISTRICT.

I, G.M. Rushing , a physician , on oath state that I attended on Mrs. Lorena M Morgan , wife of Dick Morgan on the 5 day of May , 1904; that there was born to her on said date a female child; that said child was living March 4, 1905, and is said to have been named Sallie Puryear Morgan

G.M. Rushing

Witnesses To Mark:
{

Subscribed and sworn to before me this 17 day of Apl , 1905

(Name Illegible)
Notary Public.

NEW-BORN AFFIDAVIT.

Number

Choctaw Enrolling Commission.

IN THE MATTER OF THE APPLICATION FOR ENROLLMENT, as a citizen of the Choctaw   Nation, of   Sallie Puryear Morgan

born on the fifth   day of   May   190 4

Name of father   Dick Morgan   a citizen of   Choctaw Nation
Nation final enrollment No   152

Name of mother   Lorena M Morgan   a citizen of   Choctaw Nation
Nation final enrollment No   9648

Applications for Enrollment of Choctaw Newborn
Act of 1905   Volume XVI

Postoffice

AFFIDAVIT OF MOTHER.

UNITED STATES OF AMERICA,
   INDIAN TERRITORY,
  Central   DISTRICT

I   Lorena M Morgan   on oath state that I am   Thirty-three   years of age and a citizen by   blood   of the   Choctaw   Nation, and as such have been placed upon the final roll of the   Choctaw   Nation, by the Honorable Secretary of the Interior my final enrollment number being   9648   ; that I am the lawful wife of   Dick Morgan   , who is a citizen of the   Choctaw   Nation, and as such has been placed upon the final roll of said Nation by the Honorable Secretary of the Interior, his final enrollment number being   152   and that a   Female   child was born to me on the   fifth   day of   May   190 2 ; that said child has been named   Sallie Puryear Morgan   , and is now living.

                                          Lorena M Morgan

WITNESSETH:
  Must be two
  Witnesses who   William M Harkin
  are Citizens.   E.E. Dyer

Subscribed and sworn to before me this   16   day of   January   190 5

                                    (Name Illegible)
                                           Notary Public.

My commission expires   Nov 18-1907

Affidavit of Attending Physician or Midwife.

UNITED STATES OF AMERICA
INDIAN TERRITORY
                DISTRICT

I,   _____ a _____ on oath state that I attended on Mrs.   Lorena M Morgan   wife of _____ on the   5   day of   May   , 190 4 , that there was born to her on said date a   Female   child, that said child is now living, and is said to have been named _____

                             GM Rushing   M.D.

Subscribed and sworn to before me this, the   16   day of   Jan   190 5

                                 James Bower
                                       Notary Public.

WITNESSETH:
  Must be two witnesses
  who are citizens and   William M Harkin

Applications for Enrollment of Choctaw Newborn
Act of 1905   Volume XVI

know the child.   E.E. Dyer

We hereby certify that we are well acquainted with ....
a .... and know .... to be reputable and of good standing in the community.

William M Harkin

E.E. Dyer

Choc New Born 1164
   Georgia E. Cullar
   (Born Nov. 4, 1903)

NEW BORN AFFIDAVIT

No ....

CHOCTAW ENROLLING COMMISSION

IN THE MATTER OF THE APPLICATION FOR ENROLLMENT as a citizen of the Choctaw Nation, of   Georgia Eugene Cullar   born on the 4th day of   November   190 3

Name of father J.C. Cullar   a citizen of ————   Nation, final enrollment No. ———   Cullar
Name of mother Birdie Carroll now   a citizen of   Choctaw   Nation, final enrollment No. 15267

Caddo I.T.   Postoffice.

AFFIDAVIT OF MOTHER

UNITED STATES OF AMERICA
   INDIAN TERRITORY
DISTRICT   Central

I   Birdie Carroll, now Cullar   , on oath state that I am   21   years of age and a citizen by   blood   of the   Choctaw   Nation, and as such have been placed upon the final roll of the   Choctaw   Nation, by the Honorable Secretary of the Interior my final enrollment number being 15267   ; that I am the lawful wife of   J.C. Cullar   , who is a citizen of the   ————   Nation, and as such has been placed upon the

Applications for Enrollment of Choctaw Newborn
Act of 1905   Volume XVI

final roll of said Nation by the Honorable Secretary of the Interior, his final enrollment number being ―― and that a Female child was born to me on the 4th day of November 190 3; that said child has been named Georgia Eugene Cullar , and is now living.

Birdie Carroll, now *Cullar*

WITNESSETH:
  Must be two witnesses { F. Manning
  who are citizens   { Laura Carroll
                          W T Smith

Subscribed and sworn to before me this, the 9th day of February , 190 5

A.E. Folsom
Notary Public.

My Commission Expires:
Jan 9 1909

Affidavit of Attending Physician or Midwife

UNITED STATES OF AMERICA, }
  INDIAN TERRITORY,
  Central   DISTRICT

I, W.J. Melton   a   Practicing Physician on oath state that I attended on Mrs. Birdie Carroll now Cullar   wife of J.C. Cullar on the 4th day of November , 190 3, that there was born to her on said date a Female child, that said child is now living, and is said to have been named Georgie Eugene Cullar

W.J. Melton   M. D.

Subscribed and sworn to before me this the 11th day of February 1905

A.E. Folsom
Notary Public.

WITNESSETH:
  Must be two witnesses   { W T Smith
  who are citizens and   { F Manning
  know the child.   Laura Carroll

We hereby certify that we are well acquainted with W.J. Melton a Physician and know him to be reputable and of good standing in the community.

F Manning
Must be two citizen { Laura Carroll
witnesses.   { W T Smith

Applications for Enrollment of Choctaw Newborn
Act of 1905   Volume XVI

DEPARTMENT OF THE INTERIOR,
Commission to the Five Civilized Tribes.
FILED
APR 21 1905
Tams Bixby CHAIRMAN.

No. 169

Certificate of Record of Marriages.

UNITED STATES OF AMERICA,
INDIAN TERRITORY,   SCT:
Central   DISTRICT.

I,   E.J. Fannin   , Clerk of the United States Court in the Indian Territory and District aforesaid, do hereby CERTIFY, that the License for and Certificate of the Marriage of

Mr.   J.C. Cullar   and

Miss   B.M. Carroll   was

filed in my office in said Territory and District the 5 day of February A.D., 190 3 and duly recorded in Book I of Marriage Record, Page 85

WITNESS my hand and seal of said Court, at   Durant   , this 5 day of   February   , A.D. 190 3

E.J. Fannin
Clerk.
By   WB Stone   *Deputy.*

No. 169   FORM NO. 598.

MARRIAGE LICENSE.

UNITES STATES OF AMERICA,
THE INDIAN TERRITORY,   ss:
Central   DISTRICT.

To any Person Authorized by Law to Solemnize Marriage—Greeting:

You are hereby commanded to solemnize the Rite and publish the Banns of Matrimony *between*
Mr.   J.C. Cullr   *of*   Caddo   *in the*

Applications for Enrollment of Choctaw Newborn
Act of 1905 Volume XVI

Indian Territory, aged 24 *years, and Miss* B.M. Carroll *of* Caddo *in the Indian Territory, aged* 19 *years, according to law, and do you officially sign and return this License to the parties therein named.*

WITNESS my hand and official seal, this 31 day of January A. D. 190 3

EJ Fannin
Clerk of the United States Court.
WB Stone   Deputy

CERTIFICATE OF MARRIAGE.

UNITES STATES OF AMERICA,
THE INDIAN TERRITORY, } ss: I, I.T. Underwood
..................DISTRICT.   a   Minister of the Gospel

do hereby CERTIFY, that on the 1st day of Feb. A, D. 190 3 ; I did duly and according to law, as commanded in the foregoing License, solemnize the Rite and publish the BANNS OF MATRIMONY between the parties therein named.

Witness my hand this 2nd day of Feb , A. D. 190 3

My credentials are recorded in the office of the Clerk of the United States Court in the Indian Territory, Central District, Book "B" Page 284

I.T. Underwood Pastor
First Baptist Church
Caddo I.T.

BIRTH AFFIDAVIT.

DEPARTMENT OF THE INTERIOR.
COMMISSION TO THE FIVE CIVILIZED TRIBES.

IN RE APPLICATION FOR ENROLLMENT, as a citizen of the Choctaw Nation, of Georgia E. Cullar , born on the 4th day of November , 1903

Name of Father: J. C. Cullar   a citizen of the Choctaw Nation.
Name of Mother: Birdie Cullar (nee Carroll)   a citizen of the Choctaw Nation.

Postoffice   Caddo Indian Territory

Applications for Enrollment of Choctaw Newborn
Act of 1905 Volume XVI

AFFIDAVIT OF MOTHER.

UNITED STATES OF AMERICA, Indian Territory, }
Central   DISTRICT.

I, Birdie Cullar (nee Carroll), on oath state that I am 21 years of age and a citizen by blood, of the Choctaw Nation; that I am the lawful wife of J. C. Cullar, who is a citizen, by marriage of the Choctaw Nation; that a Female child was born to me on 4th day of November, 1903; that said child has been named Georgia E. Cullar, and was living March 4, 1905.

                                  Birdie Cullar

Witnesses To Mark:

Subscribed and sworn to before me this 20th day of April, 1905

                                  JL Rappolee
                                  Notary Public.

AFFIDAVIT OF ATTENDING PHYSICIAN OR MID-WIFE.

UNITED STATES OF AMERICA, Indian Territory, }
Central   DISTRICT.

I, W. J. Melton, a Physician, on oath state that I attended on Mrs. Birdie Cullar (nee Carroll), wife of J. C. Cullar on the 4th day of November, 1903; that there was born to her on said date a Female child; that said child was living March 4, 1905, and is said to have been named Georgia E. Cullar

                                  W.J. Melton

Witnesses To Mark:

Subscribed and sworn to before me this 20th day of April, 1905

                                  JL Rappolee
                                  Notary Public.

7-3607

Applications for Enrollment of Choctaw Newborn
Act of 1905   Volume XVI

Muskogee, Indian Territory, April 25, 1905.

J. C. Cullar,
  Caddo, Indian Territory.

Dear Sir:

Receipt is hereby acknowledged of the affidavits of Birdie Cullar and W. J. Melton to the birth of Georgia E. Cullar, daughter of J. C. and Birdie Cullar (nee Carroll), November 4, 1903, and the same have been filed with the records of our office as an application for the enrollment of said child.

Receipt is also acknowledged of the license and certificate of marriage between J. C. Cullar and B. M. Carroll, and the same have been filed in the matter of the enrollment of said child.

Respectfully,

Chairman.

Choc New Born 1165
  Levenia Blue
  (Born April 15, 1903)

NEW BORN AFFIDAVIT

No ....

CHOCTAW ENROLLING COMMISSION

IN THE MATTER OF THE APPLICATION FOR ENROLLMENT as a citizen of the Choctaw Nation, of   Levina Blue   born on the 15 day of   April   190 3

Name of father   Willy Blue   a citizen of   Choctaw   Nation, final enrollment No. 8816
Name of mother   Melvina Blue   a citizen of   Choctaw   Nation, final enrollment No. 8817

Bengal I.T.   Postoffice.

Applications for Enrollment of Choctaw Newborn
Act of 1905 Volume XVI

AFFIDAVIT OF MOTHER

UNITED STATES OF AMERICA
INDIAN TERRITORY
DISTRICT   Central

I   Melvina Blue   , on oath state that I am   25   years of age and a citizen by   blood   of the   Choctaw   Nation, and as such have been placed upon the final roll of the   Choctaw   Nation, by the Honorable Secretary of the Interior my final enrollment number being   8817   ; that I am the lawful wife of   Willy Blue   , who is a citizen of the   Choctaw   Nation, and as such has been placed upon the final roll of said Nation by the Honorable Secretary of the Interior, his final enrollment number being   8816   and that a   Female   child was born to me on the   15   day of   April   190 3; that said child has been named   Levina Blue   , and is now living.

WITNESSETH: Melvina Blue
Must be two witnesses { Joseph Leflore
who are citizens   { Ned Sockey

Subscribed and sworn to before me this, the   17   day of   February   , 190 5

James Bower
Notary Public.

My Commission Expires:
Sept 23 - 1909

Affidavit of Attending Physician or Midwife

UNITED STATES OF AMERICA,
INDIAN TERRITORY,
Central   DISTRICT

I,   Selina Leflore   a   Midwife
on oath state that I attended on Mrs. Melvina Blue   wife of Willie[sic] Blue
on the   15   day of   April   , 190 3, that there was born to her on said date a   Female
child, that said child is now living, and is said to have been named   Levina Blue

          her
        Selina x Leflore   M. D.
          mark
Subscribed and sworn to before me this the   17   day of   Feb   1905

James Bower
Notary Public.

WITNESSETH:
Must be two witnesses { Joseph Leflore

Applications for Enrollment of Choctaw Newborn
Act of 1905   Volume XVI

who are citizens and know the child.   Ned Sockey

We hereby certify that we are well acquainted with   Selina Leflore   a   midwife   and know   her   to be reputable and of good standing in the community.

Must be two citizen witnesses. { Joseph Leflore
Ned Sockey

BIRTH AFFIDAVIT.

DEPARTMENT OF THE INTERIOR.
COMMISSION TO THE FIVE CIVILIZED TRIBES.

IN RE APPLICATION FOR ENROLLMENT, as a citizen of the   Choctaw   Nation, of   Levenia Blue   , born on the 15   day of   April   , 1903

Name of Father: Willy Blue   a citizen of the   Choctaw   Nation.
Name of Mother: Melvina Blue   a citizen of the   Choctaw   Nation.

Postoffice   Bengal I.T.

AFFIDAVIT OF MOTHER.

UNITED STATES OF AMERICA, Indian Territory,
Central   DISTRICT.

I,   Melvina Blue   , on oath state that I am   Twenty-five   years of age and a citizen by   blood   , of the   Choctaw   Nation; that I am the lawful wife of   Willy Blue   , who is a citizen, by   blood   of the   Choctaw   Nation; that a   female   child was born to me on   15   day of   April   , 1903; that said child has been named   Levenia Blue   , and was living March 4, 1905.

Melvina Blue

Witnesses To Mark:
{

Subscribed and sworn to before me this   19   day of   April   , 1905

My Com Exp 7/8/08   W L Harris
Notary Public.

AFFIDAVIT OF ATTENDING PHYSICIAN OR MID-WIFE.

Applications for Enrollment of Choctaw Newborn
Act of 1905   Volume XVI

UNITED STATES OF AMERICA, Indian Territory,
Central   DISTRICT.

    I, Selina Leflore, a ...., on oath state that I attended on Mrs. Melvina Blue, wife of Willy Blue on the 15 day of April, 1905; that there was born to her on said date a female child; that said child was living March 4, 1905, and is said to have been named Levenia Blue

                                her
Witnesses To Mark: Selina x Leflore
   C.L. Holcomb   mark
   W.S Harris

    Subscribed and sworn to before me this 19 day of April, 1905

My Com Exp 7/8/08   W L Harris
                          Notary Public.

                                7-3010

        Muskogee, Indian Territory, April 25, 1905.

Willie Blue,
    Bengal, Indian Territory.

Dear Sir:

    Receipt is hereby acknowledged of the affidavits of Melvina Blue and Selina LeFlore to the birth of Levenia Blue, Indian Territory daughter of Willy and Melvina Blue, April 15, 1903, and the same have been filed with our records as an application for the enrollment of said child.

                        Respectfully,

                                     Chairman.

Substitute

7 NB 1165

Applications for Enrollment of Choctaw Newborn
Act of 1905   Volume XVI

Muskogee, Indian Territory, July 22, 1905.

Willie Blue,
    Bengal, Indian Territory.

Dear Sir:

Receipt is hereby acknowledged of your letter of July 17, asking in regard to the selection of an allotment for your child, Levenia Blue.

In reply to your letter you are advised that the name of your child, Levenia Blue, has been placed upon a schedule of citizens by blood of the Choctaw Nation, which has been forwarded to the Secretary of the Interior, and you will be notified when her enrollment is approved by the Department. Until the approval of her enrollment, however, no selection of allotment can be made in her behalf.

Respectfully,

Commissioner.

Choc New Born 1166
    Mary Ann Graham
    (Born Dec 12, 1902)

BIRTH AFFIDAVIT.
DEPARTMENT OF THE INTERIOR.
COMMISSION TO THE FIVE CIVILIZED TRIBES.

IN RE APPLICATION FOR ENROLLMENT, as a citizen of the   Choctaw   Nation, of Mary Ann Graham   , born on the   12 day of December , 1902

Name of Father: Thomas Graham   a citizen of the Choctaw Nation.
Name of Mother: Motsey Graham   a citizen of the Choctaw Nation.

Postoffice   Muse I.T.

E. P. Pitchlynn Interpreter

AFFIDAVIT OF MOTHER.

UNITED STATES OF AMERICA, Indian Territory,

Applications for Enrollment of Choctaw Newborn
Act of 1905   Volume XVI

Central   **DISTRICT.**

I, Motsey Graham, on oath state that I am about 45 years of age and a citizen by Blood, of the Choctaw Nation; that I am the lawful wife of Thomas Graham, who is a citizen, by Blood of the Choctaw Nation; that a female child was born to me on 12 day of December, 1902; that said child has been named Mary Ann Graham, and was living March 4, 1905.

                her
          Motsey x Graham

Witnesses To Mark: mark
{ E P Pitchlynn
{ D. Thomas

Subscribed and sworn to before me this 19 day of April, 1905

          Sam T Roberts
          Notary Public.

No midwife attended by Husband

7-2119

Applications for Enrollment of Choctaw Newborn
Act of 1905   Volume XVI

Muskogee, Indian Territory, April 25, 1905.

Thomas Graham,
 News[sic], Indian Territory.

Dear Sir:

Receipt is hereby acknowledged of the affidavits of Motsey Graham, Sarah Anderson and E. P. Pitchlynn to the birth of M[sic] Mary Ann Graham, daughter of Thomas and Motsey Graham, December 12, 1902, and the same have been filed with our records as an application for the enrollment of said child.

Receipt is also acknowledged of your affidavit and the affidavit of Deliah White to the death of your son, Hardy Graham, a citizen by blood of the Choctaw Nation, which occurred May 9, 1902, and the same have been filed with our records as proof of death of the above named person.

Respectfully,

Chairman.

7--NB--1166

Muskogee, Indian Territory, June 2, 1905.

Thomas Graham,
 Muse, Indian Territory.

Dear Sir:

Referring to the application for the enrollment of your infant child, Mary Ann Graham, born December 12, 1902, it is noted from the affidavits heretofore filed in this office that you were the only one in attendance upon your wife at the time of the birth of the applicant.

In this event it will be necessary that the affidavits of two persons, who are disinterested and not related to the applicant, who have actual knowledge of the facts that the child was born, the date of her birth; that she was living on March 4, 1905, and that Motsey Graham is her mother be filed in this office.

The affidavit of Sarah Anderson and Ellington P. Pitchlynn heretofore filed in the matter of the application for the enrollment of this applicant do not show the date of birth. It will, therefore, be necessary that you secure the affidavits of two persons to these facts.

Applications for Enrollment of Choctaw Newborn
Act of 1905   Volume XVI

This matter should receive your immediate attention as no further action can be taken relative to the enrollment of your said child until the Commission is furnished with these affidavits.

Respectfully,

[sic]

7-NB-1166

Muskogee, Indian Territory, July 26, 1905.

Thomas Graham,
  Muse, Indian Territory.

Dear Sir:

Receipt is hereby acknowledged of the affidavits of E. P. Pitchlynn and Sarah Anderson, executed April 19, 1905, before Sam T. Roberts, which you offer in support of the application for the enrollment of your infant child, Mary Ann Graham, born December 12, 1902.

The same are returned to you herewith for the reason that they are deficient in that they do not show the date of birth of the applicant.

You are requested to supply the affidavits of two disinterested persons who are not related to the applicant, and who have actual knowledge of the facts, that Mary Ann Graham was born, the date of her birth, that she was living March 4, 1905, and that Motsey Graham is her mother.

This matter should have your immediate attention, as no further action can be taken relative to the enrollment of your said child until the evidence requested has been supplied.

Respectfully,

LM 26/2   Commissioner.

Applications for Enrollment of Choctaw Newborn
Act of 1905 Volume XVI

7-NB-1166

Muskogee, Indian Territory, August 23, 1905.

John J. Thomas,
    Talihina, Indian Territory.

Dear Sir:

    Receipt is hereby acknowledged of the affidavits of Benjamin Willis and B. J. Woods to the birth of Mary Ann Graham daughter of Thomas and Motsy[sic] Graham, December 12, 1902, and the same have been filed with the records of this office in the matter of the enrollment of said child.

                    Respectfully,

                                  Commissioner.

(The affidavit below typed as given.)

UNITED STATES OF America,) ss.
Central District, Ind Ter,)

    Benjamin Willis comes upon oath and states as follows.I reside near Talihina,I am 40 years old, I am acquainted with Thomas Graham and his wife, Motsey Graham.I know that on December 12th 1902 there was a Female child born to Motsy Graham,that said child was living on March 4th 1905,that I am not related to either of the Faher or Mother and that I am not interested in the prosecution of this claim.

                                    Benjamin Willis

Subscribed and sworn to before me this 19th day of August 1905.

                                    Jno J Thomas
Mycommission expires Mch 30th 1909.

(The affidavit below typed as given.)

United States of America) ss.
ntral District,Ind Ter.)

    B J woods comes upon oath and makes the following statement.I reside near Talihina,I am 64 Years old.I am acquainted with Thomas Graham and his wife,Motsy Graham,I know that there was a Female child born to them on December 12th 1902 and that said Child was named Mary Ann Graham, that said child was living on March 4th

Applications for Enrollment of Choctaw Newborn
Act of 1905   Volume XVI

1905,that I am not related to either of the claimants nor am I interested in the prsecution of this claim.

B J Woods

Subscribed and sworn to before me this the 19th day August 1905.

Jno J Thomas

My commission expires Mch 30th 1909.

Choc New Born 1167
    Maude Kathryn Semple
    (Born Aug. 6, 1904)

NEW BORN AFFIDAVIT

No

CHOCTAW ENROLLING COMMISSION

IN THE MATTER OF THE APPLICATION FOR ENROLLMENT as a citizen of the Choctaw Nation, of Maude K Semple born on the 6th day of August 190 4

Name of father Frank P. Semple a citizen of Choctaw Nation, final enrollment No. 13540
Name of mother Hellen Mae Semple a citizen of Choctaw Nation, final enrollment No. 595

Caddo I.T. Postoffice.

AFFIDAVIT OF MOTHER

UNITED STATES OF AMERICA
    INDIAN TERRITORY
DISTRICT   Central

I Hellen Mae Semple , on oath state that I am 24 years of age and a citizen by Intermarriage of the Choctaw Nation, and as such have been placed upon the final roll of the Choctaw Nation, by the Honorable Secretary of the

Applications for Enrollment of Choctaw Newborn
Act of 1905   Volume XVI

Interior my final enrollment number being 595 ; that I am the lawful wife of Frank P Semple , who is a citizen of the Choctaw Nation, and as such has been placed upon the final roll of said Nation by the Honorable Secretary of the Interior, his final enrollment number being 13540 and that a Female child was born to me on the 6th day of August 190 4; that said child has been named Maud[sic] K Semple , and is now living.

Helen[sic] Mae Semple

WITNESSETH:
Must be two witnesses who are citizens { Finis Ewing Folsom
Rhoda F Morris

Subscribed and sworn to before me this, the 9th day of February , 190 5

A.E. Folsom
Notary Public.

My Commission Expires:
Jan 9-1909

Affidavit of Attending Physician or Midwife

UNITED STATES OF AMERICA,
INDIAN TERRITORY,
Central   DISTRICT

I, Bettie Guess a Mid Wife on oath state that I attended on Mrs. Hellen Mae Semple wife of Frank P. Semple on the 6th day of August , 190 4, that there was born to her on said date a Female child, that said child is now living, and is said to have been named Maud K Semple

Bettie Guess   M. D.

Subscribed and sworn to before me this the 14th day of February 1905

A E Folsom
Notary Public.

WITNESSETH:
Must be two witnesses who are citizens and know the child. { Finis Ewing Folsom
Rhoda F. Morris

We hereby certify that we are well acquainted with Bettie Guess a Mid Wife and know her to be reputable and of good standing in the community.

Exp
Jan 9-1909

Must be two citizen witnesses. { Finis Ewing Folsom
Rhoda F Morris

Applications for Enrollment of Choctaw Newborn
Act of 1905   Volume XVI

BIRTH AFFIDAVIT.

DEPARTMENT OF THE INTERIOR.
COMMISSION TO THE FIVE CIVILIZED TRIBES.

IN RE APPLICATION FOR ENROLLMENT, as a citizen of the   Choctaw   Nation, of   Maude Kathryn Semple   , born on the 6th day of August , 1904

Name of Father: Frank P Semple   a citizen of the Choctaw Nation.
Name of Mother: Helen Mae Semple   a citizen of the Choctaw Nation.

Postoffice   Caddo Ind. Ter.

AFFIDAVIT OF MOTHER.

UNITED STATES OF AMERICA, Indian Territory,
Central   DISTRICT.

I, Helen Mae Semple , on oath state that I am 24 years of age and a citizen by Intermarriage , of the Choctaw Nation; that I am the lawful wife of Frank P. Semple , who is a citizen, by blood of the Choctaw Nation; that a female child was born to me on 6th day of August , 1904; that said child has been named Maude Kathryn Semple , and was living March 4, 1905.

Helen Mae Semple

Witnesses To Mark:
{

Subscribed and sworn to before me this 20th day of April , 1905

Sol. J. Homer
Notary Public.

AFFIDAVIT OF ATTENDING PHYSICIAN OR MID-WIFE.

UNITED STATES OF AMERICA, Indian Territory,
Central   DISTRICT.

I, Bettie Guess , a Mid Wife , on oath state that I attended on Mrs. Hellen Mae Semple , wife of Frank P. Semple on the 6th day of August , 1904; that there was born to her on said date a Female child; that said child was living March 4, 1905, and is said to have been named Maud Kathryn Semple

Bettie Guess

Applications for Enrollment of Choctaw Newborn
Act of 1905   Volume XVI

Witnesses To Mark:
{

Subscribed and sworn to before me this 19 day of April , 1905

B F Maddox
Notary Public.

My com exp 24 Feb 1909

7-5346

Muskogee, Indian Territory, April 25, 1905.

Frank P. Semple,
    Caddo, Indian Territory.

Dear Sir:

Receipt is hereby acknowledged of the affidavits of Helen Mae Semple and Bettie Guess to the birth of Maude Kathryn Semple, daughter of Frank P. and Helen Mae Semple, August 6, 1904, and the same have been filed with our records as an application for the enrollment of said child.

Respectfully,

Chairman.

Choc New Born 1168
    Fabie Sharkey
    (Born Dec. 29, 1904)
    Thomas Sharkey
    (Born Feb. 4, 1903)

No. 1. dismissed - June 28, 1905
No. 2. dismissed - Oct. 6, 1905

Applications for Enrollment of Choctaw Newborn
Act of 1905   Volume XVI

DEPARTMENT OF THE INTERIOR,
COMMISSION TO THE FIVE CIVILIZED TRIBES.

Record in the matter of the application for enrollment as a citizen by blood of the Choctaw Nation of:

        FABIE SHARKEY   7-NB-1168.

BIRTH AFFIDAVIT.

DEPARTMENT OF THE INTERIOR.
COMMISSION TO THE FIVE CIVILIZED TRIBES.

IN RE APPLICATION FOR ENROLLMENT, as a citizen of the   Choctaw   Nation, of   Fabie Sharkey   , born on the   29   day of   December   , 1904

Name of Father: Isreal Sharkey   a citizen of the   Choctaw   Nation.
Name of Mother: Luiza Sharkey   a citizen of the   Choctaw   Nation.

        Postoffice   Caney I.T.

AFFIDAVIT OF MOTHER.

UNITED STATES OF AMERICA, Indian Territory,
    Central   DISTRICT.

I,   Lueza[sic] Sharkey   , on oath state that I am   24   years of age and a citizen by   blood   , of the   Choctaw   Nation; that I am the lawful wife of   Isreal Sharkey   , who is a citizen, by blood   of the   Choctaw   Nation; that a   Female   child was born to me on   29   day of   December   , 1904; that said child has been named   Fabie Sharkey   , and was living March 4, 1905.

                Louisa Sharkey

Witnesses To Mark:

Subscribed and sworn to before me this   8   day of   April   , 1905

                A Denton Phillips
                Notary Public.

Applications for Enrollment of Choctaw Newborn
Act of 1905   Volume XVI

AFFIDAVIT OF ATTENDING PHYSICIAN OR MID-WIFE.

UNITED STATES OF AMERICA, Indian Territory,
Central   DISTRICT.

 I, Siney Robinson, a midwife, on oath state that I attended on Mrs. Luiza Sharkey, wife of Isreal Sharkey on the 29 day of December, 1904; that there was born to her on said date a Female child; that said child was living March 4, 1905, and is said to have been named Fabie Sharkey

            her
          Siney x Robinson
Witnesses To Mark: mark
 { A Denton Phillips
   Wallace Robinson

 Subscribed and sworn to before me this 8 day of April, 1905

         A Denton Phillips
          Notary Public.

7-NB-1168.

DEPARTMENT OF THE INTERIOR,
COMMISSION TO THE FIVE CIVILIZED TRIBES.
CHOCTAW LAND OFFICE.

Atoka, Indian Territory, June 15, 1905.

 In the matter of the enrollment of infant child, Fabie Sharkey.

 Louisa[sic] Sharkey, being first duly sworn, testified as follows:-

   EXAMINATION BY THE COMMISSION.

 James Culberson, official interpreter.

Q What is your name ?
A Louisa Sharkey.
Q What is your postoffice address ?
A Caney.
Q What is the name of your father ?
A Eastman Tehumba.
Q How old are you ?
A 24.
Q Are you a full blood Choctaw ?
A Yes, sir.

Applications for Enrollment of Choctaw Newborn
Act of 1905   Volume XVI

Q Are you married ?
A Yes, sir.
Q What is the name of your husband ?
A Israel Sharkey.
Q Is your husband a full blood Choctaw ?
A Yes, sir.
Q Did you on April 8, 1905, before A. Denton Phillips, a notary public, execute an affidavit to the birth of your child, Fabie Sharkey, born December 29, 1904 ?
A Yes, sir.
Q Is this child living at this time ?
A No, sir.
Q When did it die ?
A January, 1905.
Q This last January ?
A Yes, sir.
Q Was the child a male or a female ?
A Girl.
Q In this affidavit that you executed on April 8, 1905, you allege that this child was living on March 4, 1905; did you tell the notary public that this child was living at that time ?
A No, sir.
Q Did you tell him the child was dead ?
A Yes, sir.
Q And that it died in January, 1905 ?
A Yes, sir.
Q What day in January did the child die ?
A First day of the year.
Q New Years day ?
A Yes, sir.
Q Who attended you at the birth of this child ?
A Siney Robinson.
Q She went before A. Denton Phillips and made an affidavit at the same time ?
A Yes, sir.
Q In her affidavit she alleges that Fabie Sharkey was living on the 4th day of March, 1905,-did she tell him she was living on March 4, 1905 ?
A No, sir.
Q Did she tell him that she was dead on January 1, 1905 ?
A Yes, sir.
Q The allegations in these affidavits that your child, Fabie Sharkey, was living on March 4, 1905, are incorrect ?
A Yes, sir.
Q And Fabie Sharkey died on January 1, 1905 ?
A Yes sir.
Q When was Fabie Sharkey born ?
A December 29, 1904.
Q Just lived three days ?
A Yes, sir.

Applications for Enrollment of Choctaw Newborn
Act of 1905   Volume XVI

Israel Sharkey, being first duly sworn, testified as follow:-

Q What is your name ?
A Israel Sharkey.
Q What is your postoffice address ?
A Caney.
Q How old are you ?
A 56.
Q Are you a full blood Choctaw ?
A Yes, sir.
Q What is the name of your father ?
A Sharkey.
Q What is the name of your mother ?
A Lettie.
Q Are you married ?
A Yes, sir.
Q What is your wife's name ?
A Louisa.
Q Are you the father of Fabie Sharkey who was born December 29, 1904 ?
A Yes, sir.
Q Is Fabie Sharkey living at this time ?
A No, sir.
Q When did Fabie Sharkey die ?
A First day of January, 1905.
Q Louisa Sharkey, your wife, appeared before a notary public on April 8, 1905, and made affidavit that she was your wife and the mother of Fabie Sharkey, born December 29, 1904, and that Fabie Sharkey was living on March 4, 1904,- you know anything about that ?
A No, sir.
Q Fabie Sharkey only lived about three days after its birth ?
A Yes, sir.
Q Did you have an infant child living on March 4, 1905 ?
A No, sir.

Wm. L. Martin, stenographer to the Commission to the Five Civilized Tribes, upon oath states that the above and foregoing is a full, true and correct transcript of his stenographic notes taken in said cause on said date.

W^{m}LMartin

Subscribed and sworn to before me this the 19th day of June, 1905.

W.H. Angell
Notary Public.

Applications for Enrollment of Choctaw Newborn
Act of 1905   Volume XVI

W.J.
7-NB-1168.

DEPARTMENT OF THE INTERIOR,
COMMISSION TO THE FIVE CIVILIZED TRIBES.

In the matter of the application for the enrollment of Fabie Sharkey as a citizen by blood of the Choctaw Nation.

---oOo---

It appears from the record herein that on April 26, 1905, there was filed with the Commission application for the enrollment of Fabie Sharkey as a citizen by blood of the Choctaw Nation.

It further appears from the record herein and the records of the Commission that the applicant was born December 29, 1904; that she is a daughter of Israel Sharkey and Louisa Sharkey, recognized and enrolled citizens by blood of the Choctaw Nation whose names appear opposite numbers 10889 and 10890, respectively, upon the final roll of citizens by blood of the Choctaw Nation, approved by the Secretary of the Interior February 4, 1903; and that said applicant died prior to March 4, 1905.

The Act of Congress approved March 3, 1905 (Public No. 212) among other things provides:

"That the Commission to the Five Civilized Tribes is authorized for sixty days after the date of the approval of this act to receive and consider applications for enrollment of children born subsequent to September twenty-fifth, nineteen hundred and two, and prior to March fourth, nineteen hundred and five, and who were living on said latter date, to citizens by blood of the Choctaw and Chickasaw tribes of Indians whose enrollment has been approved by the Secretary of the Interior prior to the date of the approval of this act; and to enroll and make allotments to such children."

It is, therefore, hereby ordered that the application for the enrollment of Fabie Sharkey as a citizen by blood of the Choctaw Nation be dismissed in accordance with the order of the Commission of March 31, 1905.

COMMISSION TO THE FIVE CIVILIZED TRIBES,

Tams Bixby
Chairman.

Muskogee, Indian Territory.
JUN 28 1905

Applications for Enrollment of Choctaw Newborn
Act of 1905 Volume XVI

7-NB-1168.

Muskogee, Indian Territory, June 28, 1905.

Isreal Sharkey, **COPY.**
    Caney, Indian Territory.

Dear Sir:

    Inclosed herewith you will find a copy of the order of this Commission, dated June 28, 1905, dismissing the application for the enrollment of Fabie Sharkey as a citizen by blood of the Choctaw Nation.

Respectfully,

SIGNED

Tams Bixby
Registered. Chairman.
Incl. 7-NB-1168.

7-NB-1168.

Muskogee, Indian Territory, June 28, 1905.

Mansfield, McMurray & Cornish, **COPY.**
    Attorneys for Choctaw and Chickasaw Nations,
        South McAlester, Indian Territory.

Gentlemen:

    Inclosed herewith you will find a copy of the order of this Commission, dated June 28, 1905, dismissing the application for the enrollment of Fabie Sharkey as a citizen by blood of the Choctaw Nation.

Respectfully,

SIGNED

Tams Bixby
Incl. 7-NB-1168. Chairman.

Applications for Enrollment of Choctaw Newborn
Act of 1905 Volume XVI

DEPARTMENT OF THE INTERIOR,
COMMISSION TO THE FIVE CIVILIZED TRIBES.

Record in the matter of the application for enrollment as a citizen by blood of the Choctaw Nation of:

THOMAS SHARKEY   7-NB-1168.

BIRTH AFFIDAVIT.

DEPARTMENT OF THE INTERIOR.
COMMISSION TO THE FIVE CIVILIZED TRIBES.

IN RE APPLICATION FOR ENROLLMENT, as a citizen of the   Choctaw   Nation, of Thomas Sharkey   , born on the 4 day of February , 1903

Name of Father: Isreal Sharkey   a citizen of the   Choctaw   Nation.
Name of Mother: Luiza Sharkey   a citizen of the   Choctaw   Nation.

Postoffice   Caney Ind Ter

AFFIDAVIT OF MOTHER.

UNITED STATES OF AMERICA, Indian Territory,
    Central   DISTRICT.

I, Luiza Sharkey , on oath state that I am 24 years of age and a citizen by blood , of the Choctaw Nation; that I am the lawful wife of Isreal Sharkey , who is a citizen, by blood of the Choctaw Nation; that a Male child was born to me on 4 day of February , 1903; that said child has been named Thomas Sharkey , and ~~was living~~ March 4, 1905. *died about February 24 1903*[sic]

                                Louisa Sharkey
Witnesses To Mark:
{
    Subscribed and sworn to before me this 8 day of April , 1905

                                A Denton Phillips
                                Notary Public.

Applications for Enrollment of Choctaw Newborn
Act of 1905 Volume XVI

AFFIDAVIT OF ATTENDING PHYSICIAN OR MID-WIFE.

UNITED STATES OF AMERICA, Indian Territory, }
Central   DISTRICT. }

I, Mary Wilson , a Midwife , on oath state that I attended on Mrs. Luiza Sharkey , wife of Isreal Sharkey on the 4 day of February, 1903; that there was born to her on said date a male child; that said child ~~was living March 4, 1905~~, *died about February 24-1905*[sic] and is said to have been named Thomas Sharkey

Mary Wilson

Witnesses To Mark:
{

Subscribed and sworn to before me this 8 day of April , 1905

A Denton Phillips
Notary Public.

7-NB-1168.

DEPARTMENT OF THE INTERIOR,
COMMISSION TO THE FIVE CIVILIZED TRIBES.
CHOCTAW LAND OFFICE.
---:---
Atoka, Indian Territory, June 15, 1905.
---:---

In the matter of the enrollment of infant child, Thomas Sharkey.

Louisa[sic] Sharkey, being first duly sworn, testified as follows:-

EXAMINATION BY THE COMMISSION.

Q What is your name ?
A Louisa Sharkey.
Q What is your postoffice address ?
A Caney.
Q What is the name of your father ?
A Eastman Tehumba.
Q How old are you ?
A 24.
Q Are you a full blood Choctaw ?
A Yes, sir.

Applications for Enrollment of Choctaw Newborn
Act of 1905   Volume XVI

Q Are you married ?
A Yes, sir.
Q What is the name of your husband ?
A Israel Sharkey.
Q Is your husband a full blood Choctaw ?
A Yes, sir.
Q Did you on April 8, 1905, before A. Denton Phillips, a notary public, execute an affidavit to the birth of your child, Thomas Sharkey ?
A Yes, sir.
Q When was Thomas Sharkey born ?
A 1902.
Q What month ?
A February.
Q What day ?
A February 4, 1902.
Q Is Thomas Sharkey living now ?
A No, sir.
Q When did he die ?
A He lived about two weeks.
Q He would have died then about the 18th or 20th of February, 1902 ?
A Yes, sir.
Q In your affidavit that you made before A. Denton Phillips, you allege that Thomas Sharkey, your child, was born on February 3, 1903, and that he died on February 24, 1903: are these dates incorrect and he was born on the 4th day of February, 1902, and died about two weeks afterwards ?
A Yes, sir.
Q Thomas Sharkey was not living on March 4, 1905, then, was he ?
A No, sir.
Q Who attended you at the birth of Thomas Sharkey ?
A Mary Wilson.
Q At the time you went before this notary public did Mary Wilson go with you and make the same affidavit ?
A Yes, sir.
Q And the correct dates are that he was born on February 4, 1902, and died about two weeks afterwards ?
A Yes, sir.
Q And was not living on March 4, 1905 ?
A No, sir.

Israel Sharkey, being first duly sworn, testified as follow:-

Q What is your name ?
A Israel Sharkey.
Q What is your postoffice address ?
A Caney.
Q How old are you ?
A 56.

Applications for Enrollment of Choctaw Newborn
Act of 1905   Volume XVI

Q Are you a full blood Choctaw ?
A Yes, sir.
Q What is the name of your father ?
A Sharkey.
Q What is the name of your mother ?
A Lettie.
Q Are you married ?
A Yes, sir.
Q What is your wife's name ?
A Louisa.
Q Are you the father of Thomas Sharkey ?
A Yes, sir.
Q When was Thomas Sharkey born ?
A 1903.
Q What day and what month ?
A February; I have forgotten, but I think February 3rd.
Q Your wife, Louisa Sharkey, testified that Thomas Sharkey was born on the 4th day of February, 1903, and you say he was born on the 3rd day of February, 1902; which is the correct date?
A I said 1903.
Q But your wife said 1902 ?
A I suppose I made a mistake.
Q You think your wife would know more about the correct date than you do ?
A Yes, sir; I think she would know more about it.
Q Is Thomas Sharkey living now ?
A No, sir.
Q When did he die ?
A I think he died 10th of February.
Q Sam year he was born ?
A Yes, sir.
Q How long did he live; how many days ?
A About 8 days, I think.?[sic]
Q You had no child living on the 4th day of March, 1905 ?
A No, sir.

Wm. L. Martin, stenographer to the Commission to the Five Civilized Tribes, upon oath states that the above and foregoing is a full, true and correct transcript of his stenographic notes taken in said cause on said date.

W^m L Martin

Subscribed and sworn to before me this the 19th day of June, 1905.

W.H. Angell
Notary Public.

Applications for Enrollment of Choctaw Newborn
Act of 1905   Volume XVI

W.F.
7-NB-1168.

DEPARTMENT OF THE INTERIOR,
COMMISSIONER TO THE FIVE CIVILIZED TRIBES.

In the matter of the application for the enrollment of Thomas Sharkey as a citizen by blood of the Choctaw Nation.

----oOo----

It appears from the record herein that on April 21, 1905 there was filed with the Commission to the Five Civilized Tribes application for the enrollment of Thomas Sharkey as a citizen by blood of the Choctaw Nation.

It appears from said application filed on April 21, 1905 that the applicant, Thomas Sharkey, was born February 4, 1903; that he is a son of Israel Sharkey and Louisa Sharkey, recognized and enrolled citizens by blood of the Choctaw Nation whose names apear opposite numbers 10889 and 10890, respectively, upon the final roll of citizens by blood of the Choctaw Nation, approved by the Secretary of the Interior February 4, 1903, and that said applicant died on February 24, 1903. However, on June 15, 1905 said Israel Sharkey and Louisa Sharkey, parents of the applicant herein, appeared before the Commission to the Five Civilized Tribes and from their testimony taken on that date it appears that the date of birth of said applicant as given in said application filed on April 21, 1905 is incorrect and that in fact said applicant was born on February 4, 1902 and died about two weeks thereafter.

The Act of Congress approved March 3, 1905 (Public No. 212) among other things provides:

"That the Commission to the Five Civilized Tribes is authorized for sixty days after the date of the approval of this act to receive and consider applications for enrollment of children born subsequent to September twenty-fifth, nineteen hundred and two, and prior to March fourth, nineteen hundred and five, and who were living on said latter date, to citizens by blood of the Choctaw and Chickasaw tribes of Indians whose enrollment has been approved by the Secretary of the Interior prior to the date of the approval of this act; and to enroll and make allotments to such children."

It is therefore hereby ordered that the application for the enrollment of Thomas Sharkey as a citizen by blood of the Choctaw Nation be dismissed.

Tams Bixby Commissioner.

Muskogee, Indian Territory.
OCT 6- 1905

Applications for Enrollment of Choctaw Newborn
Act of 1905   Volume XVI

7-NB-1168.

Muskogee, Indian Territory, October 6, 1905.

Israel Sharkey,
    Caney, Indian Territory.

Dear Sir:

    Inclosed herewith you will find a copy of the order of the Commissioner to the Five Civilized Tribes, dated October 6, 1905, dismissing the application for the enrollment of your minor son Thomas Sharkey as a citizen by blood of the Choctaw Nation.

                  Respectfully,

                                                Commissioner.

Register.
    7-NB-1168.

7-NB-1168.

Muskogee, Indian Territory, October 6, 1905.

Mansfield, McMurray & Cornish,
    Attorneys for Choctaw and Chickasaw Nations,
        South McAlester, Indian Territory.

Gentlemen:

    Inclosed herewith you will find a copy of the order of the Commissioner to the Five Civilized Tribes, dated October 6, 1905, dismissing the application for the enrollment of Thomas Sharkey as a citizen by blood of the Choctaw Nation.

                    Respectfully,

                                                Commissioner.

7-NB-1168.

Applications for Enrollment of Choctaw Newborn
Act of 1905   Volume XVI

7-3864

Muskogee, Indian Territory, April 25, 1905.

Isreal Shockey[sic],
    Caney, Indian Territory.

Dear Sir:

    Receipt is hereby acknowledged of the affidavits of Louisa Shockey and Siney Robenson[sic] to the birth of Tabie[sic] Shockey, daughter of Isreal and Louisa Shockey, December 29, 1904.

    Receipt is also acknowledged of the affidavits of Louisa Shockey and Mary Wilson to the birth of Thomas Shockey, son of Isreal and Louisa Shockey, February 4, 1903. It appears in the affidavit of the mother that this child died about February 24, 1903.

    You are advised that under the provisions of the act of Congress approved July 1, 1902, the provisions of the act of Congress approved March 3, 1905, the Commission is authorized for a period of sixty days from that date, to receive applications for the enrollment of children born to enrolled citizens by blood of the Choctaw and Chickasaw Nations, between September 25, 1902, and March 4, 1905, and living on the latter date. You will, therefore, see the Commission is without authority to enroll children born to citizens of said nations, subsequent to September 25, 1902, who were not living on March 4, 1905.

                                                    Respectfully,

                                                                 Chairman.

<u>Choc New Born 1169</u>
    Sarah[sic] McIntosh
    (Born Sept. 17, 1904)

Applications for Enrollment of Choctaw Newborn
Act of 1905   Volume XVI

AFFIDAVIT OF ATTENDING PHYSICIAN OR MIDWIFE

UNITED STATES OF AMERICA
INDIAN TERRITORY
Western   DISTRICT

I, Malinda[sic] Sawyers   a   Mid Wife on oath state that I attended on Mrs. Catherine McIntosh wife of Joseph McIntosh on the 17 day of September, 190 4, that there was born to her on said date a Female child, that said child is now living, and is said to have been named Sarrah McIntosh

Melinda Sawyers

Subscribed and sworn to before me this, the   27   day of January   190 5

WITNESSETH: John M Lintz   Notary Public.
Must be two witnesses   { L B Holland
who are citizens   Newt Sanders

We hereby certify that we are well acquainted with   Malinda Sawyers a   Mid Wife   and know   her   to be reputable and of good standing in the community.

L B Holland   P.O. Enterprise I.T.

Newt Sanders   Brooken I.T.

BIRTH AFFIDAVIT.

DEPARTMENT OF THE INTERIOR.
COMMISSION TO THE FIVE CIVILIZED TRIBES.

IN RE APPLICATION FOR ENROLLMENT, as a citizen of the   Choctaw   Nation, of Sarrah McIntosh   , born on the 17 day of September , 1904

Name of Father: Joseph McIntosh   a citizen of the   Choctaw   Nation.
Name of Mother: Catharine McIntosh   a citizen of the   Choctaw   Nation.

Postoffice   Enterprise Ind. T.

Applications for Enrollment of Choctaw Newborn
Act of 1905   Volume XVI

AFFIDAVIT OF MOTHER.

UNITED STATES OF AMERICA, Indian Territory,
    Western   DISTRICT.

    I, Catharine McIntosh, on oath state that I am 41 years of age and a citizen by Blood, of the Choctaw Nation; that I am the lawful wife of Joseph McIntosh, who is a citizen, by In=termarriage of the Choctaw Nation; that a Female child was born to me on 17 day of September, 1904; that said child has been named Sarrah McIntosh, and was living March 4, 1905.

                                                her
                                 Catharine x McIntosh
Witnesses To Mark: mark
  { C H Boyd
    CD Fowler

    Subscribed and sworn to before me this 20 day of April, 1905

                                 J. M. White
                                      Notary Public.

AFFIDAVIT OF ATTENDING PHYSICIAN OR MID-WIFE.

UNITED STATES OF AMERICA, Indian Territory,
    Western   DISTRICT.

    I, Malinda Sawyers, a Midwife, on oath state that I attended on Mrs. Catharine McIntosh, wife of Joseph McIntosh on the 17 day of September, 1904; that there was born to her on said date a Female child; that said child was living March 4, 1905, and is said to have been named Sarrah McIntosh

                                 Melindie Sawyers
Witnesses To Mark:
{

    Subscribed and sworn to before me this 20 day of April, 1905

                                 J. M. White
                                      Notary Public.

Applications for Enrollment of Choctaw Newborn
Act of 1905 Volume XVI

NEW-BORN AFFIDAVIT.

Number..............

...Choctaw Enrolling Commission...

IN THE MATTER OF THE APPLICATION FOR ENROLLMENT, as a citizen of the Choctaw Nation, of Sarrah McIntosh

born on the 17 day of __September__ 190 4

Name of father Joseph McIntosh   a citizen of Creek Nation final enrollment No............
Name of mother Catharine McIntosh   a citizen of Choctaw Nation final enrollment No. 12418

Postoffice   Enterprise I T

AFFIDAVIT OF MOTHER.

UNITED STATES OF AMERICA
INDIAN TERRITORY
Western   DISTRICT

I Catharine McIntosh , on oath state that I am 41 years of age and a citizen by Blood of the Choctaw Nation, and as such have been placed upon the final roll of the Choctaw Nation, by the Honorable Secretary of the Interior my final enrollment number being 12418 ; that I am the lawful wife of Joseph McIntosh , who is a citizen of the Creek Nation, and as such has been placed upon the final roll of said Nation by the Honorable Secretary of the Interior, his final enrollment number being .... and that a Female child was born to me on the 17 day of September 190 4; that said child has been named Sarrah McIntosh , and is now living.

                                                 her
                                  Catharine x McIntosh

Witnesseth.   mark

Must be two Witnesses who are Citizens.
     Thomas J Walls Jr
     Wallace Durant

Subscribed and sworn to before me this 27 day of Jan 190 5

                                 John M Lintz
                                    Notary Public.

My commission expires: Nov 27 1907

Applications for Enrollment of Choctaw Newborn
Act of 1905   Volume XVI

7-4473

Muskogee, Indian Territory, April 25, 1905.

Joseph McIntosh,
    Enterprise, Indian Territory.

Dear Sir:

    Receipt is hereby acknowledged of the affidavits of Catharine McIntosh and Malindie Sawyers to the birth of Sarrah McIntosh, September 17, 1904, and the same have been filed with our records as an application for the enrollment of said child.

        Respectfully,

                              Chairman.

Choc New Born 1170
    Vincenta W. Finns[sic]
    (Born July 28, 1904)

BIRTH AFFIDAVIT.

DEPARTMENT OF THE INTERIOR.
COMMISSION TO THE FIVE CIVILIZED TRIBES.

IN RE APPLICATION FOR ENROLLMENT, as a citizen of the Choctaw Nation, of Vincenta W Tims, born on the 28 day of July, 1904

Name of Father: Mitchell Tims   a citizen of the Choctaw Nation.
Name of Mother: Mildred Tims   a citizen of the Choctaw Nation.

        Postoffice   Fort Towson Ind Ter

AFFIDAVIT OF MOTHER.

UNITED STATES OF AMERICA, Indian Territory, }
    Central   DISTRICT.

    I, Mildred Tims, on oath state that I am 23 years of age and a citizen by Blood, of the Choctaw Nation; that I am the lawful wife of Mitchell Tims, who is a citizen, by Blood of the Choctaw Nation; that a Male child

Applications for Enrollment of Choctaw Newborn
Act of 1905   Volume XVI

was born to me on   28   day of   July , 1904; that said child has been named Vincenta W. Tims, and was living March 4, 1905.

Mildred Tims

Witnesses To Mark:
{

Subscribed and sworn to before me this 25th   day of   March   , 1905

Thomas Fennell
Notary Public.

AFFIDAVIT OF ATTENDING PHYSICIAN OR MID-WIFE.

UNITED STATES OF AMERICA, Indian Territory,
   Central   DISTRICT.

I,   Emeline Tims   , a   midwife   , on oath state that I attended on Mrs.   Mildred Tims   , wife of   Mitchell Tims   on the   28   day of   July , 1904; that there was born to her on said date a   male   child; that said child was living March 4, 1905, and is said to have been named   Vincenta W Tims

Emeline Tims

Witnesses To Mark:
{

Subscribed and sworn to before me this   19th   day of   March   , 1905

Thomas Fennell
Notary Public.

---

7 NB 1170

Muskogee, Indian Territory, June 15, 1905.

Mishel[sic] Tims,
   Fort Towson, Indian Territory.

Dear Sir:

Receipt is hereby acknowledged of your letter of June 10, 1905, asking if the birth certificate of Vincenta W. Tims was received.

In reply to your letter you are informed that the affidavits heretofore forwarded to the birth of your child Vincenta W. Tims have been filed as an application for the

Applications for Enrollment of Choctaw Newborn
Act of 1905   Volume XVI

enrollment of said child and you will be notified of such further action as is taken in this case.

                Respectfully,

                              Chairman.

Choc New Born 1171
    Arthur Wilson
    (Born March 23, 1903)

BIRTH AFFIDAVIT.

DEPARTMENT OF THE INTERIOR.
COMMISSION TO THE FIVE CIVILIZED TRIBES.

IN RE APPLICATION FOR ENROLLMENT, as a citizen of the Choctaw Nation, of Auther[sic] Wilson, born on the 23 day of March, 1903

Name of Father: James Wilson   a citizen of the Choctaw Nation.
Name of Mother: Rosanna Wilson   a citizen of the Choctaw Nation.

                Postoffice   Fort Towson, Ind. Ter

AFFIDAVIT OF MOTHER.

UNITED STATES OF AMERICA, Indian Territory,
    Central   DISTRICT.

    I, Rosanna Wilson, on oath state that I am 23 years of age and a citizen by Blood, of the Choctaw Nation; that I am the lawful wife of James Wilson, who is a citizen, by Blood of the Choctaw Nation; that a Male child was born to me on 23 day of March, 1903; that said child has been named Auther Wilson, and was living March 4, 1905.

                                her
                        Rosanna x Wilson
Witnesses To Mark: mark
    { James Wilson
      John Aaron

Applications for Enrollment of Choctaw Newborn
Act of 1905 Volume XVI

Subscribed and sworn to before me this 25th day of March , 1905

                Thomas Fennell
                Notary Public.

AFFIDAVIT OF ATTENDING PHYSICIAN OR MID-WIFE.

UNITED STATES OF AMERICA, Indian Territory,
    Central Dis   DISTRICT.

I, Emeline Tims , a midwife , on oath state that I attended on Mrs. Rosanna Wilson , wife of James Wilson on the 23 day of March , 1903; that there was born to her on said date a male child; that said child was living March 4, 1905, and is said to have been named Auther Wilson

                Emeline Tims

Witnesses To Mark:

Subscribed and sworn to before me this 19th day of March , 1905

                Thomas Fennell
                Notary Public.

Choc New Born 1172
    Anna Adams
    (Born June 5, 1903)

BIRTH AFFIDAVIT.
DEPARTMENT OF THE INTERIOR.
COMMISSION TO THE FIVE CIVILIZED TRIBES.

IN RE APPLICATION FOR ENROLLMENT, as a citizen of the Choctaw Nation, of Anna Adams , born on the 5 day of June , 1903

Name of Father: Reuben Adams   a citizen of the Choctaw Nation.
Name of Mother: Selena Adams *nee Colbert*   a citizen of the Choctaw Nation.

            Postoffice   LeFlore I.T.

Applications for Enrollment of Choctaw Newborn
Act of 1905 Volume XVI

AFFIDAVIT OF MOTHER.

UNITED STATES OF AMERICA, Indian Territory,
Central DISTRICT.

I, Selena Adams nee Colbert , on oath state that I am 19 years of age and a citizen by blood , of the Choctaw Nation; that I am the lawful wife of Reuben Adams , who is a citizen, by blood of the Choctaw Nation; that a female child was born to me on 5 day of June , 1903; that said child has been named Anna Adams , and was living March 4, 1905.

                          her
                 Selena x Adams, nee Colbert
Witnesses To Mark: mark
  Thomas McCurtain
  Sarphim Atoko

Subscribed and sworn to before me this 21 day of April , 1905

                          Robert E Lee
My com ex 1-11-1906   Notary Public.

AFFIDAVIT OF ATTENDING PHYSICIAN OR MID-WIFE.

UNITED STATES OF AMERICA, Indian Territory,
Central DISTRICT.

I, Betsey Atoko , a midwife , on oath state that I attended on Mrs. Selena Adams, nee Colbert , wife of Reuben Adams on the 5 day of June , 1903; that there was born to her on said date a female child; that said child was living March 4, 1905, and is said to have been named Anna Adams

                        her
                 Betsey x Atoko
Witnesses To Mark: mark
  Thomas McCurtain
  Sarphim Atoko

Subscribed and sworn to before me this 21 day of April , 1905

                          Robert E Lee
My com ex 1-11-1906   Notary Public.

Final enrollment no of Reuben Adams being No 8507
   "   "   " " Selena Adams, nee Colbert being No 8881

Applications for Enrollment of Choctaw Newborn
Act of 1905 Volume XVI

Muskogee, Indian Territory, April 25, 1905.

Reuben Adams,
    Leflore, Indian Territory.

Dear Sir:

    Receipt is hereby acknowledged of the affidavits of Selena Adams, nee Colbert and Betsey Atoko, to the birth of Anna Adams daughter of Reuben and Selena Adams, June 5, 1903, and the same have been filed with our records as an application for the enrollment of said child.

                  Respectfully,

                                Chairman.

Choc New Born 1173
    Georgia May Roebuck
    (Born Oct. 21, 1904)

NEW BORN AFFIDAVIT

No ....

CHOCTAW ENROLLING COMMISSION

IN THE MATTER OF THE APPLICATION FOR ENROLLMENT as a citizen of the Choctaw Nation, of Georgia May Roebuck born on the 21^{St} day of October 190 4

Name of father David E Roebuck   a citizen of   Choctaw   Nation, final enrollment No. 4728
Name of mother Carrie Roebuck   a citizen of   Choctaw   Nation, final enrollment No. 5014

                        Antlers I.T.   Postoffice.

Applications for Enrollment of Choctaw Newborn
Act of 1905   Volume XVI

AFFIDAVIT OF MOTHER

UNITED STATES OF AMERICA
    INDIAN TERRITORY
DISTRICT   Central

I   Carrie Roebuck   , on oath state that I am   24   years of age and a citizen by blood of the   Choctaw   Nation, and as such have been placed upon the final roll of the   Choctaw   Nation, by the Honorable Secretary of the Interior my final enrollment number being   5014   ; that I am the lawful wife of   David E Roebuck , who is a citizen of the   Choctaw   Nation, and as such has been placed upon the final roll of said Nation by the Honorable Secretary of the Interior, his final enrollment number being   4728   and that a   Female   child was born to me on the   21st   day of   October   190 4; that said child has been named   Georgia May Roebuck   , and is now living.

                                              Carrie Roebuck

WITNESSETH:
Must be two witnesses { Eden Nelson
who are citizens { Laura Nelson

Subscribed and sworn to before me this, the   4   day of   March   , 190 5

                                              A J Arnote
                                                 Notary Public.

My Commission Expires: May 16th 1907

Affidavit of Attending Physician or Midwife

UNITED STATES OF AMERICA,
    INDIAN TERRITORY,
Central   DISTRICT

I,   Elizabeth Carter   a   Mid-wife   on oath state that I attended on Mrs.   Carrie Roebuck   wife of   David E Roebuck   on the   21st   day of   October   , 190 4, that there was born to her on said date a   Female   child, that said child is now living, and is said to have been named   Georgia May Roebuck

                                        Elizabeth Carter   *Midwife*

Subscribed and sworn to before me this the   4th   day of   March   1905

                                              A J Arnote
                                               Notary Public.

WITNESSETH:
Must be two witnesses { Eden Nelson
who are citizens and
know the child. { Laura Nelson

Applications for Enrollment of Choctaw Newborn
Act of 1905 Volume XVI

We hereby certify that we are well acquainted with   Elizabeth Carter   a   Mid-wife   and know   her   to be reputable and of good standing in the community.

Must be two citizen witnesses. { Eden Nelson / Laura Nelson }

BIRTH AFFIDAVIT.

DEPARTMENT OF THE INTERIOR.
COMMISSION TO THE FIVE CIVILIZED TRIBES.

IN RE APPLICATION FOR ENROLLMENT, as a citizen of the   Choctaw   Nation, of Georgia May Roebuck   , born on the 21st day of Oct , 1904

Name of Father: David E Roebuck   a citizen of the   Choctaw   Nation.
Name of Mother: Carrie Roebuck   a citizen of the   Choctaw   Nation.

Postoffice   Antlers I.T.

AFFIDAVIT OF MOTHER.

UNITED STATES OF AMERICA, Indian Territory,
Central   DISTRICT.

I, Carrie Roebuck , on oath state that I am 24   years of age and a citizen by   blood , of the   Choctaw   Nation; that I am the lawful wife of   David E Roebuck   , who is a citizen, by blood   of the   Choctaw   Nation; that a female   child was born to me on   21st day of   October   , 1904; that said child has been named   Georgie May Roebuck   , and was living March 4, 1905.

Carrie Roebuck

Witnesses To Mark:

Subscribed and sworn to before me this   21st day of   April   , 1905

John Cocke
Notary Public.

Applications for Enrollment of Choctaw Newborn
Act of 1905   Volume XVI

AFFIDAVIT OF ATTENDING PHYSICIAN OR MID-WIFE.

UNITED STATES OF AMERICA, Indian Territory,
Central   DISTRICT.

I, Mrs Elizabeth Carter, a midwife, on oath state that I attended on Mrs. Carrie Roebuck, wife of David E Roebuck on the 21st day of October, 1904; that there was born to her on said date a female child; that said child was living March 4, 1905, and is said to have been named Georgia May Roebuck

Elizabeth Carter

Witnesses To Mark:

Subscribed and sworn to before me this 21st day of April, 1905

John Cocke
Notary Public.

7-1768

Muskogee, Indian Territory, April 15, 1905.

David E. Roebuck,
Antlers, Indian Territory.

Dear Sir:

Receipt is hereby acknowledged of your letter of April 8, 1905, in which you state that sometime ago you forwarded affidavits to the birth of Georgia May Roebuck to James Bowers at Spiro, Indian Territory and have not heard from it and you wish to know if she has been enrolled.

In reply to your letter you are informed that it does not appear from our records that affidavits to the birth of Georgia May Roebuck have been forwarded this office and for your convenience there is inclosed you herewith blank for the enrollment of an infant child which you should have executed and returned to this office within sixty days from March 3, 1905.

Respectfully,

B.C.   Chairman.

Applications for Enrollment of Choctaw Newborn
Act of 1905   Volume XVI

Choc New Born 1174
   Narciss Quinton
   (Born Aug. 4, 1903)

NEW-BORN AFFIDAVIT.

Number..............

...Choctaw Enrolling Commission...

IN THE MATTER OF THE APPLICATION FOR ENROLLMENT, as a citizen of the Choctaw   Nation, of   Narciss Quinton

born on the   4th day of __August__   190 3

Name of father   James M Quinton   a citizen of   Choctaw
Nation final enrollment No.   8862
Name of mother   Sallie Quinton   a citizen of   white
Nation final enrollment No.   ———

                                                      Postoffice

AFFIDAVIT OF MOTHER.
UNITED STATES OF AMERICA
INDIAN TERRITORY
   Western   DISTRICT

I   Sallie Quinton   , on oath state that I am   34   years of age and a citizen by   white   of the   ———   Nation, and as such have been placed upon the final roll of the   ———   Nation, by the Honorable Secretary of the Interior my final enrollment number being   ——— ; that I am the lawful wife of   James M Quinton   , who is a citizen of the   Choctaw   Nation, and as such has been placed upon the final roll of said Nation by the Honorable Secretary of the Interior, his final enrollment number being   8862   and that a   female   child was born to me on the   4th day of   August   190 3; that said child has been named   Narciss Quinton   , and is now living.   her
                                                      Sallie Quinton x
Witnesseth.   mark
   Must be two   ⎫   T.J. Walls
   Witnesses who ⎬
   are Citizens. ⎭   T. D. Dyer

Applications for Enrollment of Choctaw Newborn
Act of 1905 Volume XVI

Subscribed and sworn to before me this 4 day of Jan 190 5

John M Lintz
Notary Public.

My commission expires: Nov 27 1907

AFFIDAVIT OF ATTENDING PHYSICIAN OR MIDWIFE

UNITED STATES OF AMERICA
INDIAN TERRITORY
Western DISTRICT

I, Elizabeth Quinton a midwife on oath state that I attended on Mrs. Sallie Quinton wife of James M Quinton on the 4th day of August , 190 3 , that there was born to her on said date a female child, that said child is now living, and is said to have been named Narciss Quinton

Elizabeth Quinton

Subscribed and sworn to before me this, the 4 day of January 190 5

John M Lintz Notary Public.

WITNESSETH:
Must be two witnesses who are citizens
Katie Quinton
T.D. Dyer

We hereby certify that we are well acquainted with Elizabeth Quinton a midwife and know her to be reputable and of good standing in the community.

T.J. Walls _____

Katie Quinton _____

BIRTH AFFIDAVIT.

DEPARTMENT OF THE INTERIOR.
COMMISSION TO THE FIVE CIVILIZED TRIBES.

IN RE APPLICATION FOR ENROLLMENT, as a citizen of the Choctaw Nation, of Narciss Quinton , born on the 4th day of August , 1903

Name of Father: James Quinton   a citizen of the Choctaw Nation.
Name of Mother: Sallie Quinton   a citizen of the Choctaw Nation.

Applications for Enrollment of Choctaw Newborn
Act of 1905   Volume XVI

Postoffice   Quinton, Indian Territory

AFFIDAVIT OF MOTHER.

UNITED STATES OF AMERICA, Indian Territory,
  Western   DISTRICT.

    I, Sallie Quinton, on oath state that I am 34 years of age and a citizen by --------, of the -------------- Nation; that I am the lawful wife of James Quinton, who is a citizen, by Blood of the Choctaw Nation; that a female child was born to me on 4th day of August, 1903; that said child has been named Narciss Quinton, and was living March 4, 1905.

                                            her
Witnesses To Mark: Sallie x Quinton
{ Clark C Fowler   mark
{ L. Monk

    Subscribed and sworn to before me this 21st day of April, 1905

                                      Guy A Perry
                                      Notary Public.

AFFIDAVIT OF ATTENDING PHYSICIAN OR MID-WIFE.

UNITED STATES OF AMERICA, Indian Territory,
  Western   DISTRICT.

    I, Mary Shiew, a mid-wife, on oath state that I attended on Mrs. Sallie Quinton, wife of James Quinton on the 4th day of August, 1903; that there was born to her on said date a female child; that said child was living March 4, 1905, and is said to have been named Narciss Quinton

                                            her
Witnesses To Mark: Mary x Shiew
{ Clark C Fowler   mark
{ L. Monk

    Subscribed and sworn to before me this 21st day of April, 1905

                                      Guy A Perry
                                      Notary Public.

Applications for Enrollment of Choctaw Newborn
Act of 1905   Volume XVI

7-3025.

Muskogee, Indian Territory, April 25, 1905.

James Quinton,
    Quinton, Indian Territory.

Dear Sir:

    Receipt is hereby acknowledged of the affidavits of Sallie Quinton and Mary Shiew to the birth of Narciss Quinton, daughter of James and Sallie Quinton, August 4, 1903, and the same have been filed with our records as an application for the enrollment of said child.

        Respectfully,

                Chairman.

Choc New Born 1175
    Jesse R. Pritchard
    (Born Oct. 31, 1904)

NEW-BORN AFFIDAVIT.

    Number................

Choctaw Enrolling Commission.

    IN THE MATTER OF THE APPLICATION FOR ENROLLMENT, as a citizen of the Choctaw   Nation, of   Jesse Robert Pritchard

born on the   31   day of   October   190 4

Name of father   James Robert Pritchard   a citizen of   Choctaw
Nation final enrollment No   —
Name of mother   Jane Pritchard   a citizen of   Choctaw
Nation final enrollment No   14806

        Postoffice   Durant I.T.

Applications for Enrollment of Choctaw Newborn
Act of 1905 Volume XVI

AFFIDAVIT OF MOTHER.

UNITED STATES OF AMERICA,
INDIAN TERRITORY,
Central   DISTRICT

I Jane Pritchard on oath state that I am 34 years of age and a citizen by blood of the Choctaw Nation, and as such have been placed upon the final roll of the Choctaw Nation, by the Honorable Secretary of the Interior my final enrollment number being 14806 ; that I am the lawful wife of James Robert Pritchard , who is a citizen of the white Nation, and as such has been placed upon the final roll of said Nation by the Honorable Secretary of the Interior, his final enrollment number being —— and that a male child was born to me on the 31 day of October 190 4 ; that said child has been named Jesse Robert Pritchard , and is now living.

WITNESSETH: Jane Pritchard

Must be two
Witnesses who   E E Dyer
are Citizens.   Joseph E Nelson

Subscribed and sworn to before me this 16 day of January 190 5

James Bower
Notary Public.

My commission expires Sept 23 1907

Affidavit of Attending Physician or Midwife.

UNITED STATES OF AMERICA
INDIAN TERRITORY
Central   DISTRICT

I, W J Melton a Physician on oath state that I attended on Mrs. Jane Pritchard wife of James Robert Pritchard on the 31st day of October , 190 4 , that there was born to her on said date a Male child, that said child is now living, and is said to have been named Jesse Robert Pritchard

W.J. Melton   M.D.

Subscribed and sworn to before me this, the 18th day of January 190 5

CH Ewing
Notary Public.

WITNESSETH:

Must be two witnesses
who are citizens and   Cyrus Byington
know the child.   (Name Illegible)

89

Applications for Enrollment of Choctaw Newborn
Act of 1905   Volume XVI

We hereby certify that we are well acquainted with   W.J. Melton   a   Physician   and know   him   to be reputable and of good standing in the community.

> Cyrus Byington
> *(Name Illegible)*

BIRTH AFFIDAVIT.

DEPARTMENT OF THE INTERIOR.
COMMISSION TO THE FIVE CIVILIZED TRIBES.

IN RE APPLICATION FOR ENROLLMENT, as a citizen of the   Choctaw   Nation, of Jesse R Pritchard   , born on the 31st day of   October   , 1904

Name of Father: James R Pritchard   a ^non^ citizen of the   Choctaw   Nation.
Name of Mother: Jane Pritchard   a citizen of the   Choctaw   Nation.

Postoffice..

AFFIDAVIT OF MOTHER.

UNITED STATES OF AMERICA, Indian Territory, }
   Central   DISTRICT. }

I,   Jane Pritchard   , on oath state that I am   35   years of age and a citizen by   Blood   , of the   Choctaw   Nation; that I am the lawful wife of   James R Pritchard   , who is a *non* citizen, by ——— of the ————— Nation; that a   male   child was born to me on 31st day of   October   , 1904; that said child has been named   Jesse R Pritchard   , and was living March 4, 1905.

> Jane Pritchard

Witnesses To Mark:
{

Subscribed and sworn to before me this   20th day of   April   , 1905

> C.H. Ewing
> Notary Public.

Applications for Enrollment of Choctaw Newborn
Act of 1905 Volume XVI

AFFIDAVIT OF ATTENDING PHYSICIAN OR MID-WIFE.

UNITED STATES OF AMERICA, Indian Territory, } Central DISTRICT.

I, W.J. Melton , a Physician , on oath state that I attended on Mrs. Jane Pritchard , wife of James R Pritchard on the 31st day of October , 1904; that there was born to her on said date a Female[sic] child; that said child was living March 4, 1905, and is said to have been named Jesse R Pritchard

W.J. Melton

Witnesses To Mark:
{

Subscribed and sworn to before me this 20th day of April , 1905

C.H. Ewing
Notary Public.

$W^m O.B.$

COMMISSIONERS:
TAMS BIXBY,
THOMAS B. NEEDLES,
C.R. BRECKINBRIDGE.

WM. O. BEALL
Secretary

DEPARTMENT OF THE INTERIOR,
COMMISSIONER TO THE FIVE CIVILIZED TRIBES.

REFER IN REPLY TO THE FOLLOWING:

7-3485.

ADDRESS ONLY THE
COMMISSION TO THE FIVE CIVILIZED TRIBES.

Muskogee, Indian Territory, April 25, 1905.

James R. Pritchard,
    Durant, Indian Territory.

Dear Sir:

Receipt is hereby acknowledged of the affidavits of Jane Pritchard and W.J. Melton to the birth of Jesse R. Pritchard, son of James and Jane Pritchard, October 31, 1904, and the same have been filed with our records as an application for the enrollment of said child.

Respectfully,

Tams Bixby Chairman.

Applications for Enrollment of Choctaw Newborn
Act of 1905 Volume XVI

7 N. B. 1175.

Muskogee, Indian Territory, May 4, 1905.

C. Helting,
    Caddo, Indian Territory.

Dear Sir:

    Receipt is hereby acknowledged of your letter of April 29, stating that J. R. Pritchard recently forwarded proof of the birth of Jesse R. Pritchard and you ask that receipt be acknowledged.

    In reply to your letter you are advised that the affidavits heretofore forwarded to the birth of Jesse R. Pritchard have been filed with our records as an application for the enrollment of said child.

                    Respectfully,

                                Chairman.

Choc New Born 1176
    Myrtle Parks Cassell
    (Born Sept. 1, 1903)

BIRTH AFFIDAVIT.

DEPARTMENT OF THE INTERIOR.
COMMISSION TO THE FIVE CIVILIZED TRIBES.

    IN RE APPLICATION FOR ENROLLMENT, as a citizen of the Chocktaw[sic] Nation, of Myrtle Parks Cassell , born on the 1 day of Sept , 1903

Name of Father: J. T. Cassell   a citizen of the United St Nation.
Name of Mother: Serena Cassell   a citizen of the Chocktaw Nation.

                    Postoffice   Massey Mo Ter

Applications for Enrollment of Choctaw Newborn
Act of 1905 Volume XVI

AFFIDAVIT OF MOTHER.

UNITED STATES OF AMERICA, Indian Territory, }
Western   DISTRICT.

I, Serena Cassell , on oath state that I am 32 years of age and a citizen by By Blood , of the Chocktaw Nation; that I am the lawful wife of J. T. Cassell , who is a citizen, by blood of the United States Nation; that a Girl child was born to me on the 1 day of Sept 1903 , 1903; that said child has been named Myrtle Parks Cassell , and was living March 4, 1905.

Serena Cassell

Witnesses To Mark:
{

Subscribed and sworn to before me this 21 day of April , 1905

My commission expires   Jos B Henderson
Dec 19-1908   Notary Public.

AFFIDAVIT OF ATTENDING PHYSICIAN OR MID-WIFE.

UNITED STATES OF AMERICA, Indian Territory, }
Central   DISTRICT.

I, J H Bristow , a Physician , on oath state that I attended on Mrs. Serena Cassell , wife of J. F[sic] Cassell on the 1st day of Sept , 1903; that there was born to her on said date a Girl child; that said child was living March 4, 1905, and is said to have been named Myrtle Parks Cassell

J.H. Bristow

Witnesses To Mark:
{

Subscribed and sworn to before me this 20 day of April , 1905

(Name Illegible)
Notary Public.

My commission expires Jan 17-1908

Applications for Enrollment of Choctaw Newborn
Act of 1905   Volume XVI

7-4963.

Muskogee, Indian Territory, April 26, 1905.

J. T. Cassell,
    Massey, Indian Territory.

Dear Sir:

    Receipt is hereby acknowledged of the affidavits of Serena Cassell and J. H. Bristow, to the birth of Myrtle Parks Cassell, child of J. T. and Serena Cassell, September 1, 1903, and the same have been filed with our records as an application for the enrollment of said child.

                    Respectfully,

                                      Chairman.

Choc New Born 1177
    Edker Westbrook
    (Born June 23, 1904)

NEW-BORN AFFIDAVIT.

            Number_____

...Choctaw Enrolling Commission...

    IN THE MATTER OF THE APPLICATION FOR ENROLLMENT, as a citizen of the Choctaw   Nation, of   Edger[sic] Westbrook

born on the   23   day of ___June___ 190 4

Name of father A.J. Westbrook	a citizen of ———
Nation final enrollment No. 458	
Name of mother Mattie Westbrook	a citizen of Choctaw
Nation final enrollment No. 12,676	

                            Postoffice   Brooken I.T.

Applications for Enrollment of Choctaw Newborn
Act of 1905   Volume XVI

AFFIDAVIT OF MOTHER.

UNITED STATES OF AMERICA
INDIAN TERRITORY
Western   DISTRICT

I   Mattie Westbrook   , on oath state that I am 28 years of age and a citizen by blood of the Chocktaw Nation, and as such have been placed upon the final roll of the Chocktaw Nation, by the Honorable Secretary of the Interior my final enrollment number being 12676 ; that I am the lawful wife of A.J. Westbrook , who is a citizen of the ——— Nation, and as such has been placed upon the final roll of said Nation by the Honorable Secretary of the Interior, his final enrollment number being 454 and that a Male child was born to me on the 23 day of June 190 4; that said child has been named Edger Westbrook , and is now living.

Mattie Westbrook

Witnesseth.

Must be two Witnesses who are Citizens. } T.J. Walls
T.D. Dyer

Subscribed and sworn to before me this 4 day of Jan 190 5

John M Lentz
Notary Public.

My commission expires:
Nov 27 1907

AFFIDAVIT OF ATTENDING PHYSICIAN OR MIDWIFE

UNITED STATES OF AMERICA
INDIAN TERRITORY
Western   DISTRICT

I,   Nancy A Autry   a   Mid wife on oath state that I attended on Mrs. Mattie Westbrook wife of A J Westbrook on the 23 day of June , 190 3[sic] , that there was born to her on said date a male child, that said child is now living, and is said to have been named Edger Westbrook

N A Autry

Subscribed and sworn to before me this, the 4 day of January   190 5

WITNESSETH:
Must be two witnesses who are citizens { T.D. Dyer
Jess Walls

John M Lentz   Notary Public.

Applications for Enrollment of Choctaw Newborn
Act of 1905 Volume XVI

We hereby certify that we are well acquainted with_____
a _____ and know _____ to be reputable and of good standing in the community.

    Jess Walls   _____

    T.J. Walls   _____

BIRTH AFFIDAVIT.

DEPARTMENT OF THE INTERIOR.
COMMISSION TO THE FIVE CIVILIZED TRIBES.

IN RE APPLICATION FOR ENROLLMENT, as a citizen of the Choctaw Nation, of Edker Westbrook, born on the 23 day of June, 1904

Name of Father: Andy J Westbrook   a citizen of the Choctaw Nation.
Name of Mother: Mattie Westbrook   a citizen of the Choctaw Nation.

         Postoffice   Brooken I.T.

AFFIDAVIT OF MOTHER.

UNITED STATES OF AMERICA, Indian Territory,
    Western   DISTRICT.

I, Mattie Westbrook, on oath state that I am 28 years of age and a citizen by Blood, of the Choctaw Nation; that I am the lawful wife of Andy J Westbrook, who is a citizen, by intermarriage[sic] of the Choctaw Nation; that a male child was born to me on 23 day of June, 1904; that said child has been named Edker Westbrook, and was living March 4, 1905.

                              Mattie Westbrook

Witnesses To Mark:

     Subscribed and sworn to before me this 19 day of April, 1905

                              S P Davis
                                  Notary Public.

Applications for Enrollment of Choctaw Newborn
Act of 1905   Volume XVI

AFFIDAVIT OF ATTENDING PHYSICIAN OR MID-WIFE.

UNITED STATES OF AMERICA, Indian Territory,
Western   DISTRICT.

I, Nancy A Autry   , a   midwife   , on oath state that I attended on Mrs. Mattie Westbrook   , wife of Andy J Westbrook   on the 25[sic] day of June , 1904; that there was born to her on said date a   male   child; that said child was living March 4, 1905, and is said to have been named Edker Westbrook

                                        Nancy A Autry
Witnesses To Mark:

Subscribed and sworn to before me this 19 day of   April   , 1905

                                        S P Davis
                                        Notary Public.
My commission expires Feb 9-07

BIRTH AFFIDAVIT.

DEPARTMENT OF THE INTERIOR.
COMMISSION TO THE FIVE CIVILIZED TRIBES.

IN RE APPLICATION FOR ENROLLMENT, as a citizen of the   Choctaw   Nation, of Edker Westbrook   , born on the 23 day of June , 1904

Name of Father: Andrew J Westbrook   a citizen of the   Choctaw   Nation.
Name of Mother: Mattie Westbrook   a citizen of the   Choctaw   Nation.

                Postoffice   Brooken Ind Ter

AFFIDAVIT OF MOTHER.

UNITED STATES OF AMERICA, Indian Territory,
Western   DISTRICT.

I, Mattie Westbrook   , on oath state that I am   28   years of age and a citizen by   Blood   , of the   Choctaw   Nation; that I am the lawful wife of Andrew J Westbrook   , who is a citizen, by intermarriage   of the   Choctaw Nation; that a   male   child was born to me on 23   day of   June   , 1904; that said child has been named   Edker Westbrook   , and was living March 4, 1905.

                                        Mattie Westbrook

Applications for Enrollment of Choctaw Newborn
Act of 1905 Volume XVI

Witnesses To Mark:

{

    Subscribed and sworn to before me this 27 day of   June   , 1905

                              Sterling P Davis
                              Notary Public.

AFFIDAVIT OF ATTENDING PHYSICIAN OR MID-WIFE.

UNITED STATES OF AMERICA, Indian Territory,
    Western   DISTRICT.

    I, Nancie[sic] A Autry , a midwife , on oath state that I attended on Mrs. Mattie Westbrook , wife of Andrew J Westbrook on the 23 day of June , 1904; that there was born to her on said date a male child; that said child was living March 4, 1905, and is said to have been named Edker Westbrook

                              Nancy A Autry

Witnesses To Mark:

{

    Subscribed and sworn to before me this 27 day of   June   , 1905

                              Sterling P Davis
                              Notary Public.

My commission expires Feb 9-07

                                                7-4579.

Muskogee, Indian Territory, April 26, 1905.

Andy J. Westbrook,
    Brooken, Indian Territory.

Dear Sir:

    Receipt is hereby acknowledged of the affidavits of Mattie Westbrook and Nancy A. Autry, to the birth of Edker Westbrook, child of Andy J. and Mattie Westbrook, June 23, 1904, and the same have been filed with our records as an application for the enrollment of said child.

                        Respectfully,

                                                Chairman.

Applications for Enrollment of Choctaw Newborn
Act of 1905   Volume XVI

7-NB-1177.

Muskogee, Indian Territory, June 10, 1905.

Andrew J. Westbrook,
    Brooken, Indian Territory.

Dear Sir:

There is enclosed herewith for execution application for the enrollment of your infant child, Edker Westbrook.

In the affidavits of April 19, 1905, heretofore filed in this office, the date of the applicant's birth is given as June 23, 1904, while in the affidavits of January 4, 1905, the mother gives this date as June 23, 1905[sic], and the physician as June 23, 1903. In the enclosed affidavits the date of birth is left blank. Please insert the correct date, and when the affidavits are properly executed return them to this office.

In having these affidavits executed care should be exercised to see that all names are written in full, as they appear in the body of the affidavit, and in the event either of the persons signing the affidavits are unable to write, signature by mark must be attested by two witnesses. Each affidavit must be executed before a Notary Public and the notarial seal and signature of the officer must be attached to each separate affidavit.

                        Respectfully,

DeB--1/10   Chairman.

7-NB-1177

Muskogee, Indian Territory, July 5, 1905.

Andrew J. Westbrook,
    Brooken, Indian Territory.

Dear Sir:

Receipt is hereby acknowledged of the affidavits of Maite[sic] Westbrook and Nancy A. Autry to the birth of Edker Westbrook, son of Andrew J. Westbrook and Mattie Westbrook, June 23, 1904, and the same have been filed with the records of this office in the matter of the enrollment of said child.

                        Respectfully,

                                            Commissioner.

Applications for Enrollment of Choctaw Newborn
Act of 1905   Volume XVI

Choc New Born 1178
  Willie D. McKee
  (Born Oct. 9, 1904)

NEW-BORN AFFIDAVIT.

Number................

Choctaw Enrolling Commission.

IN THE MATTER OF THE APPLICATION FOR ENROLLMENT, as a citizen of the Choctaw   Nation, of   Willie D. McKee

born on the 9 day of   October   190 4

Name of father   John D. McKee   a citizen of Choc by interm.
Nation final enrollment No   641
Name of mother   Mary A McKee   a citizen of   Choctaw
Nation final enrollment No   4737

Postoffice   Nelson

AFFIDAVIT OF MOTHER.

UNITED STATES OF AMERICA,
   INDIAN TERRITORY,
Central   DISTRICT

I   Mary A McKee   on oath state that I am 37 years of age and a citizen by   Blood   of the   Choctaw   Nation, and as such have been placed upon the final roll of the   Choctaw   Nation, by the Honorable Secretary of the Interior my final enrollment number being   4737   ; that I am the lawful wife of John D. McKee   , who is a citizen of the   Choctaw by interm.   Nation, and as such has been placed upon the final roll of said Nation by the Honorable Secretary of the Interior, his final enrollment number being   641   and that a   Male   child was born to me on the 9 day of October   190 4 ; that said child has been named   Willie D. McKee , and is now living.

Mary A McKee

WITNESSETH:
  Must be two
  Witnesses who   Willy Griggs
  are Citizens.   Henry Williams

Subscribed and sworn to before me this   23   day of   Jan   190 5

W.E. Larecy
Notary Public.

My commission expires
My commission expires   *July 9th, 1908.*

Applications for Enrollment of Choctaw Newborn
Act of 1905   Volume XVI

Affidavit of Attending Physician or Midwife

UNITED STATES OF AMERICA,
   INDIAN TERRITORY,
Central   DISTRICT

I, Narcissa Smallwood a Mid-wife on oath state that I attended on Mrs. Mary A McKee wife of John D McKee on the 9th day of October , 190 5[sic], that there was born to her on said date a male child, that said child is now living, and is said to have been named Willie D McKee

                          her
                    Narcissa x Smallwood
                        mark

Subscribed and sworn to before me this the 23 day of Jan 1905

      My commission expires   W.E. Larecy
      July 9th, 1908.   Notary Public.

WITNESSETH:
Must be two witnesses who are citizens and know the child.
{ Willy Griggs
  Henry Williams }

We hereby certify that we are well acquainted with Narcissa Smallwood a Mid-wife and know her to be reputable and of good standing in the community.

                  Must be two citizen witnesses.   { Thomas Ashford
                                                      Mary Griggs }

BIRTH AFFIDAVIT.

DEPARTMENT OF THE INTERIOR.
COMMISSION TO THE FIVE CIVILIZED TRIBES.

IN RE APPLICATION FOR ENROLLMENT, as a citizen of the Choctaw Nation, of Willie D. McKee , born on the 9th day of Oct , 1904

Name of Father: John D. McKee   a citizen of the Choctaw Nation.
Name of Mother: Mary A. McKee   a citizen of the Choctaw Nation.

                  Postoffice   Nelson I.T.

Applications for Enrollment of Choctaw Newborn
Act of 1905   Volume XVI

AFFIDAVIT OF MOTHER.

UNITED STATES OF AMERICA, Indian Territory,
Central   DISTRICT.

I, Mary A. McKee, on oath state that I am 37 years of age and a citizen by Blood, of the Choctaw Nation; that I am the lawful wife of John D. McKee, who is a citizen, by Intermarriage of the Choctaw Nation; that a male child was born to me on 9th day of Oct, 1904; that said child has been named Willie D. McKee, and was living March 4, 1905.

Mary A. McKee

Witnesses To Mark:

Subscribed and sworn to before me this 20 day of April, 1905

My commission expires
July 9th, 1908.

W.E. Larecy
Notary Public.

AFFIDAVIT OF ATTENDING PHYSICIAN OR MID-WIFE.

UNITED STATES OF AMERICA, Indian Territory,
Central   DISTRICT.

I, Narcissa Smallwood, a midwife, on oath state that I attended on Mrs. Mary A McKee, wife of John D McKee on the 9th day of Oct, 1904; that there was born to her on said date a male child; that said child was living March 4, 1905, and is said to have been named Willie D. McKee

           her
         Narcissa x Smallwood
Witnesses To Mark: mark
 Willy Griggs
 Mary Griggs

Subscribed and sworn to before me this 20 day of April, 1905

My commission expires
July 9th, 1908.

W.E. Larecy
Notary Public.

Applications for Enrollment of Choctaw Newborn
Act of 1905 Volume XVI

BIRTH AFFIDAVIT.

DEPARTMENT OF THE INTERIOR.
COMMISSION TO THE FIVE CIVILIZED TRIBES.

IN RE APPLICATION FOR ENROLLMENT, as a citizen of the Choctaw Nation, of Willie D. McKee, born on the 9th day of Oct, 1904

Name of Father: John D. McKee   a citizen of the Choctaw Nation.
Name of Mother: Mary A. McKee   a citizen of the Choctaw Nation.

Postoffice   Nelson Ind Ter

AFFIDAVIT OF MOTHER.

UNITED STATES OF AMERICA, Indian Territory, }
   Central   DISTRICT. }

I, Mary A. McKee, on oath state that I am 37 years of age and a citizen by blood, of the Choctaw Nation; that I am the lawful wife of John D. McKee, who is a citizen, by intermarriage of the Choctaw Nation; that a male child was born to me on 9th day of October, 1904; that said child has been named Willie D. McKee, and was living March 4, 1905.

Mary A. McKee

Witnesses To Mark:
{

Subscribed and sworn to before me this 19th day of June, 1905

My commission expires
July 9th, 1908.

W.E. Larecy
Notary Public.

AFFIDAVIT OF ATTENDING PHYSICIAN OR MID-WIFE.

UNITED STATES OF AMERICA, Indian Territory, }
   Central   DISTRICT. }

I, Narcissa Smallwood, a Midwife, on oath state that I attended on Mrs. Mary A McKee, wife of John D McKee on the 9th day of Oct, 1904; that there was born to her on said date a male child; that said child was living March 4, 1905, and is said to have been named Willie D. McKee

                         her
                Narcissa x Smallwood
                         mark

Applications for Enrollment of Choctaw Newborn
Act of 1905   Volume XVI

Witnesses To Mark:
 { Willy Griggs
 { Mary Griggs

    Subscribed and sworn to before me this 9th   day of   June   , 1905

My commission expires
July 9th, 1908.

W.E. Larecy
Notary Public.

7-NB-1178.

Muskogee, Indian Territory, June 10, 1905.

John D. McKee,
    Nelson, Indian Territory.

Dear Sir:

    There is enclosed herewith for execution application for the enrollment of your infant child, Willie D. McKee.

    In the application filed in this office on April 26[sic], 1905, the date of the applicant's birth is given as October 9, 1904, while in the one filed on April 25[sic], 1905, the mother gives this date as October 9, 1904 and the midwife gives it as October 9, 1905. In the enclosed application the date of the birth is left blank. Please insert the correct date and when the affidavits are properly executed return them to this office.

    In having these affidavits executed care should be exercised to see that all names are written in full, as they appear in the body of the affidavit, and in the event either of the persons signing the affidavit are unable to write, signatures by mark must be attested by two witnesses. Each affidavit must be executed before a Notary Public and the notarial seal and signature of the officer must be attached to each separate affidavit.

                                       Respectfully,

DeB--2/10   Chairman.

Applications for Enrollment of Choctaw Newborn
Act of 1905   Volume XVI

7 NB 1178

Muskogee, Indian Territory, June 21, 1905.

John D. McKee,
    Nelson, Indian Territory.

Dear Sir:

    Receipt is hereby acknowledged of the affidavits of Mary A. McKee and Narcissa Smallwood to the birth of Willie D. McKee, son of John D. McKee and Mary A. McKee, October 9, 1904, and the same have been filed with our records in the matter of the enrollment of said child.

        Respectfully,

                Chairman.

Choc New Born 1179
    Samuel James Watson
    (Born Oct. 23, 1903)

NEW BORN AFFIDAVIT

No _____

CHOCTAW ENROLLING COMMISSION

IN THE MATTER OF THE APPLICATION FOR ENROLLMENT as a citizen of the Choctaw Nation, of   Samuel James Watson   born on the 23 day of   September   190 3

Name of father   Andrew Watson   a citizen of   non   Nation,
final enrollment No. ———
Name of mother   Mary Watson   a citizen of   Choctaw   Nation,
final enrollment No. 6917

                      Heavener I.T.   Postoffice.

Applications for Enrollment of Choctaw Newborn
Act of 1905   Volume XVI

AFFIDAVIT OF MOTHER

UNITED STATES OF AMERICA
   INDIAN TERRITORY
DISTRICT   Central

    I   Mary Watson   , on oath state that I am   27   years of age and a citizen by   blood   of the   Choctaw   Nation, and as such have been placed upon the final roll of the   Choctaw   Nation, by the Honorable Secretary of the Interior my final enrollment number being   6917   ; that I am the lawful wife of   Andrew Watson   , who is a citizen of the   non   Nation, and as such has been placed upon the final roll of said Nation by the Honorable Secretary of the Interior, his final enrollment number being   —   and that a   Male   child was born to me on the   23   day of   September   190 3; that said child has been named   Samuel James Watson   , and is now living.

                                                           her
WITNESSETH: Mary x Watson
   Must be two witnesses   John Folsom   mark
   who are citizens   Rhoda West

    Subscribed and sworn to before me this, the   28"   day of   Feby   , 190 5

                                       J.M. Young
                                                   Notary Public.
My Commission Expires: March 6, 1905

Affidavit of Attending Physician or Midwife

UNITED STATES OF AMERICA,
   INDIAN TERRITORY,
  Central   DISTRICT

    I,   Nancy Dudley   a   midwife on oath state that I attended on Mrs. Mary Watson   wife of Andrew Watson on the   23   day of   September , 190 3, that there was born to her on said date a   male child, that said child is now living, and is said to have been named   Samuel James Watson

                                             her
                                    Nancy x Dudley   *Midwife*
                                       mark
    Subscribed and sworn to before me this the   28"   day of   Feby   1905

My com expires March 6 - 1905   J.M. Young
                                                  Notary Public.
WITNESSETH:
   Must be two witnesses   John Folsom
   who are citizens and
   know the child.   Rhoda West

Applications for Enrollment of Choctaw Newborn
Act of 1905   Volume XVI

We hereby certify that we are well acquainted with   Nancy Dudley   a   midwife   and know   her   to be reputable and of good standing in the community.

Must be two citizen witnesses. { Rhoda West
Carnolie Runton

7-6917

BIRTH AFFIDAVIT.

DEPARTMENT OF THE INTERIOR.
COMMISSION TO THE FIVE CIVILIZED TRIBES.

IN RE APPLICATION FOR ENROLLMENT, as a citizen of the   Choctaw   Nation, of Samuel James Watson   , born on the 23   day of   October[sic]   , 1903

Name of Father: A C Watson   a citizen of the United States Nation.
Name of Mother: Mary Watson   a citizen of the   Choc   Nation.

Postoffice   Howe I.T.

AFFIDAVIT OF MOTHER.

UNITED STATES OF AMERICA, Indian Territory,
Central   DISTRICT.

I, Mary Watson   , on oath state that I am 27   years of age and a citizen by blood   , of the   Choctaw   Nation; that I am the lawful wife of   A. C. Watson   , who is a citizen, by .... of the   United States   Nation; that a   male   child was born to me on   23   day of   October[sic]   , 1903; that said child has been named   Samuel James Watson   , and was living March 4, 1905.

                                      her
                             Mary x Watson
Witnesses To Mark: mark
{ Chas T Difendafer
  OL Johnson

Subscribed and sworn to before me this 20 day of   April   , 1905

                             OL Johnson
                             Notary Public.

Applications for Enrollment of Choctaw Newborn
Act of 1905   Volume XVI

AFFIDAVIT OF ATTENDING PHYSICIAN OR MID-WIFE.

UNITED STATES OF AMERICA, Indian Territory, }
Central   DISTRICT.

    I, Nancy Dudley, a midwife, on oath state that I attended on Mrs. Mary Watson, wife of AC Watson on the 23 day of October[sic], 1903; that there was born to her on said date a male child; that said child was living March 4, 1905, and is said to have been named Samuel James Watson

                                           her
                                     Nancy x Dudley
Witnesses To Mark: mark
{ W F Ryburn
{ C J White

    Subscribed and sworn to before me this 20 day of April, 1905

                            NS Costelow
                                  Notary Public.
My com expr Mch 20 1907

BIRTH AFFIDAVIT.

DEPARTMENT OF THE INTERIOR.
COMMISSION TO THE FIVE CIVILIZED TRIBES.

    IN RE APPLICATION FOR ENROLLMENT, as a citizen of the Choctaw Nation, of Samuel James Watson, born on the 23 day of Sept, 1903

Name of Father: A. C. Watson   a citizen of the ——— Nation.
Name of Mother: Mary Watson   a citizen of the Choctaw Nation.

                        Postoffice   Howe, Ind. Ter.

AFFIDAVIT OF MOTHER.

UNITED STATES OF AMERICA, Indian Territory, }
Central   DISTRICT.

    I, Mary Watson, on oath state that I am 27 years of age and a citizen by blood, of the Choctaw Nation; that I am the lawful wife of A. C. Watson, who is a citizen, by —— of the ———Nation; that a male child was born to me on 23d day of Sept, 1903; that said child has been named Samuel James Watson, and was living March 4, 1905.

                                         her
                                 Mary x Watson
                                     mark

Applications for Enrollment of Choctaw Newborn
Act of 1905 Volume XVI

Witnesses To Mark:
{ Wm Dyer
  W.J. Dean

    Subscribed and sworn to before me this   12th day of   June   , 1905

                            W.N. Estes
                            Notary Public.

AFFIDAVIT OF ATTENDING PHYSICIAN OR MID-WIFE.

UNITED STATES OF AMERICA, Indian Territory, }
   Central   DISTRICT. }

    I,   Nancy Dudley   , a midwife   , on oath state that I attended on Mrs.   Mary Watson   , wife of   A C Watson   on the 23rd day of Sept , 1903; that there was born to her on said date a   male   child; that said child was living March 4, 1905, and is said to have been named Samuel James Watson

                              her
                        Nancy x Dudley

Witnesses To Mark: mark
{ *(Name Illegible)*
  C. Runton

    Subscribed and sworn to before me this   12 day of   June   , 1905

                            NS Costelow
                            Notary Public.
                            Heavener I.T

---

                                          7 N.B. 1179.

              Muskogee, Indian Territory, May 25, 1905.

John Begley,
    Box 83,
        Howe, Indian Territory.

Dear Sir:

    Receipt is hereby acknowledged of your letter of May 22, asking if the Department has approved the enrollment of Samuel J. Watson, child of A. C. and Mary Watson.

Applications for Enrollment of Choctaw Newborn
Act of 1905   Volume XVI

In reply to your letter you are advised that the affidavits heretofore forwarded to the birth of Samuel James Watson have been filed with our records as an application for the enrollment of said child, but his name has not yet been placed upon a schedule of citizens by blood of the Choctaw Nation prepared for forwarding to the Secretary of the Interior. In the event further evidence is necessary to determine the right to enrollment of said child Mr. Watson will be duly advised.

                Respectfully,

                              Chairman.

7-NB-1179

                Muskogee, Indian Territory, July 21, 1905.

Andrew C. Watson,
    Howe, Indian Territory.

Dear Sir:

Receipt is hereby acknowledged of your letter of July 13, 1905, asking if the enrollment of James[sic] Samuel[sic] Watson has been approved.

In reply to your letter you are advised that the name of James Samuel Watson has not yet been placed upon a schedule of citizens by blood of the Choctaw Nation, prepared for frowarding[sic] to the Secretary of the Interior, but if further evidence is necessary to determine his right to enrollment you will be notified.

                Respectfully,

                              Commissioner.

(The letter above given again.)

Applications for Enrollment of Choctaw Newborn
Act of 1905   Volume XVI

7--NB--1179

Muskogee, Indian Territory, June 2, 1905.

A. C. Watson,
    Howe, Indian Territory.

Dear Sir:

There is enclosed you herewith for execution application for the enrollment of your infant child, Samuel James Watson.

The affidavits executed under date of February 28, 1905, give the date of the applicant's birth as September 23, 1903, while the affidavits executed on April 20, 1905, give this date as October 23, 1903. In the enclosed application the date of birth is left blank. You are requested to insert the correct date and when the affidavits have been properly executed return the same to this office.

In having the affidavits executed care should be exercised to see that all names are written in full, as they appear in the body of the affidavits and in the event that either of the persons signing same are unable to write, signatures by mark must be attested by two witnesses. Each affidavit must be executed before a Notary Public and the notarial seal and signature of the officer must be attached to each separate affidavit.

This matter should receive your immediate attention as no further action can be taken relative to the enrollment of said child until the Commission is furnished these affidavits.

                        Respectfully,

                                      Commissioner.

Enc-FVK-15

---

7 NB 1179

Muskogee, Indian Territory, June 15, 1905.

A. C. Watson,
    Howe, Indian Territory.

Dear Sir:

Receipt is hereby acknowledged of the affidavits of Mary Watson and Nancy Dudley to the birth of Samuel James Watson, son of A. C. and Mary Watson, September 23, 1903, and the same have been filed with our records in the matter of the enrollment of said child.

Applications for Enrollment of Choctaw Newborn
Act of 1905   Volume XVI

Respectfully,

Chairman.

Choc New Born 1180
    Allen Jack
    (Born Feb. 7, 1905)

BIRTH AFFIDAVIT.

DEPARTMENT OF THE INTERIOR.
COMMISSION TO THE FIVE CIVILIZED TRIBES.

IN RE APPLICATION FOR ENROLLMENT, as a citizen of the   Choctaw   Nation, of Allen Jack   , born on the 7 day of Feb , 1905

Name of Father: Martin Jack   a citizen of the Choctaw   Nation.
Name of Mother: Lauina Jack nee Adams   a citizen of the Choctaw   Nation.

Postoffice   Le Flore I.T.

AFFIDAVIT OF MOTHER.

UNITED STATES OF AMERICA, Indian Territory, }
    Central   DISTRICT.

    I,   Lauina Jack nee Adams   , on oath state that I am 20 years of age and a citizen by   blood   , of the   Choctaw   Nation; that I am the lawful wife of Martin Jack   , who is a citizen, by blood   of the   Choctaw   Nation; that a   male   child was born to me on 7 day of February , 1905; that said child has been named   Allen Jack   , and was living March 4, 1905.

                                       her
                            Lauina x Jack, nee Adams
Witnesses To Mark: mark
  { Sidney Amos
    Henry Burns

    Subscribed and sworn to before me this 21 day of   April   , 1905

My com 1-11-1906   Robert E Lee
                                  Notary Public.

Applications for Enrollment of Choctaw Newborn
Act of 1905   Volume XVI

AFFIDAVIT OF ATTENDING PHYSICIAN OR MID-WIFE.

UNITED STATES OF AMERICA, Indian Territory,
Central   DISTRICT.

I, Martin Jack, a husband, on oath state that I attended on Mrs. Lauina Jack nee Adams, ~~wife of~~ *my own wife* on the 7 day of Feb, 1905; that there was born to her on said date a male child; that said child was living March 4, 1905, and is said to have been named Allen Jack

Martin Jack

Witnesses To Mark:

Subscribed and sworn to before me this 21 day of April, 1905

My com 1-11-1906   Robert E Lee
                           Notary Public.

Final enrollment no of Martin Jack being no. 8883
"   "   " " Lauina Jack nee Adams being no. 8508

Affidavit of Wilson Nicholas

Commission to the Five Civilized Tribes

In the matter of Allen Jack the applicant for the enrollment as a new born - I, Wilson Nicholas on oath state that I am not related to the said Allen Jack and in my own knowledge of the facts that the said Allen Jack was born on the 7 day of February 1905 and his father was in attendance upon Lauina Jack the mother of said Allen Jack and the said Allen Jack was living on the 4th day of March 1905 and the said Lauina Jack is the mother of said Allen Jack

Wilson Nicholas

Sworn to and subscribed before me this 1 day of Aug 1905

Robert E Lee
Notary Public
Central District
Indian Territory

My com expires Jan. 11-1906

Applications for Enrollment of Choctaw Newborn
Act of 1905   Volume XVI

Affidavit of Lillie Adams

Commission to the Five Civilized Tribes

In the matter of Allen Jack the applicant for the enrollment of a new born:- I, Lilly Adams on oath state that I am not related to the said Allen Jack and I am in actual knowledge of the facts that the said Allen Jack was born on the 7 day of February 1905 and was living on the 4th day of March 1905, and the same was named Allen Jack and that Lauina Jack is the mother of said Allen Jack.

Lillie Adams

Sworn to and subscribed before me this 1 day of Aug. 1905.

Robert E Lee
Notary Public
Central District
Indian Territory

My com expires Jan. 11-1906

7-2892.

Muskogee, Indian Territory, April 26, 1905.

Martin Jack,
LeFlore, Indian Territory.

Dear Sir:

Receipt is hereby acknowledged of the affidavits of Louina[sic] Jack and Martin Jack, to the birth of Allen Jack, child of Martin and Louina Jack, February 7, 1905, and the same have been filed with our records as an application for the enrollment of said child.

Respectfully,

Chairman.

Applications for Enrollment of Choctaw Newborn
Act of 1905   Volume XVI

7--NB--1180

7--[sic]

Muskogee, Indian Territory, June 2, 1905.

Martin Jack,
    LeFlore, Indian Territory.

Dear Sir:

    Referring to the application for the enrollment of your infant child, Allen Jack, born February 7, 1905, it is noted from the affidavits heretofore filed in this office that you were the only one in attendance upon your wife at the time of the birth of the applicant.

    In this event it will be necessary that the affidavits of two persons, who are disinterested and not related to the applicant, who have actual knowledge of the facts that the child was born, the date of his birth; that he was living on March 4, 1905, and that Louina Jack is his mother be filed in this office.

    This matter should receive your immediate attention as no further action can be taken relative to the enrollment of your said child until the Commission has been furnished these affidavits.

                      Respectfully,

                                                  [sic]

7-NB-1180

Muskogee, Indian Territory, July 26, 1905.

Martin Jack,
    LeFlore, Indian Territory.

Dear Sir:

    Your attention is called to a communication addressed to you by the Commission to the Five Civilized Tribes, under date of June 2, 1905, in which you were requested to furnish additional evidence in the matter of the enrollment of your child, Allen Jack, born February 7, 1905.

    You were informed that if you were the only one in attendance upon your wife at the time of the birth of the applicant, it was necessary that you furnish the affidavits of two persons who are disinterested and not related to the applicant, and who have actual knowledge of the facts, that the child was born, the date of his birth, that he was living

Applications for Enrollment of Choctaw Newborn
Act of 1905   Volume XVI

March 4, 1905, and that Louvina[sic] Jack is his mother. No reply to this letter has been received.

Respectfully,

Commissioner.

7-NB-1180

Muskogee, Indian Territory, August 7, 1905.

Martin Jack,
    Leflore, Indian Territory.

Dear Sir:

Receipt is hereby acknowledged of the affidavits of Wilson Nicholas and Lillie Adams to the birth of Allen Jack, February 7, 1905, and the same have been filed with the records of this office in the matter of the enrollment of said child.

Respectfully,

Commissioner.

7-NB-1180

Muskogee, Indian Territory, September 14, 1905.

Martin Jack,
    Le Flore, Indian Territory.

Dear Sir:

Replying to your letter of September 9th, you are advised that on August 26, 1905, the Commissioner to the Five Civilized Tribes transmitted to the Secretary of the Interior for his approval a schedule of new-born citizens by blood of the Choctaw Nation, the name of your child appearing upon said schedule opposite number 1509. When this office is advised of the approval of the schedule by the Secretary of the Interior, you will be notified thereof.

No allotment can be selected for the child until his enrollment has been approved by the Secretary of the Interior.

Respectfully,

Acting Commissioner.

Applications for Enrollment of Choctaw Newborn
Act of 1905 Volume XVI

Choc New Born 1181
    Lena Stephen
    (Born August 20, 1903)

BIRTH AFFIDAVIT.

DEPARTMENT OF THE INTERIOR.
COMMISSION TO THE FIVE CIVILIZED TRIBES.

IN RE APPLICATION FOR ENROLLMENT, as a citizen of the Choctaw Nation, of Lena Stephen, born on the 20th day of August, 1903

Name of Father: Lemus[sic] Stephen   a citizen of the Choctaw Nation.
Name of Mother: Linas Stephen   a citizen of the Choctaw Nation.

Postoffice   Hoche[sic] Town, I.T.

AFFIDAVIT OF MOTHER.

UNITED STATES OF AMERICA, Indian Territory, }
    Central   DISTRICT.

    I, Linas Stephen, on oath state that I am 25 years of age and a citizen by blood, of the Choctaw Nation; that I am the lawful wife of Lemus Stephen, who is a citizen, by blood of the Choctaw Nation; that a female child was born to me on 20th day of August, 1903; that said child has been named Lena Stephen, and was living March 4, 1905.

                                   her
                            Linas x Stephen
Witnesses To Mark: mark
  { Robert Anderson
    Vester Rose

    Subscribed and sworn to before me this 10th day of April, 1905

                       Wirt Franklin
                           Notary Public.

Applications for Enrollment of Choctaw Newborn
Act of 1905 Volume XVI

AFFIDAVIT OF ATTENDING PHYSICIAN OR MID-WIFE.

UNITED STATES OF AMERICA, Indian Territory, }
Central DISTRICT.

I, Stephen Outahyubbe , a doctor , on oath state that I attended on Mrs. Linas Stephen , wife of Lemus Stephen on the 20th day of August, 1903; that there was born to her on said date a female child; that said child was living March 4, 1905, and is said to have been named Lena Stephen

Stephen Outahyubbe

Witnesses To Mark:
{

Subscribed and sworn to before me this 10th day of April , 1905

Wirt Franklin
Notary Public.

7 NB 1181

Muskogee, Indian Territory, July 1, 1905.

Lamus Stephen,
Hochatown, Indian Territory.

Dear Sir:

Receipt is hereby acknowledged of your letter of June 27, 1905, asking the status of the application for the enrollment of your child Lena Stephen.

In reply to your letter you are advised that the name of your daughter Lena Stephen has been placed upon a schedule of citizens by blood of the Choctaw Nation prepared for forwarding to the Secretary of the Interior.

You will be notified when her enrollment is approved by the Department.

Respectfully,

Commissioner.

Applications for Enrollment of Choctaw Newborn
Act of 1905 Volume XVI

Choc New Born 1182
    Daisy Lily Overstreet
    (Born Nov. 4, 1903)

NEW-BORN AFFIDAVIT.

Number

Choctaw Enrolling Commission.

IN THE MATTER OF THE APPLICATION FOR ENROLLMENT, as a citizen of the Choctaw Nation, of   Daisy Lillie Overstreet

born on the 4 day of November 190 3

Name of father   WM. Newton Overstreet   a citizen of
Nation final enrollment No
Name of mother   Addie A Overstreet   a citizen of   Choctaw
Nation final enrollment No   10448

Postoffice   Ego I T

AFFIDAVIT OF MOTHER.

UNITED STATES OF AMERICA,
    INDIAN TERRITORY,
Central   DISTRICT

    I   Addie A Overstreet   on oath state that I am 25 years of age and a citizen by   Blood   of the   Choctaw   Nation, and as such have been placed upon the final roll of the   Choctaw   Nation, by the Honorable Secretary of the Interior my final enrollment number being   10448   ; that I am the lawful wife of   Wm Newton Overstreet   , who is a citizen of the   Nation, and as such has been placed upon the final roll of said Nation by the Honorable Secretary of the Interior, his final enrollment number being   and that a Female   child was born to me on the   4   day of   November   190 3 ; that said child has been named   Daisy Lillie Overstreet   , and is now living.

WITNESSETH: Addie A Overstreet
   Must be two   D S Moran
   Witnesses who
   are Citizens.   John C Izard

Subscribed and sworn to before me this   19   day of   Jan   190 5

                             J T Hoover
                                   Notary Public.

My commission expires   Feb 26-1906

Applications for Enrollment of Choctaw Newborn
Act of 1905 Volume XVI

Affidavit of Attending Physician or Midwife

UNITED STATES OF AMERICA,
INDIAN TERRITORY,
Central   DISTRICT

I,   Thos M. Morgan   a   Physician
on oath state that I attended on Mrs. Adie[sic] A Overstreet   wife of   Newt Overstreet
on the 4th   day of   November , 190 3, that there was born to her on said date a   Female
child, that said child is now living, and is said to have been named   Daisy Lillie Overstreet

                                        Thos. M. Morgan   M. D.

Subscribed and sworn to before me this the   18   day of   January   1905

                                        J.T. Hoover
                                                Notary Public.

WITNESSETH:
Must be two witnesses { D S Moran
who are citizens and
know the child.   John C Izard

We hereby certify that we are well acquainted with   Thos M Morgan
a   Physician   and know him   to be reputable and of good standing in the
community.

                        Must be two citizen { D S Moran
                        witnesses.   John C Izard

BIRTH AFFIDAVIT.

DEPARTMENT OF THE INTERIOR.
COMMISSION TO THE FIVE CIVILIZED TRIBES.

IN RE APPLICATION FOR ENROLLMENT, as a citizen of the   Choctaw   Nation, of
Daisy Lily Moran[sic]   , born on the 4th   day of November , 1903

Name of Father: Wm Newton Overstreet   a citizen of the   U.S.   Nation.
Name of Mother: Addie A Overstreet   a citizen of the   Choctaw   Nation.

                    Postoffice   Ego IT

Applications for Enrollment of Choctaw Newborn
Act of 1905   Volume XVI

AFFIDAVIT OF MOTHER.

UNITED STATES OF AMERICA, Indian Territory,
Central   DISTRICT.

I, Addie A Overstreet, on oath state that I am 19 years of age and a citizen by Blood, of the Choctaw Nation; that I am the lawful wife of Wm Newton Overstreet, who is a citizen, by _____ of the U.S. Nation; that a Female child was born to me on 4th day of November, 1903; that said child has been named Daisy Litty[sic] Overstreet, and was living March 4, 1905.

Addie A Overstreet

Witnesses To Mark:
{ Fred Sammons
  HY Morgan

Subscribed and sworn to before me this 11th day of April, 1905

J T Hoover
Notary Public.

AFFIDAVIT OF ATTENDING PHYSICIAN OR MID-WIFE.

UNITED STATES OF AMERICA, Indian Territory,
Central   DISTRICT.

I, Thos. M. Morgan, a Physician, on oath state that I attended on Mrs. Addie A Overstreet, wife of Wm Newton Overstreet on the 4th day of November, 1903; that there was born to her on said date a female child; that said child was living March 4, 1905, and is said to have been named Daisy Lillie Overstreet

Thos M. Morgan

Witnesses To Mark:
{

Subscribed and sworn to before me this 10th day of April, 1905

J.T. Hoover
Notary Public.

Applications for Enrollment of Choctaw Newborn
Act of 1905   Volume XVI

BIRTH AFFIDAVIT.

DEPARTMENT OF THE INTERIOR.
COMMISSION TO THE FIVE CIVILIZED TRIBES.

IN RE APPLICATION FOR ENROLLMENT, as a citizen of the   Choctaw   Nation, of Daisy Lillie Overstreet   , born on the 4th day of November   , 1903

Name of Father: Wm Newton Overstreet   a citizen of the   U.S.   Nation.
Name of Mother: Addie A Overstreet   a citizen of the   Choctaw   Nation.

Postoffice   Ego I.T.

AFFIDAVIT OF MOTHER.

UNITED STATES OF AMERICA, Indian Territory,
Central   DISTRICT.

I,   Addie A Overstreet   , on oath state that I am   19   years of age and a citizen by   blood   , of the   Choctaw   Nation; that I am the lawful wife of   Wm Newton Overstreet   , who is a citizen, ~~by~~ ——— of the   United States   Nation; that a   female   child was born to me on   4th day of   November   , 1903; that said child has been named   Daisy Lillie Overstreet   , and was living March 4, 1905.

Addie A Overstreet

Witnesses To Mark:

Subscribed and sworn to before me this   30 day of   June   , 1905

J G Reeder
Notary Public.

AFFIDAVIT OF ATTENDING PHYSICIAN OR MID-WIFE.

UNITED STATES OF AMERICA, Indian Territory,
Central   DISTRICT.

I,   Thos. M. Morgan   , a physician   , on oath state that I attended on Mrs.   Addie Overstreet   , wife of Wm Newton Overstreet   on the   4th day of November   , 1903; that there was born to her on said date a   Female   child; that said child was living March 4, 1905, and is said to have been named   Daisy Lillie Overstreet

Thos M. Morgan M.D.

Witnesses To Mark:

Applications for Enrollment of Choctaw Newborn
Act of 1905   Volume XVI

Subscribed and sworn to before me this   30   day of   June   , 1905

J G Reeder
Notary Public.

Muskogee, Indian Territory, April 15, 1905.

William Newton Overstreet,
Ego, Indian Territory.

Dear Sir:

Receipt is hereby acknowledged of the affidavits of Addie A. Overstreet and Thos. M. Morgan to the birth of Daisy Lillie Overstreet, daughter of William Newton and Addie A. Overstreet, November 4, 1903.

It is stated in the affidavit of the mother that she is a citizen by blood of the Choctaw Nation. If this is correct, you are requested to state the name under which che[sic] was enrolled, the names of her parents and, if she has selected her allotment of the lands of the Choctaw and Chickasaw Nations, give her roll number as the same appears upon her certificate of allotment.

This matter should receive immediate attention in order that proper disposition may be made of the application for the enrollment of your child, Daisy Lillie Overstreet.

Respectfully,

Chairman.

Choctaw 3693.

Muskogee, Indian Territory, April 27, 1905.

Addie A. Overstreet,
Ego, Indian Territory.

Dear Madam:

Receipt is hereby acknowledged of your letters of April 19, and 20, relative to the application for the enrollment of your child, Daisy Lillie Overstreet.

In reply to your letter you are advised that the information contained therein has enabled us to identify you upon our records as an enrolled citizen by blood of the Choctaw Nation, and the affidavits heretofore forwarded to the birth of your child, Daisy

Applications for Enrollment of Choctaw Newborn
Act of 1905   Volume XVI

Lily Overstreet, have been filed with our records as an application for the enrollment of said child.

                    Respectfully,

                                        Chairman.

                                        7--NB--1182.

                    Muskogee, Indian Territory, June 3, 1905.

William Newton Overstreet,
    Ego, Indian Territory.

Dear Sir:

      There is enclosed herewith for execution application for the enrollment of your infant child, born November 4, 1903.

      In the affidavit of the mother of this applicant executed April 11, 1905, the name of the applicant is given as "Daisy Litty Overstreet", while in the affidavit of the attending physician dated April 10, 1905, the name is given as "Daisy Lillie Overstreet". In the enclosed affidavits the name of the child has been left blank. Please insert the correct name of the applicant and when the affidavits have been properly executed return the same to this office.

      In having these affidavits executed care should be exercised to see that all names are written in full, as they appear in the body of the affidavit, and in the event that either of the persons signing the affidavit are unable to write, signatures by mark must be attested by two witnesses. Each affidavit must be executed before a Notary Public and the notarial seal and signature of the officer must be attached to each separate affidavit.

      This matter should receive your immediate attention as no further action can be taken relative to the enrollment of said child until these affidavits have been furnished the Commission.

                    Respectfully,

                    Ch[sic]

Choc New Born 1183
    Rosey Butler
    (Born Nov. 19, 1903)

Applications for Enrollment of Choctaw Newborn
Act of 1905   Volume XVI

BIRTH AFFIDAVIT.

DEPARTMENT OF THE INTERIOR.
COMMISSION TO THE FIVE CIVILIZED TRIBES.

IN RE APPLICATION FOR ENROLLMENT, as a citizen of the   Choctaw   Nation, of Rosey Butler   , born on the 19th   day of   November   , 1903

Name of Father: J F Butler   a citizen of the   non citizen   Nation.
Name of Mother: Lizzie Butler Roll 10385   a citizen of the   Choctaw   Nation.

Postoffice   Cade Ind Ter

AFFIDAVIT OF ATTENDING PHYSICIAN OR MID-WIFE.

UNITED STATES OF AMERICA, Indian Territory,
Central   DISTRICT.

am acquainted with

I,   D A Russey   , a ...., on oath state that I ~~attended on~~ Mrs.   Lizzie Butler   , wife of   J F Butler; *that on or about* the 19th day of November   , 1903; that there was born to her on said date a   female   child; that said child was living March 4, 1905, and is said to have been named   Rosey Butler, *and that I am not related to the parents of said child.*

D A Russey

Witnesses To Mark:

Subscribed and sworn to before me this   12 day of   June   , 1905

T.M. Sullivan
Notary Public.

BIRTH AFFIDAVIT.

DEPARTMENT OF THE INTERIOR.
COMMISSION TO THE FIVE CIVILIZED TRIBES.

IN RE APPLICATION FOR ENROLLMENT, as a citizen of the   Choctaw   Nation, of Rosey Butler   , born on the 19th   day of   November   , 1903

Name of Father: J F Butler   a citizen of the   non citizen   Nation.
Name of Mother: Lizzie Butler Roll 10385   a citizen of the   Choctaw   Nation.

Applications for Enrollment of Choctaw Newborn
Act of 1905   Volume XVI

Postoffice   Cade Ind Ter

AFFIDAVIT OF ATTENDING PHYSICIAN OR MID-WIFE.

UNITED STATES OF AMERICA, Indian Territory,
Central   DISTRICT.

I, Katie Maddox   , a ...., *am acquainted with* on oath state that I ~~attended on~~ Mrs. Lizzie Butler   , wife of   J F Butler   on the   19th   day of   November   , 1903; that there was born to her on said date a   female   child; that said child was living March 4, 1905, and is said to have been named Rosey Butler, *that I am not related to the parents of said child.*

Katie Maddox

Witnesses To Mark:

Subscribed and sworn to before me this   12   day of   June   , 1905

T.M. Sullivan
Notary Public.

BIRTH AFFIDAVIT.

Department of the Interior,
COMMISSION TO THE FIVE CIVILIZED TRIBES.

IN RE APPLICATION FOR ENROLLMENT, as a citizen of the   Choctaw   Nation, of   Rosey Buttler[sic]   , born on the   19   day of   Nov   , 190 3

Name of Father: J F Buttler   a citizen of the   U.S.   ~~Nation~~.
Name of Mother: Lizzie Buttler   a citizen of the   Choctaw   Nation.

Post-Office: Cade Ind. Ter

AFFIDAVIT OF MOTHER.

UNITED STATES OF AMERICA,
INDIAN TERRITORY,
Central   District.

I, Lizzie Buttler   , on oath state that I am   21   years of age and a citizen by   Birth   , of the   Choctaw   Nation; that I am the lawful wife of   J F Buttler   , who is a citizen, by Birth   of the   U.S.   ~~Nation~~; that a   female   child was born to me on   19   day of   November   , 190 3, that said child has been named   Rosey Buttler   , and is now living.

Applications for Enrollment of Choctaw Newborn
Act of 1905   Volume XVI

her
Lizzie x Buttler
mark

WITNESSES TO MARK:
{ J.L. Lightfoot
{ W.E. Townley

Subscribed and sworn to before me this 12 day of   April , 1905

T.M. Sullivan
Notary Public.

(The letter below typed as given.)

Dear Sirs on January 20th 1905 I Enclosed the affidavit of J H Hargraves the attending physician at the here in name child & we are unable to get his affidavit this time haveing move to new orleans tho I supose the affidavit that was sent to you January 20 1905 will answer yours respt

J L. Butler

7-3675

Muskogee, Indian Territory, January 28, 1905.

T. M. Sullivan,
   Bennington, Indian Territory.

Dear Sir:

Receipt is hereby acknowledged of your letter of January 20, 1905, addressed to the United States Indian Agent which has been by him referred to the Commission to the Five Civilized Tribes for appropriate action. Therewith you enclose the affidavits of Lizzie Butler and J. H. Hargrove to the birth of Rosey Butler, daughter of J. F. and Lizzie Butler, November 29[sic], 1903, which it is presumed have been forwarded as an application for the enrollment of said child.

You are advised that under the provisions of the act of Congress approved July 1, 1902, no children born to citizens of the Choctaw and Chickasaw Nations subsequent to September 25, 1902, the date of the ratification of said act, are entitled to enrollment and allotment in the Choctaw and Chickasaw Nations.

Respectfully,

Chairman.

Applications for Enrollment of Choctaw Newborn
Act of 1905   Volume XVI

Choctaw 3675.

Muskogee, Indian Territory, April 27, 1905.

J. F. Butler,
Cade, Indian Territory.

Dear Sir:

Receipt is hereby acknowledged of your letter of April 21, giving the roll number of your wife, Lizzie Butler, and the affidavit heretofore forwarded to the birth of Rosey Butler, daughter of J. F. and Lizzie Butler has been filed with our records as an application for the enrollment of said child.

Respectfully,

Chairman.

Muskogee, Indian Territory, April 15, 1905.

J. F. Butler,
Cade, Indian Territory.

Dear Sir:

Receipt is hereby acknowledged of the affidavits of Lizzie Butler to the birth of Rasey[sic] Buttler, daughter of J. F. and Lizzie Buttler, March 19, 1903.

It is stated in the affidavit of Lizzie Buttler that she is a citizen by blood of the Choctaw Nation. If this is correct you are requested to state the name under which she was enrolled, the names of her parents, and if she has selected an allotment of the lands of the Choctaw and Chickasaw Nation[sic] please give her roll number as it appears upon her allotment certificate.

Respectfully,

Chairman.

Applications for Enrollment of Choctaw Newborn
Act of 1905   Volume XVI

7 NB 1183

Muskogee, Indian Territory, June 15, 1905.

J. F. Butler,
    Cade, Indian Territory.

Dear Sir:

    Receipt is hereby acknowledged of the affidavits of D. A. Russey and Hatie[sic] Maddox to the birth of Rosey Butler, daughter of J. F. and Lizzie Butler, November 19, 1903, and the same have been filed in the matter of the enrollment of said child.

Respectfully,

Chairman.

7-NB-1183

Muskogee, Indian Territory, June 1, 1905.

J. F. Butler,
    Cade, Indian Territory.

Dear Sir:

    There are enclosed you herewith two affidavits to be executed by disinterested persons in the matter of the enrollment of your infant child, Rosey Butler, born November 19, 1903.

    The affidavit of the physician heretofore filed with the Commission shows the child was living on January 22, 1905. It is necessary, for the child to be enrolled, that affidavits other than that of the mother show that she was living on March 4, 1905.

    In having these affidavits executed care should be exercised to see that all names are written in full, as they appear in the body of the affidavit, and in the event that either of the persons signing the affidavit are unable to write, signatures by mark must be attested by two witnesses. Each affidavit must be executed before a Notary Public and the notarial seal and signature of the officer must be attached to each separate affidavit.

    This matter should receive your immediate attention as no further action can be taken relative to the enrollment of your said child until the Commission has been furnished with this information.

Respectfully,

FVK-21

Chairman.

Applications for Enrollment of Choctaw Newborn
Act of 1905   Volume XVI

7-NB-1183

Muskogee, Indian Territory, January 15, 1906.

J. F. Butler,
    Cade, Indian Territory.

Dear Sir:

    Receipt is hereby acknowledged of your letter of January 5, 1906, asking if you can file on land for your daughter Rosey Butler.

    In reply to your letter you are advised that the enrollment of Rosey Butler as a new born citizen of the Choctaw Nation was approved by the Secretary of the Interior, August 22, 1905, and selection of allotment may be made in her behalf in accordance with the rules and regulations governing the selection of allotments and the designation of homesteads in the Choctaw and Chickasaw Nations.

                Respectfully,

                              Commissioner.

Choc New Born 1184
    Israel Kemp
    (Born Dec. 8, 1903)

BIRTH AFFIDAVIT.

DEPARTMENT OF THE INTERIOR.
COMMISSION TO THE FIVE CIVILIZED TRIBES.

IN RE APPLICATION FOR ENROLLMENT, as a citizen of the   Choctaw   Nation, of Israel Kemp   , born on the   8th   day of   Dec , 1903

Name of Father: Nelson Kemp   a citizen of the   Choctaw   Nation.
Name of Mother: Ellen Kemp nee Going   a citizen of the   Choctaw   Nation.

                Postoffice   Goodwater I.T.

Applications for Enrollment of Choctaw Newborn
Act of 1905   Volume XVI

AFFIDAVIT OF MOTHER.

UNITED STATES OF AMERICA, Indian Territory,
Central   DISTRICT.

I, Ellen Kemp, on oath state that I am 21 years of age and a citizen by Blood, of the Choctaw Nation; that I am the lawful wife of Nelson Kemp, who is a citizen, by Blood of the Choctaw Nation; that a male child was born to me on 8th day of December, 1903; that said child has been named Israel Kemp, and was living March 4, 1905.

            her
           Ellen x Kemp
Witnesses To Mark: mark
 { LL Battiest
   Daniel Jefferson

Subscribed and sworn to before me this 10th day of April, 1905

          (Name Illegible)
          Notary Public.

AFFIDAVIT OF ATTENDING PHYSICIAN OR MID-WIFE.

UNITED STATES OF AMERICA, Indian Territory,
Central   DISTRICT.

I, Elima Kemp, a mid-wife, on oath state that I attended on Mrs. Ellen Kemp, wife of Nelson Kemp on the 8th day of December, 1903; that there was born to her on said date a male child; that said child was living March 4, 1905, and is said to have been named Israel Kemp

            her
          Elima x Kemp
Witnesses To Mark: mark
 { LL Battiest
   Daniel Jefferson

Subscribed and sworn to before me this 10th day of April, 1905

          (Name Illegible)
          Notary Public.

Applications for Enrollment of Choctaw Newborn
Act of 1905   Volume XVI

Choc New Born 1185
  (Ellis Bybee)
  (Born Sept. 21, 1904)

BIRTH AFFIDAVIT.

DEPARTMENT OF THE INTERIOR.
COMMISSION TO THE FIVE CIVILIZED TRIBES.

IN RE APPLICATION FOR ENROLLMENT, as a citizen of the   Choctaw   Nation, of Ellis Bybee   , born on the 21st day of   Sept   , 1904

Name of Father: Will D. Bybee   a citizen of the   U. S.   Nation.
Name of Mother: Nora Bybee nee Williams   a citizen of the   Choctaw   Nation.

Postoffice   Valliant, I.T.

AFFIDAVIT OF MOTHER.

UNITED STATES OF AMERICA, Indian Territory,
  Central   DISTRICT.

I, Nora Bybee nee Williams , on oath state that I am 19 years of age and a citizen by   blood , of the   Choctaw   Nation; that I am the lawful wife of Will D. Bybee   , who is a citizen, ~~by~~ *of the U.S.* of the .... Nation; that a   male   child was born to me on   21st day of   September , 1904; that said child has been named   Ellis Bybee   , and was living March 4, 1905.

Nora Bybee vs Williams
Witnesses To Mark:
{

Subscribed and sworn to before me this   18   day of   April   , 1905

H L Fowler
Notary Public.

AFFIDAVIT OF ATTENDING PHYSICIAN OR MID-WIFE.

UNITED STATES OF AMERICA, Indian Territory,
.... DISTRICT.

I, Josephine Fowler   , a ...., on oath state that I attended on Mrs. Nora Bybee nee Williams , wife of   Will D. Bybee   on the 21st day of

Applications for Enrollment of Choctaw Newborn
Act of 1905 Volume XVI

September   , 1904; that there was born to her on said date a   male   child; that said child was living March 4, 1905, and is said to have been named Ellis Bybee

Witnesses To Mark:
{

Josephine Fowler

Subscribed and sworn to before me this 18 day of   April   , 1905

H L Fowler
Notary Public.

7-948
7-NB-1185

Muskogee, Indian Territory, January 23, 1907.

Nora Bybee,
Sawyer, Indian Territory.

Dear Madam:

Receipt is hereby acknowledged of your letter of January 15, 1907, asking if your[sic] can get your child born in November on the rolls.

In reply to your letter you are advised that you do not give the name of your child nor the date of its birth, and it is impracticable to advise you whether an application has been made for its enrollment.

You are informed that the name of Ellis Bybee, appears upon Choctaw New Born card No. 1185 as a new born citizen of the Choctaw Nation under the Act of Congress approved March 3, 1905, and his enrollment as such was approved by the Secretary of the Interior July 22, 1905.

You are further advised that the time within which applications could be received under the Act of Congress approved April 26, 1906, for the enrollment of minor children of citizens of the Choctaw and Chickasaw Nations expired July 25, 1906, and since that time there is no authority for the reception of applications.

Respectfully,

Commissioner.

Applications for Enrollment of Choctaw Newborn
Act of 1905 Volume XVI

Choc New Born 1186
   Lizzie Kaneubbe[sic]
   (Born Feb. 18, 1905)

BIRTH AFFIDAVIT.

DEPARTMENT OF THE INTERIOR.
COMMISSION TO THE FIVE CIVILIZED TRIBES.

IN RE APPLICATION FOR ENROLLMENT, as a citizen of the   Choctaw   Nation, of Lizzie Kaniubbe   , born on the 18th day of February   , 1905

Name of Father: Moses Kaniubbe   a citizen of the   Choctaw   Nation.
Name of Mother: Betsy Kaniubbe   a citizen of the   Choctaw   Nation.

   Postoffice   Lenton, Ind. Ter.

AFFIDAVIT OF MOTHER.

UNITED STATES OF AMERICA, Indian Territory, ⎫
   Central   DISTRICT. ⎭

I,   Betsy Kaniubbe   , on oath state that I am about 30   years of age and a citizen by   blood   , of the   Choctaw   Nation; that I am the lawful wife of Moses Kaniubbe   , who is a citizen, by blood   of the   Choctaw   Nation; that a   female   child was born to me on   18th day of February   , 1905; that said child has been named Lizzie Kaniubbe   , and was living March 4, 1905.

   Betsy x Kaniubbe

Witnesses To Mark:
{ Robert Anderson
{ Vester Rose

Subscribed and sworn to before me this 20th day of   April   , 1905

   Wirt Franklin
   Notary Public.

Applications for Enrollment of Choctaw Newborn
Act of 1905   Volume XVI

AFFIDAVIT OF ATTENDING PHYSICIAN OR MID-WIFE.

UNITED STATES OF AMERICA, Indian Territory,
Central   DISTRICT.

 I, Laura McLaughlin   , a   mid-wife   , on oath state that I attended on Mrs.   Betsy Kaniubbe   , wife of   Moses Kaniubbe   on the   18th   day of   February   , 1905; that there was born to her on said date a   female   child; that said child was living March 4, 1905, and is said to have been named   Lizzie Kaniubbe

            her
          Laura x McLaughlin
Witnesses To Mark: mark
 { Robert Anderson
  Vester Rose

 Subscribed and sworn to before me this   20th day of   April   , 1905

        Wirt Franklin
        Notary Public.

Choc New Born 1187
 Cornelius Tilly
 (Born Aug 2, 1904)

NEW-BORN AFFIDAVIT.

   Number............

Choctaw Enrolling Commission.

 IN THE MATTER OF THE APPLICATION FOR ENROLLMENT, as a citizen of the Choctaw   Nation, of   Cornelius Tilly

born on the 2nd day of   August   190 4

Name of father   Jim Tilly   a citizen of   white
Nation final enrollment No ....
Name of mother   Mable Standley Tilly   a citizen of   Choctaw
Nation final enrollment No   15488

     Postoffice   Hugo I.T.

Applications for Enrollment of Choctaw Newborn
Act of 1905   Volume XVI

AFFIDAVIT OF MOTHER.

UNITED STATES OF AMERICA,
INDIAN TERRITORY,
Central   DISTRICT

I   Mable Standley now Tilly   on oath state that I am   17   years of age and a citizen by   Blood   of the   Choctaw   Nation, and as such have been placed upon the final roll of the   Choctaw   Nation, by the Honorable Secretary of the Interior my final enrollment number being   15488   ; that I am the lawful wife of   Jim Tilly   , who is a citizen of the   ~~Choctaw~~   Nation, and as such has been placed upon the final roll of said Nation by the Honorable Secretary of the Interior, his final enrollment number being _____ and that a   Male   child was born to me on the   1[sic]   day of   August   190 4 ; that said child has been named   Cornelius Tilly, and is now living.

Mabel Standley

WITNESSETH:
Must be two Witnesses who are Citizens.   Susie Hall
Joshua Yota

Subscribed and sworn to before me this   19   day of   Jany   190 5

W.T. Glenn
Notary Public.

My commission expires   1907

Affidavit of Attending Physician or Midwife

UNITED STATES OF AMERICA,
INDIAN TERRITORY,
Central   DISTRICT

I,   Perry Fling   a   Physician   on oath state that I attended on Mrs. Mabel Standley now Tilley[sic]   wife of   Jim Tilley on the   2   day of   August   , 190 4, that there was born to her on said date a   male   child, that said child is now living, and is said to have been named   Cornelius Tilley

Perry Fling   M. D.

Subscribed and sworn to before me this the   26   day of   Jany   1905

WT Glenn
Notary Public.

WITNESSETH:
Must be two witnesses who are citizens and know the child.   John McIntosh
Susie Hall

Applications for Enrollment of Choctaw Newborn
Act of 1905 Volume XVI

We hereby certify that we are well acquainted with Perry Fling a Physician and know him to be reputable and of good standing in the community.

Must be two citizen witnesses. { John McIntosh
J.T. Jeter

BIRTH AFFIDAVIT.

DEPARTMENT OF THE INTERIOR.
COMMISSION TO THE FIVE CIVILIZED TRIBES.

IN RE APPLICATION FOR ENROLLMENT, as a citizen of the Choctaw Nation, of Cornelius Tilly , born on the 2nd day of August , 1904

Name of Father: Jim Tilly   a citizen of the United States Nation.
Name of Mother: Mabel Tilly   a citizen of the Choctaw Nation.

Postoffice Hugo, Ind. Ter.

AFFIDAVIT OF MOTHER.

UNITED STATES OF AMERICA, Indian Territory,
Central   DISTRICT.

I, Mabel Tilly , on oath state that I am 18 years of age and a citizen by blood , of the Choctaw Nation; that I am the lawful wife of Jim Tilly , who is a citizen, ~~by~~ of the United States ~~Nation~~; that a male child was born to me on 2nd day of August , 1904; that said child has been named Cornelius Tilly , and was living March 4, 1905.

Mable Tilly

Witnesses To Mark:

Subscribed and sworn to before me this 20th day of April , 1905

Wirt Franklin
Notary Public.

Applications for Enrollment of Choctaw Newborn
Act of 1905   Volume XVI

AFFIDAVIT OF ATTENDING PHYSICIAN OR MID-WIFE.

UNITED STATES OF AMERICA, Indian Territory, }
   Central   DISTRICT. }

    I, Perry E. A. Fling , a physician , on oath state that I attended on Mrs. Mabel Tilly , wife of Jim Tilly on the 2nd day of August , 1904; that there was born to her on said date a male child; that said child was living March 4, 1905, and is said to have been named Cornelius Tilly

                                    Perry E.A. Fling

Witnesses To Mark:

    Subscribed and sworn to before me this 20th day of April , 1905

                                    Wirt Franklin
                                    Notary Public.

Choc New Born 1188
    Harmon J. Bohanan, Jr.
    (Born June 8, 1903)

NEW-BORN AFFIDAVIT.

        Number......

...Choctaw Enrolling Commission...

    IN THE MATTER OF THE APPLICATION FOR ENROLLMENT, as a citizen of the Choctaw Nation, of Harmon J Bohanan

born on the 8 day of ___June___ 190 3

Name of father Harmon J Bohanan   a citizen of   Choctaw
Nation final enrollment No. 4462
Name of mother   Lula Bohanan   a citizen of   Choctaw
Nation final enrollment No. 814

                             Postoffice   Hugo I.T.

Applications for Enrollment of Choctaw Newborn
Act of 1905   Volume XVI

AFFIDAVIT OF MOTHER.

UNITED STATES OF AMERICA
INDIAN TERRITORY
   Central   DISTRICT

        I   Lula Bohanan   , on oath state that I am 23 years of age and a citizen by Ind Ma of the Choctaw Nation, and as such have been placed upon the final roll of the Choctaw Nation, by the Honorable Secretary of the Interior my final enrollment number being 814 ; that I am the lawful wife of Harmon J Bohanan , who is a citizen of the Choctaw Nation, and as such has been placed upon the final roll of said Nation by the Honorable Secretary of the Interior, his final enrollment number being 4462 and that a Male child was born to me on the 8 day of June 190 3; that said child has been named Harmon J Bohanan , and is now living.

                                              her
                                  Lula Bohanan x
Witnesseth.   mark

Must be two Witnesses who are Citizens.   { JH Everidge
                                   J W MᶜIntosh

    Subscribed and sworn to before me this 25 day of Jany   190 5

                                W.T. Glenn
                                       Notary Public.
My commission expires:

AFFIDAVIT OF ATTENDING PHYSICIAN OR MIDWIFE

UNITED STATES OF AMERICA
INDIAN TERRITORY
   Central   DISTRICT

    I, M.E. Grubbs a mid wife on oath state that I attended on Mrs. Harmon J Bohanan wife of Harmon J Bohanan on the 8 day of June , 190 3 , that there was born to her on said date a male child, that said child is now living, and is said to have been named Harmon J Bohanan

        Subscribed and sworn to before me this, the 25 day of Jany 190 5

                              M E Grubbs
WITNESSETH: W.T. Glenn   Notary Public.
Must be two witnesses who are citizens { JH Everidge
                           JW MᶜIntosh

Applications for Enrollment of Choctaw Newborn
Act of 1905   Volume XVI

We hereby certify that we are well acquainted with M.E. Grubbs a Mid wife and know her to be reputable and of good standing in the community.

J H Everidge   _____

JW McIntosh   _____

BIRTH AFFIDAVIT.

DEPARTMENT OF THE INTERIOR.
COMMISSION TO THE FIVE CIVILIZED TRIBES.

IN RE APPLICATION FOR ENROLLMENT, as a citizen of the Choctaw Nation, of Harmon J Bohanan Jr , born on the 8 day of June , 1903

Name of Father: Harmon J Bohanan   a citizen of the Choctaw Nation.
Name of Mother: Lula Bohanan   a citizen of the Choctaw Nation.

Postoffice   Hugo I.T.

AFFIDAVIT OF MOTHER.

UNITED STATES OF AMERICA, Indian Territory,
Central   DISTRICT.

I, Lula Bohanan , on oath state that I am 23 years of age and a citizen by marriage , of the Choctaw Nation; that I am the lawful wife of Harmon J Bohanan , who is a citizen, by blood of the Choctaw Nation; that a male child was born to me on 8th day of June , 1903; that said child has been named Harmon J Bohanan, Jr , and was living March 4, 1905.

                                    her
                            Lula x Bohanan
Witnesses To Mark: mark
  Robert Anderson
  Vester Rose

Subscribed and sworn to before me this 20th day of April , 1905

                        Wirt Franklin
                            Notary Public.

Applications for Enrollment of Choctaw Newborn
Act of 1905   Volume XVI

AFFIDAVIT OF ATTENDING PHYSICIAN OR MID-WIFE.

UNITED STATES OF AMERICA, Indian Territory,
Central   DISTRICT.

I, Nannie Day , a Mid wife , on oath state that I attended on Mrs. Lula Bohanan , wife of Harmon J Bohanan on the 8 day of June , 1903; that there was born to her on said date a male child; that said child was living March 4, 1905, and is said to have been named Harmon J Bohanan

Nannie Day

Witnesses To Mark:

Subscribed and sworn to before me this 17 day of April , 1905

W.T. Glenn
Notary Public.

Choc New Born 1189
    Edgar Everidge
    (Born Jan. 26, 1904)

NEW-BORN AFFIDAVIT.

Number

Choctaw Enrolling Commission.

IN THE MATTER OF THE APPLICATION FOR ENROLLMENT, as a citizen of the Choctaw Nation, of   Egar Everidge

born on the 26th day of Jan   190 4

Name of father   Edward M. Everidge   a citizen of   Choctaw
Nation final enrollment No   5017
Name of mother   Lula Everidge   a citizen of   Choctaw
Nation final enrollment No   642

Postoffice   Grant, Ind. Ter.

Applications for Enrollment of Choctaw Newborn
Act of 1905   Volume XVI

AFFIDAVIT OF MOTHER.

UNITED STATES OF AMERICA,
  INDIAN TERRITORY,
Central   DISTRICT

I   Lula Everidge   on oath state that I am   24   years of age and a citizen by   adoption (marriage)   of the   Choctaw   Nation, and as such have been placed upon the final roll of the   Choctaw   Nation, by the Honorable Secretary of the Interior my final enrollment number being   642   ; that I am the lawful wife of   Edward M Everidge   , who is a citizen of the   Choctaw   Nation, and as such has been placed upon the final roll of said Nation by the Honorable Secretary of the Interior, his final enrollment number being   5017   and that a   male   child was born to me on the 26th day of   Jan   190 4 ; that said child has been named   Egar Everidge   , and is now living.

Lula Everidge

WITNESSETH:
Must be two Witnesses who are Citizens.   Bin F Ervin
     Robert M Raulston

Subscribed and sworn to before me this   18   day of   Jan   190 5

Chas G Shull
Notary Public.

My commission expires   Dec 14-1906

Affidavit of Attending Physician or Midwife

UNITED STATES OF AMERICA,
  INDIAN TERRITORY,
Central   DISTRICT

I,   Perry Fling   a   Physician   on oath state that I attended on Mrs. Lula Everidge   wife of   Edward M Everidge   on the   26   day of   Jan   , 190 4, that there was born to her on said date a   male   child, that said child is now living, and is said to have been named   Egar Everidge

Perry Fling   M. D.

Subscribed and sworn to before me this the   18   day of   Jan   1905

Chas G Shull
Notary Public.

WITNESSETH:
Must be two witnesses who are citizens and know the child.   Arabella M Raulston
    Bin F Ervin

Applications for Enrollment of Choctaw Newborn
Act of 1905 Volume XVI

We hereby certify that we are well acquainted with Perry Fling a physician and know him to be reputable and of good standing in the community.

Must be two citizen witnesses. { Robert M Raulston
Bin F Ervin

BIRTH AFFIDAVIT.

DEPARTMENT OF THE INTERIOR.
COMMISSION TO THE FIVE CIVILIZED TRIBES.

IN RE APPLICATION FOR ENROLLMENT, as a citizen of the Choctaw Nation, of Edgar Everidge, born on the 26th day of January, 1904

Name of Father: Edward M Everidge   a citizen of the Choctaw Nation.
Name of Mother: Lula Everidge   a citizen of the Choctaw Nation.

Postoffice   Grant, Ind. Ter.

AFFIDAVIT OF MOTHER.

UNITED STATES OF AMERICA, Indian Territory, } Central DISTRICT.

I, Lula Everidge, on oath state that I am 23 years of age and a citizen by marriage, of the Choctaw Nation; that I am the lawful wife of Edward M Everidge, who is a citizen, by blood of the Choctaw Nation; that a male child was born to me on 26th day of January, 1904; that said child has been named Edgar Everidge, and was living March 4, 1905.

Lula Everidge

Witnesses To Mark:
{

Subscribed and sworn to before me this 20th day of April, 1905.

Wirt Franklin
Notary Public.

Applications for Enrollment of Choctaw Newborn
Act of 1905 Volume XVI

AFFIDAVIT OF ATTENDING PHYSICIAN OR MID-WIFE.

UNITED STATES OF AMERICA, Indian Territory, }
Central　　　　　　　　DISTRICT. }

　　　I,　Perry E. A. Fling　　, a　physician　, on oath state that I attended on Mrs.　Lula Everidge　, wife of　Edward M Everidge　on the　26th day of January　, 1904; that there was born to her on said date a　male　child; that said child was living March 4, 1905, and is said to have been named　Edgar Everidge

　　　　　　　　　　　　　　　　　　　Perry E.A. Fling
Witnesses To Mark:
{

　　Subscribed and sworn to before me this　20th day of　April　, 1905

　　　　　　　　　　　　　　　Wirt Franklin
　　　　　　　　　　　　　　　　Notary Public.

Choc New Born 1190
　　　Emm[sic] May Ervin
　　　(Born May 7, 1903)

BIRTH AFFIDAVIT.
　　　　　　　　　　DEPARTMENT OF THE INTERIOR.
　　　　　　　COMMISSION TO THE FIVE CIVILIZED TRIBES.

　　　IN RE APPLICATION FOR ENROLLMENT, as a citizen of the　　Choctaw　　Nation, of Emma May Ervin　　, born on the　7th　day of　May　, 1903

Name of Father: W.J. Ervin　　　　a citizen of the United States Nation.
Name of Mother: Nellie Ervin　　　　a citizen of the　Choctaw　Nation.

　　　　　　　　　　Postoffice　　Hugo, Ind. Territory

Applications for Enrollment of Choctaw Newborn
Act of 1905   Volume XVI

AFFIDAVIT OF MOTHER.

UNITED STATES OF AMERICA, Indian Territory, }
Central   DISTRICT.

I,   Nellie Ervin   , on oath state that I am   31   years of age and a citizen by blood   , of the   Choctaw   Nation; that I am the lawful wife of   W. J. Ervin   , who is a citizen, by birth   of the   United States   ~~Nation~~; that a   female   child was born to me on   7th day of   May   , 1903; that said child has been named   Emma May Ervin   , and was living March 4, 1905.

Nellie Ervin

Witnesses To Mark:
{

Subscribed and sworn to before me this   19th day of   April   , 1905.

Chas. G. Shull
Notary Public.

AFFIDAVIT OF ATTENDING PHYSICIAN OR MID-WIFE.

UNITED STATES OF AMERICA, Indian Territory, }
Central   DISTRICT.

I,   Cassie Davis   , a   mid wife   , on oath state that I attended on Mrs.   Nellie Ervin   , wife of   W.J. Ervin   on the 7th day of   May   , 1903; that there was born to her on said date a   female   child; that said child was living March 4, 1905, and is said to have been named   Emma May Ervin

her
Cassie x Davis
mark

Witnesses To Mark:
{ Hugh Davis
  W E Fuller

Subscribed and sworn to before me this   19th day of   April   , 1905.

Chas. G. Shull
Notary Public.

Applications for Enrollment of Choctaw Newborn
Act of 1905   Volume XVI

Choc New Born 1191
   Willie Ahekatubby
   (Born Nov. 23, 1903)

NEW-BORN AFFIDAVIT.

   Number

Choctaw Enrolling Commission.

IN THE MATTER OF THE APPLICATION FOR ENROLLMENT, as a citizen of the Choctaw   Nation, of   Willie Ahekatubby

born on the   23   day of   November   190 3

Name of father   John Ahekatubby   a citizen of   Choctaw
Nation final enrollment No   1544
Name of mother   Emma Ahekatubby   a citizen of   Choctaw
Nation final enrollment No

   Postoffice   Grant I T

AFFIDAVIT OF MOTHER.

UNITED STATES OF AMERICA,
   INDIAN TERRITORY,
   Central   DISTRICT

   I   Emma Ahekatubby   on oath state that I am   25   years of age and a citizen by   blood   of the   Choctaw   Nation, and as such have been placed upon the final roll of the   Choctaw   Nation, by the Honorable Secretary of the Interior my final enrollment number being   ; that I am the lawful wife of   John Ahekatubby   , who is a citizen of the   Choctaw   Nation, and as such has been placed upon the final roll of said Nation by the Honorable Secretary of the Interior, his final enrollment number being   1544   and that a   male   child was born to me on the   23   day of   November   190 3 ; that said child has been named   Willie Ahekatubby   , and is now living.

   Emma Ahekatubby

WITNESSETH:
   Must be two
   Witnesses who
   are Citizens.
   (Name Illegible)
   Thomas B Bohanon

Applications for Enrollment of Choctaw Newborn
Act of 1905 Volume XVI

Subscribed and sworn to before me this   17   day of   Jany   190 5

                                         W.T. Glenn

                                                             Notary Public.

My commission expires   1907

Affidavit of Attending Physician or Midwife

UNITED STATES OF AMERICA,
    INDIAN TERRITORY,
Central   DISTRICT

    I,   Prince Butler   a   was present on oath state that I attended on Mrs. Emma Ahekatubby   wife of   John Ahekatubby on the   23   day of   November , 190 3, that there was born to her on said date a   male child, that said child is now living, and is said to have been named   Willie Ahekatubby

                                                 his
                               Prince Butler   M.X.D.
                                                 mark

Subscribed and sworn to before me this the   17   day of   Jany   1905

                                       W.T. Glenn

                                                 Notary Public.

WITNESSETH:

Must be two witnesses who are citizens and know the child.   { (Name Illegible)
                                     Thomas B Bohanon

    We hereby certify that we are well acquainted with   Prince Butler a   ———   and know   him   to be reputable and of good standing in the community.

                               Must be two citizen { (Name Illegible)
                               witnesses.   Thomas B Bohanon

Applications for Enrollment of Choctaw Newborn
Act of 1905 Volume XVI

United States of America,)
)
Indian Territory,) ss.
)
Central District.)

    I, Mary Butler, on oath state that I am thirty-five years of age and a Chickasaw freedman; that my post office address is Grant, Indian Territory; that I am personally acquainted with Emma Ahekatubby, wife of John Ahekatubby, and have known said parties all their lives; that on or about the 23rd day of November, 1903, there was born to the said Emma Ahekatubby a male child; that said child is now living and has been named Willie Ahekatubby; that the way I know the circumstances attending the birth of this child is that I came by and stopped at their house and saw said child the next day after it's[sic] birth.

                                                                     her
                                            Mary x Butler
                                              mark

Subscribed and sworn to before me this 20th day of April, 1905.

                                            Wirt Franklin
                                            Notary Public.

Witnesses to mark.
    Robert Anderson
    Vester Rose

United States of America,)
)
Indian Territory,) ss.
)
Central District.)

    I, Prince Butler, on oath state that I am thirty-three years of age and a Choctaw freedman; that my post office address is Grant, Indian Territory; that I am personally acquainted with Emma Ahekatubby, wife of John Ahekatubby, and have known said parties about ten years; that I have lived within two miles of where they live, near Grant, Indian Territory, for the last eight years; that on or about the 23rd day of November, 1903, there was born to the said Emma Ahekatubby a male child; that said child is now living and has been named Willie Ahekatubby; that the way I know of the circumstances attending the birth of this child is, that I came by and stopped at their house about a half hour after said child was born.

                                              his
                                      Prince x Butler
                                         mark

Applications for Enrollment of Choctaw Newborn
Act of 1905 Volume XVI

Subscribed and sworn to before me this 20th day of April, 1905.

Wirt Franklin
Notary Public.

Witnesses to mark.
Robert Anderson
Vester Rose

BIRTH AFFIDAVIT.

DEPARTMENT OF THE INTERIOR.
COMMISSION TO THE FIVE CIVILIZED TRIBES.

IN RE APPLICATION FOR ENROLLMENT, as a citizen of the Choctaw Nation, of Willie Ahekatubby, born on the 23rd day of November, 1903

Name of Father: John Ahekatubby   a citizen of the Choctaw Nation.
Name of Mother: Emma Ahekatubby   a citizen of the Choctaw Nation.

Postoffice   Grant, Ind. Ter.

AFFIDAVIT OF MOTHER.

UNITED STATES OF AMERICA, Indian Territory,
Central DISTRICT.

I, Emma Ahekatubby, on oath state that I am 28 years of age and a citizen by blood, of the Choctaw Nation; that I am the lawful wife of John Ahekatubby, who is a citizen, by blood of the Choctaw Nation; that a male child was born to me on 23rd day of November, 1903; that said child has been named Willie Ahekatubby, and was living March 4, 1905. *and that no physician or mid-wife attended me at the birth of said child.*

her
Emma x Ahekatubby
mark

Witnesses To Mark:
{ Vester W Rose
{ Robert Anderson

Subscribed and sworn to before me this 20th day of April, 1905

Wirt Franklin
Notary Public.

Applications for Enrollment of Choctaw Newborn
Act of 1905   Volume XVI

AFFIDAVIT OF ATTENDING PHYSICIAN OR MID-WIFE.

UNITED STATES OF AMERICA, Indian Territory,
Central DISTRICT.

I, John Ahekatubby, ~~a~~ _____, on oath state that I attended on Mrs. Emma Ahekatubby, ~~wife of~~ *my wife* on the 23rd day of November, 1903; that there was born to her on said date a male child; that said child was living March 4, 1905, and ~~is said to have~~ *has* been named Willie Ahekatubby *and that no one else was present when said child was born*

John Ahekatubby

Witnesses To Mark:

Subscribed and sworn to before me this 20th day of April, 1905

Wirt Franklin
Notary Public.

Choc New Born 1192
    Willie Lee Howze
    (Born April 13, 1903)
    Jessie Myrtle Howze
    (Born Feb. 1, 1905)

BIRTH AFFIDAVIT.

DEPARTMENT OF THE INTERIOR.
COMMISSION TO THE FIVE CIVILIZED TRIBES.

IN RE APPLICATION FOR ENROLLMENT, as a citizen of the Choctaw Nation, of Jessie Myrtle Howze, born on the 1st day of February, 1905

Name of Father: Morris L. Howze   a citizen of the United States ~~Nation~~.
Name of Mother: Sophronia Howze   a citizen of the Choctaw Nation.

Postoffice   Atoka I.T.

Applications for Enrollment of Choctaw Newborn
Act of 1905   Volume XVI

AFFIDAVIT OF MOTHER.

UNITED STATES OF AMERICA, Indian Territory, }
Central   DISTRICT.

I, Sophronia, on oath state that I am 24 years of age and a citizen by blood, of the Choctaw Nation; that I am the lawful wife of Morris L. Howze, who is a citizen, ~~by~~ .... of the United States ~~Nation~~; that a female child was born to me on 1st day of February, 1905; that said child has been named Jessie Myrtle Howze, and was living March 4, 1905.

                                        Sophronia Howze

Witnesses To Mark:
{

Subscribed and sworn to before me this 20ᵗʰ day of April, 1905

                                        C G Bozarth
                                        Notary Public.

AFFIDAVIT OF ATTENDING PHYSICIAN OR MID-WIFE.

UNITED STATES OF AMERICA, Indian Territory, }
Central   DISTRICT.

I, Mrs J L. Rainey aged 53 years, on oath state that I attended on Mrs. Sophronia Howze, wife of Morris L. Howze on the 1st day of February, 1905; that there was born to her on said date a female child; that said child was living March 4, 1905, and ~~is said to have~~ *has* been named Jessie Myrtle Howze

                                          her
                                  Mrs J.L. x Rainey

Witnesses To Mark: mark
{ JG Ralls
  (Name Illegible)

Subscribed and sworn to before me this 20th day of April, 1905

                                        C G Bozarth
                                        Notary Public.

Applications for Enrollment of Choctaw Newborn
Act of 1905   Volume XVI

BIRTH AFFIDAVIT.

DEPARTMENT OF THE INTERIOR.
COMMISSION TO THE FIVE CIVILIZED TRIBES.

IN RE APPLICATION FOR ENROLLMENT, as a citizen of the Choctaw Nation, of Willie Lee Howze, born on the 13th day of April, 1903

Name of Father: Morris L. Howze   a citizen of the United States Nation.
Name of Mother: Sophronia Howze   a citizen of the Choctaw Nation.

Postoffice   Atoka Ind. Ter.

AFFIDAVIT OF MOTHER.

UNITED STATES OF AMERICA, Indian Territory,
Central   DISTRICT.

I, Sophronia Howze, on oath state that I am 24 years of age and a citizen by blood, of the Choctaw Nation; that I am the lawful wife of Morris L. Howze, who is a citizen, ~~by~~ of the United States ~~Nation~~; that a male child was born to me on 13th day of April, 1903; that said child has been named William[sic] Lee Howze, and was living March 4, 1905.

Sophronia Howze

Witnesses To Mark:

Subscribed and sworn to before me this 20th day of April, 1905

C G Bozarth
Notary Public.

AFFIDAVIT OF ATTENDING PHYSICIAN OR MID-WIFE.

UNITED STATES OF AMERICA, Indian Territory,
Central   DISTRICT.

I, Mrs J L. Rainey aged 53 years, on oath state that I attended on Mrs. Sophronia Howze, wife of Morris L. Howze on the 13th day of April, 1903; that there was born to her on said date a male child; that said child was living March 4, 1905, and ~~is said to have~~ has been named Willie Lee Howze

her
Mrs J.L. x Rainey
mark

Applications for Enrollment of Choctaw Newborn
Act of 1905 Volume XVI

Witnesses To Mark:
{ JG Ralls
{ (Name Illegible)

Subscribed and sworn to before me this 20th day of April , 1905

C G Bozarth
Notary Public.

Choctaw 424.

Muskogee, Indian Territory, April 27, 1905.

J. G. Ralls,
    Attorney at Law,
        Atoka, Indian Territory.

Dear Sir:

    Receipt is hereby acknowledged of your letter of April 20, enclosing the affidavits of Sophronia Howze and Mrs. J. L. Rainey to the birth of Willie Lee Howze and Jessie Myrtle Howze, children of Morris L. and Sophronia Howze, April 13, 1903, and February 1, 1905, respectively, and the same have been filed with our records as an application for the enrollment of said children.

Choc New Born 1193
    Annie Battiest
    (Born Dec. 26, 1904)

BIRTH AFFIDAVIT.

DEPARTMENT OF THE INTERIOR.
COMMISSION TO THE FIVE CIVILIZED TRIBES.

IN RE APPLICATION FOR ENROLLMENT, as a citizen of the Choctaw Nation, of Annie Battiest , born on the 26th day of December , 1904

Name of Father: Osborne Battiest   a citizen of the Choctaw Nation.
Name of Mother: Louisa Battiest   a citizen of the Choctaw Nation.

Postoffice   Hugo, Ind. Ter.

Applications for Enrollment of Choctaw Newborn
Act of 1905   Volume XVI

AFFIDAVIT OF MOTHER.

UNITED STATES OF AMERICA, Indian Territory,
Central   DISTRICT.

I, Louisa Battiest , on oath state that I am 29 years of age and a citizen by blood , of the Choctaw Nation; that I am the lawful wife of Osborne Battiest , who is a citizen, by blood of the Choctaw Nation; that a female child was born to me on 26th day of December , 1904; that said child has been named Annie Battiest , and was living March 4, 1905.

            her
          Louisa x Battiest
Witnesses To Mark: mark
 { Robert Anderson
  Vester Rose

Subscribed and sworn to before me this 21st day of April , 1905

          Wirt Franklin
           Notary Public.

AFFIDAVIT OF ATTENDING PHYSICIAN OR MID-WIFE.

UNITED STATES OF AMERICA, Indian Territory,
Central   DISTRICT.

I, Annie Snowton , a mid-wife , on oath state that I attended on Mrs. Louisa Battiest , wife of Osborne Battiest on the 26th day of December , 1904; that there was born to her on said date a female child; that said child was living March 4, 1905, and is said to have been named Annie Battiest

            her
          Annie x Snowton
Witnesses To Mark: mark
 { Robert Anderson
  Vester Rose

Subscribed and sworn to before me this 21st day of April , 1905

          Wirt Franklin
           Notary Public.

Applications for Enrollment of Choctaw Newborn
Act of 1905 Volume XVI

7-NB-1193

Muskogee, Indian Territory, September 9, 1905.

E. W. Dodd,
    Grant, Indian Territory.

Dear Sir:

Replying to your letter of August 25th, you are advised that on July 22, 1905, the Secretary of the Interior approved the enrollment of Annie Battiest as a citizen by blood of the Choctaw Nation and the name of said child appears upon the final roll of new-born citizens by blood of the Choctaw Nation opposite number 1063.

The child is now entitled to an allotment and selection thereof should be made without delay at the land office for the nation in which the prospective allotment is located.

                         Respectfully,

                                 Acting Commissioner.

Choc New Born 1194
    Earl Spring
    (Born Feb. 5, 1905)

BIRTH AFFIDAVIT.

DEPARTMENT OF THE INTERIOR.
COMMISSION TO THE FIVE CIVILIZED TRIBES.

IN RE APPLICATION FOR ENROLLMENT, as a citizen of the Choctaw Nation, of Earl Spring , born on the 5th day of February , 1905

Name of Father: Eli Spring   a citizen of the Choctaw Nation.
Name of Mother: Mollie Spring   a citizen of the Choctaw Nation.

                      Postoffice   Hugo, Ind. Ter.

Applications for Enrollment of Choctaw Newborn
Act of 1905   Volume XVI

AFFIDAVIT OF MOTHER.

UNITED STATES OF AMERICA, Indian Territory,
Central   DISTRICT.

I, Mollie Spring , on oath state that I am 20 years of age and a citizen by blood , of the Choctaw Nation; that I am the lawful wife of Eli Spring , who is a citizen, by blood of the Choctaw Nation; that a male child was born to me on 5th day of February , 1905; that said child has been named Earl Spring , and was living March 4, 1905.

Mollie Spring

Witnesses To Mark:

Subscribed and sworn to before me this 21st day of April , 1905

Wirt Franklin
Notary Public.

AFFIDAVIT OF ATTENDING PHYSICIAN OR MID-WIFE.

UNITED STATES OF AMERICA, Indian Territory,
Central   DISTRICT.

I, Josie Bohanan , a mid-wife , on oath state that I attended on Mrs. Mollie Spring , wife of Eli Spring on the 5th day of February , 1905; that there was born to her on said date a male child; that said child was living March 4, 1905, and is said to have been named Earl Spring

Josie Bohanan

Witnesses To Mark:

Subscribed and sworn to before me this 21st day of April , 1905

Wirt Franklin
Notary Public.

Applications for Enrollment of Choctaw Newborn
Act of 1905 Volume XVI

Choc New Born 1195
    John Noah
    (Born May 2, 1904)

BIRTH AFFIDAVIT.

DEPARTMENT OF THE INTERIOR.
COMMISSION TO THE FIVE CIVILIZED TRIBES.

IN RE APPLICATION FOR ENROLLMENT, as a citizen of the Choctaw Nation, of John Noah, born on the 2nd day of May, 1904

Name of Father: Numan Noah   a citizen of the ChoctawNation Nation.
Name of Mother: _____ a citizen of the ChoctawNation Nation.

        Postoffice   Bethel Ind Teritoy[sic]

AFFIDAVIT OF MOTHER.

UNITED STATES OF AMERICA, Indian Territory, }
                          DISTRICT. }

    I, Emma Noah, on oath state that I am 30 years of age and a citizen by Blood, of the Choctaw Nation; that I am the lawful wife of Numan Noah, who is a citizen, by Blood of the Choctaw Nation Nation; that a male child was born to me on May 2nd day of May 1904, 1 _____; that said child has been named John Noah, and was living March 4, 1905.

                              Emma x Noah
Witnesses To Mark: her mark
{ Frank Hill
{ Mary x Mashentuby
   her mark
Subscribed and sworn to before me this 18 day of April, 1905

                              J H Matthews
                                Notary Public.

Applications for Enrollment of Choctaw Newborn
Act of 1905   Volume XVI

AFFIDAVIT OF ATTENDING PHYSICIAN OR MID-WIFE.

UNITED STATES OF AMERICA, Indian Territory,
Central   DISTRICT.

I, Mary Mashentuby, a ...., on oath state that I attended on Mrs. Emma Noah, wife of Numan Noah on the 2nd day of May 1904, 1......; that there was born to her on said date a male child; that said child was living March 4, 1905, and is said to have been named John Noah

                           Mary x Mashentuby
Witnesses To Mark: her mark
   Frank Hill Noah Ind Territory
   Tracy Matthews Bethel Ind Territory

Subscribed and sworn to before me this 18 day of April, 1905

                         J H Matthews
                              Notary Public.

BIRTH AFFIDAVIT.

DEPARTMENT OF THE INTERIOR.
COMMISSION TO THE FIVE CIVILIZED TRIBES.

IN RE APPLICATION FOR ENROLLMENT, as a citizen of the Choctaw Nation, of John Noah, born on the 2^{d} day of May, 1904

Name of Father: Newman Noah   a citizen of the Choctaw Nation.
Name of Mother: Emma Noah   a citizen of the non citizen Nation.

                    Postoffice   Bethel Ind Ter

AFFIDAVIT OF MOTHER.

UNITED STATES OF AMERICA, Indian Territory,
Central   DISTRICT.

I, Emma Noah, on oath state that I am 30 years of age and a ~~citizen by~~ non citizen ~~Nation~~; that I am the lawful wife of Newman Noah, who is a citizen, by blood of the Choctaw Nation; that a male child was born to me on 2^{d} day of May, 1904; that said child has been named John Noah, and was living March 4, 1905.

                         her
                   Emma x Noah
                       mark

Applications for Enrollment of Choctaw Newborn
Act of 1905   Volume XVI

Witnesses To Mark:
{ Holton J Hicks   Bethel IT
{ Tracy Matthews   Bethel IT

Subscribed and sworn to before me this   29   day of   Aug   , 1905

J H Matthews
Notary Public.

AFFIDAVIT OF ATTENDING PHYSICIAN OR MID-WIFE.

UNITED STATES OF AMERICA, Indian Territory, }
   Central   DISTRICT. }

I,   Mary Meashentubbee   , a   midwife   , on oath state that I attended on Mrs.   Emma Noah   , wife of   John[sic] Noah   on the 2 ^{d} day of May ,1904; that there was born to her on said date a   male   child; that said child was living March 4, 1905, and is said to have been named   John Noah

                                      her
                              Mary x Meashentubbee
Witnesses To Mark: mark
{ Holton J Hicks   Bethel IT
{ Sarah Matthews   Bethel IT

Subscribed and sworn to before me this   29   day of   Aug   , 1905

J H Matthews
Notary Public.

7-NB-1195.

Muskogee, Indian Territory, June 10, 1905.

Newman Noah,
    Bethel, Indian Territory.

Dear Sir:

Referring to the application for the enrollment of your infant child, John Newman[sic], born May 2, 1904, it is noted from the affidavits heretofore filed in this office that your wife claims to be a citizen by blood of the Choctaw Nation.

If this is correct you are requested to state when, where and under what name she was listed for enrollment, the names of her parents and other members of her family for

Applications for Enrollment of Choctaw Newborn
Act of 1905 Volume XVI

whom application was made at the same time and if she has selected an allotment please give her roll number as the same appears upon her allotment certificate.

                Respectfully,

                              Chairman.

7-NB-1195

                Muskogee, Indian Territory, July 26, 1905.

Newman Noah,
    Bethel, Indian Territory.

Dear Sir:

    There is inclosed you herewith for execution application for the enrollment of your infant child, John Noah, born May 2, 1904.

    It is noted in the affidavits of April 18, 1905, heretofore filed with the Commission to the Five Civilized Tribes, that the affidavits of Emma Noah is signed by mark, and that Mary Meashintubbee, one of the witnesses to her mark, also signs by mark.

    In having these affidavits executed care should be exercised to see that all names are written in full, as they appear in the body of the affidavit, and in the event that the persons signing the affidavits can write, they should do so in their own hand, otherwise, signatures by mark must be attested by two witnesses. When the affidavits are properly executed return to this office immediately, as no further action can be taken relative to the enrollment of your said child until the evidence requested is supplied.

                Respectfully,

LM 26/4   Commissioner.

Choc New Born 1196
    Mary E. Carroll
    (Born Dec. 2, 1904)

Applications for Enrollment of Choctaw Newborn
Act of 1905 Volume XVI

NEW BORN AFFIDAVIT

No _____

CHOCTAW ENROLLING COMMISSION

IN THE MATTER OF THE APPLICATION FOR ENROLLMENT as a citizen of the Choctaw Nation, of Mary Ernestine Carroll   born on the 2nd day of December   190 4

Name of father Ernest Carroll   a citizen of Choctaw   Nation,
final enrollment No. 15271
Name of mother Laura Carroll   a citizen of Choctaw   Nation,
final enrollment No. — —

Caddo I.T.   Postoffice.

AFFIDAVIT OF MOTHER

UNITED STATES OF AMERICA
INDIAN TERRITORY
DISTRICT   Central

I   Laura Carroll   , on oath state that I am 23 years of age and a citizen by intermrg of the Choctaw   Nation, and as such have been placed upon the final roll of the Choctaw   Nation, by the Honorable Secretary of the Interior my final enrollment number being _____ ; that I am the lawful wife of Ernest Carroll , who is a citizen of the Choctaw   Nation, and as such has been placed upon the final roll of said Nation by the Honorable Secretary of the Interior, his final enrollment number being 15271   and that a Female child was born to me on the 2nd day of December 190 4; that said child has been named Mary Ernestine Carroll , and is now living.

Laura Carroll

WITNESSETH:
Must be two witnesses   F Manning
who are citizens   Birdie Carroll now Cullar

Subscribed and sworn to before me this, the 9" day of February , 190 5

A.E. Folsom
Notary Public.
My Commission Expires:
Jan 9-1909

161

Applications for Enrollment of Choctaw Newborn
Act of 1905 Volume XVI

Affidavit of Attending Physician or Midwife

UNITED STATES OF AMERICA,
INDIAN TERRITORY,
Central DISTRICT

I, H.E Rappolee a Practicing Physician on oath state that I attended on Mrs. Laura Carroll wife of Ernest Carroll on the 2 day of December, 190 4, that there was born to her on said date a Female child, that said child is now living, and is said to have been named Mary Ernestine Carroll

H E Rappolee M. D.

Subscribed and sworn to before me this the 24" day of February 1905

AE Folsom
Notary Public.

WITNESSETH:
Must be two witnesses who are citizens and know the child.
{ F Manning
Birdie Carroll now Cullar }

We hereby certify that we are well acquainted with H E Rappolee a Physician and know him to be reputable and of good standing in the community.

Must be two citizen witnesses.
{ Birdie Carroll now Cullar
F. Manning }

BIRTH AFFIDAVIT.

DEPARTMENT OF THE INTERIOR.
COMMISSION TO THE FIVE CIVILIZED TRIBES.

IN RE APPLICATION FOR ENROLLMENT, as a citizen of the Choctaw Nation, of Mary E. Carroll, born on the 2ed[sic] day of December, 1904

Name of Father: Ernest Carroll a citizen of the Choctaw Nation.
Name of Mother: Laura L. Carroll a citizen of the Choctaw Nation.

Postoffice Caddo, Indian Territory

Applications for Enrollment of Choctaw Newborn
Act of 1905   Volume XVI

AFFIDAVIT OF MOTHER.

UNITED STATES OF AMERICA, Indian Territory,
Central   DISTRICT.

I,   Laura L. Carroll , on oath state that I am   24   years of age and a citizen by   marriage , of the   Choctaw   Nation; that I am the lawful wife of   Ernest Carroll , who is a citizen, by blood   of the   Choctaw   Nation; that a female   child was born to me on   2ed   day of   December   , 1904; that said child has been named   Mary E. Carroll   , and was living March 4, 1905.

Laura L Carroll

Witnesses To Mark:

Subscribed and sworn to before me this   21st day of   April   , 1905

JL Rappolee
Notary Public.

AFFIDAVIT OF ATTENDING PHYSICIAN OR MID-WIFE.

UNITED STATES OF AMERICA, Indian Territory,
Central   DISTRICT.

I,   H.E. Rappolee   , a   Physician   , on oath state that I attended on Mrs.   Laura L. Carroll   , wife of   Ernest Carroll   on the   2ed   day of   December   , 1904; that there was born to her on said date a   female   child; that said child was living March 4, 1905, and is said to have been named   Mary E. Carroll

H.E. Rappolee

Witnesses To Mark:

Subscribed and sworn to before me this   21st day of   April   , 1905

JL Rappolee
Notary Public.

Applications for Enrollment of Choctaw Newborn
Act of 1905   Volume XVI

7-5751.

Muskogee, Indian Territory, April 26, 1905.

J. L. Rappolee,
    Attorney at Law,
        Caddo, Indian Territory.

Dear Sir:

    Receipt is hereby acknowledged of your letter without date transmitting affidavits of Laura L. Carroll and H. E. Rappolee to the birth of Mary E. Carroll, daughter of Ernest and Laura L. Carroll, December 2, 1904, and the same have been filed with our records as an application for the enrollment of said child.

        Respectfully,

        Chairman.

Choc New Born 1197
    William Burns
    (Born Jan. 9, 1905)

BIRTH AFFIDAVIT.

DEPARTMENT OF THE INTERIOR.
COMMISSION TO THE FIVE CIVILIZED TRIBES.

IN RE APPLICATION FOR ENROLLMENT, as a citizen of the Choctaw Nation, of William Burns, born on the 9 day of Jan, 1905

Name of Father: Jackson Burns   a citizen of the Choctaw Nation.
Name of Mother: Laura Burns   a citizen of the Choctaw Nation.

        Postoffice   Massey I.T.

Applications for Enrollment of Choctaw Newborn
Act of 1905 Volume XVI

AFFIDAVIT OF MOTHER.

UNITED STATES OF AMERICA, Indian Territory, }
Central DISTRICT.

I, Laura Burns, on oath state that I am 23 years of age and a citizen by marriage, of the Choctaw Nation; that I am the lawful wife of Jackson Burns, who is a citizen, by Blood of the Choctaw Nation; that a male child was born to me on 9 day of Jan, 1905; that said child has been named William Burns, and was living March 4, 1905.

Laura Burns

Witnesses To Mark:
{

Subscribed and sworn to before me this 22 day of April, 1905

O.P. Swisher
Notary Public.

My commission expires Jan 14-1908

AFFIDAVIT OF ATTENDING PHYSICIAN OR MID-WIFE.

UNITED STATES OF AMERICA, Indian Territory, }
Central DISTRICT.

I, Sarah Williams, a Mid Wife, on oath state that I attended on Mrs. Laura Burns, wife of Jackson Burns on the 9 day of Jan, 1905; that there was born to her on said date a male child; that said child was living March 4, 1905, and is said to have been named William Burns

her
Sarah x Williams
mark

Witnesses To Mark:
{ J.G. Hatfield
{ Edmon Massey

Subscribed and sworn to before me this 22 day of April, 1905

O.P. Swisher
Notary Public.

My commission expires Jan 14-1908

Applications for Enrollment of Choctaw Newborn
Act of 1905   Volume XVI

Choc New Born 1198
    Eulah Cordelia Hulsey
    (Born July 20, 1904)

BIRTH AFFIDAVIT.

DEPARTMENT OF THE INTERIOR.
COMMISSION TO THE FIVE CIVILIZED TRIBES.

IN RE APPLICATION FOR ENROLLMENT, as a citizen of the Choctaw Nation, of Eulah Cordelia Hulsey, born on the 20 day of July, 1904

Name of Father: Henry Hulsey   a citizen of the Choctaw Nation.
Name of Mother: Lilly Hulsey   a citizen of the Choctaw Nation.

    Postoffice Stigler, Ind. Ter.

AFFIDAVIT OF MOTHER.

UNITED STATES OF AMERICA, Indian Territory,
    Central   DISTRICT.

    I, Lilly Hulsey, on oath state that I am 18 years of age and a citizen by intermarriage, of the Choctaw Nation; that I am the lawful wife of Henry Hulsey, who is a citizen, by blood of the Choctaw Nation; that a female child was born to me on 20 day of July, 1904; that said child has been named Eulah Cordelia Hulsey, and was living March 4, 1905.

                Lilly Hulsey
Witnesses To Mark:

    Subscribed and sworn to before me this 21 day of April, 1905

                Edwin O. Clark
                Notary Public.

AFFIDAVIT OF ATTENDING PHYSICIAN OR MID-WIFE.

UNITED STATES OF AMERICA, Indian Territory,
    Central   DISTRICT.

    I, C. C. Jones, a physician, on oath state that I attended on Mrs. Lilly Hulsey, wife of Henry Hulsey on the 20 day of July,

Applications for Enrollment of Choctaw Newborn
Act of 1905 Volume XVI

1904; that there was born to her on said date a   female   child; that said child was living March 4, 1905, and is said to have been named   Eulah Cordelia Hulsey

                            C. C. Jones

Witnesses To Mark:
{

Subscribed and sworn to before me this 20 day of   April , 1905

                            Edwin O. Clark
                            Notary Public.

No. 2086

Certificate of Record of Marriages.

United States of America,
The Indian Territory,   } sct.
Central   District.

I,   E. J. Fannin   Clerk of the United States Court, in the Indian Territory and District aforesaid, do hereby CERTIFY, that the License for and Certificate of the Marriage of

Mr.   Henry Hulsey   and
M iss Lillie McCaslin   was

filed in my office in said Territory and District the
6   day of   April
A.D., 190 4 , and duly recorded in Book 2
of Marriage Record, Page   425

WITNESS my hand and Seal of said Court, at
        Poteau
this   6"   day of   April
A.D. 190 4
              EJ Fannin
                    Clerk.
By   T.T. Vurnor   Deputy.

P. O.   Garland

DEPARTMENT OF THE INTERIOR,
COMMISSION TO THE FIVE CIVILIZED TRIBES.
FILED
APR 24 1905

Tams Bixby CHAIRMAN.

INDIAN TERRITORY, CENTRAL DISTRICT, AT POTEAU. I hereby certify that the within is a true and correct copy of the original.	
EJ Fannin	Clerk
By T.T. Vurnor	D.C.

Applications for Enrollment of Choctaw Newborn
Act of 1905   Volume XVI

No. 2086

MARRIAGE LICENSE

United States of America,   The Indian Territory,
                                                          Central   DISTRICT, SS.

To any Person Authorized by Law to Solemnize Marriage, Greeting:

You are hereby commanded to Solemnize the Rite and publish the Banns of Matrimony between Mr.   Henry Hulsey
of   Garland   in the Indian Territory, aged   20   years,
and Miss Lillie McCaslin   of   Garland
in the Indian Territory., aged   17   years, according to law, and do you officially sign and return this License to the parties therein named.

WITNESS my hand and official seal, this   6th   day
of   April   A. D. 190 4

E.J. Fannin
Clerk of the United States Court.

By T.T. Vurnor   Deputy

Certificate of Marriage.

United States of America, ⎫
  The Indian Territory,   ⎬ ss.
  Central   District.   ⎭   I,   John R Smith

a   Minister   , do hereby certify, that on the   6"   day of
April   A. D. 190 4 , I did, duly and according to law, as commanded in the foregoing License, solemnize the Rite and publish the Banns of Matrimony between the parties therein named.

Witness my hand, this   6   day of   April   A. D. 190 4

My credentials are recorded in the office of the Clerk of ⎫   J.R. Smith
  the United States Court in the Indian Territory,   ⎬
  Central District, Book — , Page   —   ⎭   a   Minister

Note—This License and Certificate of Marriage must be returned to the Office of the Clerk of the United States Court of the Indian Territory, from whence it was issued, within sixty days from the date thereof, or the party to whom the License was issued will be liable in the amount of the One Hundred Dollars ($100.00)

Applications for Enrollment of Choctaw Newborn
Act of 1905 Volume XVI

(The below typed as written.)

Indoresed on back.
No 2086
CERTIFIcATE OF RECORD OF MARRIAGES.
United States of America
The Indian Territory
Central District, S.S.:
I E. J. Fannin Clerk fo the United States Court in the Indian Territory, do hereby c ertify that the License for and Certificate of the Marriage of Mr. Henry Hulsey and Miss Lillie McCCushin was filed in my office in said Territory and District the 6th day of April A D. 1904, and duly recorded in Book 2 of Marriage Record, Page 425.
   Witness my hand and seal of said Court, at Poteau this 6 day of April A. D. 1904.

E. J. Fannin, Clerk.
By T. T. Vurnor, Deputy.

P.O.Garland.
(SEAL)

   Department of the Interior?
Commission to the Five Civilized Tribes.
F I L E D .

Apr. 24, 1905.
Tams Bixby, Chairman.

7-N.B. 1198.
DEPARTMENT OF THE INTERIOR,
COMMISSIONER TO THE FIVE CIVILIZED TRIBES.
Muskogee, Ind. Ter., November 14, 1905.

   In the matter of the application for the enrollment of Eulah Cordelia Hulsey as a citizen by blood of the Choctaw Nation.
   Fowler & Bolger of Poteau, Indian Territory, appearing as attorneys for the applicant.

   Lilly Hulsey being first duly sworn testified as follows:
Examination by the Commissioner:
Q What is your name? A Lilly Hulsey.
Q How old are you? A I was 18 last May.
Q What is your postoffice address? A Stigler, Ind. Ter.
Q You wish to give testimony relative to the enrollment of your child, Eulah Cordelia Hulsey as a citizen of the Choctaw Nation? A I do.
Q What is the child's name? A Eulah Cordelia.
Q When was she born? A July 20, 1904.
Q You are not a citizen of the Choctaw Nation[sic] A No sir.

Applications for Enrollment of Choctaw Newborn
Act of 1905   Volume XVI

Q Who is the father of this baby? A Henry H. Hulsey.
Q Were you married to him at the time this child was born? A Yes, before.
Q You way that you were married to him before the child was born? A Yes, before.
Q How long before? A I was married April 6, 1904, and the child was born July 20, 1904--from April until July.
Q You say that Henry Hulsey is the father of this child? A Yes sir.
Q Were you keeping company with him before you married him? A Yes sir.
Q For how long? A You will have to let me study just a minute over that. Can you tell me what year we moved up here? Let me see. I had been going with him a little over two years.
Q Continuously? A Yes sir.
Q Had you been keeping company with any other men? A Oh, yes, before I went with him I did.
Q This child was born four months after you were married. You are certain that Henry Hulsey is the father of this baby are you? A Yes sir, most surely.
Q For how long a period prior to the birth of this child had you been going with this Henry Hulsey? A Little over two years.
Q In the mean time, had you been keeping company with anyone else, did you say? A No,--how lately do you mean? Do you mean here lately? A No, I mean before the birth of the child.
A No, not after we moved up there. Before we went there I kept company with young me.

By Mr. Bogler[sic]:
Q He means before you married him, for two years you had been going with him, had you been keeping company with anyone else except Henry Hulsey? A No sir.

By the Commissioner:
Q For over a year before the birth of this child had you been keeping company with anyone else? A No one else; no one.
Q Has Henry Hulsey recognized this child as his child since its birth? A Yes, he says its[sic] his of course, but him and I don't live together.
Q Haven't you lived together at all since your marriage?
A No sir.
Q No at all? A (No answer)
Q Has he recognized this child in any way? A Why no, nothing only in speaking of her.
Q Is the child, in the community in which you live, recognized as the child of Henry Hulsey? (No answer.)

By Mr. Bolger:
Q Do the people in the community where you live recognize that child as the child of Henry Hulsey? A Yes, certainly.
Q In that other question he asked you--has he ever come to see the child? A Not but one time.

By the Commissioner.
Q When was that? A Been just a little bit over a year ago. A few days over a year.

Applications for Enrollment of Choctaw Newborn
Act of 1905 Volume XVI

Q Since this child was born has he contributed anything towards its support? A No, because I wouldn't allow it.

Q How is it that you happened to marry him then? A It was because I thought he loved me and I wanted to live with him, and after we got married his mother put in and he didn't come on as he promised he would, and then I wouldn't live with him.

Q Havn't[sic] you lived with him at all since you married him? A I don't know whether I would have lived with him if he wanted me to or not after his mother put in.

Q As soon as you were married did each one of you go your own way? A Yes, business called him to go to Cowlington and I was coming straight home. It was absolutely necessary for him to go to Cowlington and when he come home his mother put in and wouldn't let him come--or so they say; I don't know that she put in but that's what I was told.

Q Where does Henry Hulsey live? A Garland, Indian Territory is his postoffice. He lives in the country.

Q Had Henry Hulsey ever-been married before he married you? A No

Q Had you ever been married before you married him? A No sir.

    Frances R. Lane upon oath states that as stenographer to the Commission to the Five Civilized Tribes she correctly reported the testimony in the above entitled cause and that the foregoing is an accurate transcript of her stenographic notes thereof.

Frances R. Lane

Subscribed and sworn to before me this November 15, 1905.

Myron White
Notary Public.

DEPARTMENT OF THE INTERIOR,
COMMISSIONER TO THE FIVE CIVILIZED TRIBES.

South McAlester, Indian Territory, November 7, 1908.
----------------oOo-----------------

    In the matter of the application for the enrollment, as a citizen by blood of the Choctaw Nation, of Eulah Cordelia Hulsey, 7-N. B. 1198.

    Testimony taken in Garland, Indian Territory, August 10, 1906.

    J. C. HULSEY , being duly sworn, by Lacey P. Bobo, Notary Public in and for the Central District of Indian Territory, testified as follows:

BY THE COMMISSIONER:

Q What is your name? A J. C. Hulsey.
Q How old are you? A 54 years old.
Q What is your post office address? A Garland, I. T.

Applications for Enrollment of Choctaw Newborn
Act of 1905   Volume XVI

Q Is your wife a citizen by blood of the Choctaw Nation?
A Yes, sir.
Q What is her name? A Lovicey Hulsey.
Q What degree of blood is your wife?
A I guess she is about a quarter-blood.
Q Is Henry Hulsey your and Lovicey Hulsey's son? A Yes, sir.
Q What is his present age? A I think he is 22.
Q Is he a duly enrolled and recognized citizen by blood of the Choctaw Nation? A Yes, sir, and has allotted his land, every foot of it.
Q Is he a married man? A Yes, sir.
Q Has he a child or children? A Yes, sir, one.
Q When was the child born? A July 20, 1904.1
Q Whom did Henry Hulsey marry?? A Lillie McCaslin.
Q Did your son keep company with this woman as much as a year prior to the birth of that child? A Yes, sir, and longer.
Q Did this woman receive his attentions and keep company with him for more than a year prior to the birth of this child to the exclusion of other men?
A I never had any knowledge of anybody else going to see her while my son was going to see her. I know she threw off some of her old acquaintances in Arkansas.
Q She kept his company to the exclusion of all others? A Yes, sir.
Q It appears from the records of the Commission to the Five Civilized Tribes that Lillie Hulsey, on July 20, 1904, gave birth to a female child, since named Eulah Cordelia Hulsey: Do you positively consider that Henry Hulsey, your son, is the father of that child? A Yes, sir, I do; the reason why I think so is because no one else kept the woman's company, an at all the meetings, etc., it was noticed she would not pay any attention to any other boy but my son, and the child is just the image of my son.
Q Did you son ever state to you that he was the father of this child? A Yes, sir, when he was arrested I went down to see some lawyers about getting up hus[sic] bond and I took him and had a talk with him and he said it was his child, and I asked him if the girl ever had anything to do with anybody else and he said he thought not he worked with her about a week before he done anything.
   She is not a loose woman by any means.
Q Do you know additional facts that cause you to know this child to be Henry Hulsey's?
A When Henry came back from Oklahoma his mother carried him in a room and told him he would either have to marry Lillie or go the penitentiary, as the Marshal would get him, and he told his mother that if he did have to marry Lillie it was his child, and his mother asked him if anybody else had had anything to do with the woman and he said he did not believe they had.
Q The records of the Commission to the Five Civilized Tribes further show that on the 15th day of November 1905, the Commissioner addressed a letter to Henry Hulsey notifying him to appear and give testimony relative to the parentage of the aforesaid child before any further action could be taken in the matter of the application of her enrollment: Why did not Henry Hulsey appear in response to the Commission's request?
A When Henry received that letter he went over to see Lillie the mother of the child and her father came to the door and told him that they could enroll the child without any of his (Henry's) help, so my son came back home and did not do anything else about it.

Applications for Enrollment of Choctaw Newborn
Act of 1905   Volume XVI

Q Has Henry Hulsey ever contributed anything to the support of this child?
A Henry went over there and offered to give her money to by clothing for the child, but the mother said "Henry, I would be glad to take anything but my father would not let me receive anything from you and would be made if he know I spoke to you." I think he has smuggled a few things through her half-sister.
Q Does Henry Hulsey make his home with you?
A Yes, sir, he lives at home.
Q Where is he at the present time? A I sent him to Cowlington twenty miles below here; he said he was going to Ft. Smith and was coming back last night, but the waters are up and he can't get back yet.

Witness Excused.

W. P. Covington under oath states that he correctly reported the proceedings had in the above case on the date set forth, and that the foregoing is a complete transcript of said stenographic notes.   W.P. Covington

Subscribed and sworn to before me, this 8" day of Nov 1906.

Lacey P Bobo
Notary Public.

7-NB-1198.

DEPARTMENT OF THE INTERIOR,
COMMISSIONER TO THE FIVE CIVILIZED TRIBES.
MUSKOGEE, INDIAN TERRITORY, JANUARY 29, 1907.

In the matter of the application for the enrollment of Eulah Cordelia Hulsey, as a citizen by blood of the Choctaw Nation.

HENRY HULSEY,-being first duly sworn, testified as follows:

(Examination by the Commissioner)
Q What is your name? A Henry Hulsey.
Q How old are you? A 23 the 14th of December.
Q What is your post office address? A Garland.
Q Are you a citizen by blood of the Choctaw Nation.[sic[sic] A Yes sir.
Q Been finally enrolled? A Yes sir.
Q Selected your allotment? A Yes sir.
Q Are you acquainted with Lillie Hulsey? A Yes sir.
Q Is she any relation to you? A My wife.
Q When were you married to her? A I was married two years, the sixth of next April.
Q Last April, wasn't it April, 1904? A 1905.

Applications for Enrollment of Choctaw Newborn
Act of 1905   Volume XVI

Q The certificate of marriage filed with the application for the enrollment of Henry[sic] Hulsey, state that you were married on the 6th day of April, 1904, is that correct?
A Yes, it was two years, two years the 6th of last April.
Q On July 20, 1904, there was born to Lillie Hulsey a child named Henry[sic] Hulsey. That child was born to her after you married her, wasn't it? A Yes sir.
Q Did you live with Lillie Hulsey after you married her?
A No sir.
Q Have you recognized this child as yours? A Yes sir.
Q How long had you know Lillie Hulsey before you married her? A I had know her for about two years
Q Had you been going to see her continuously during that time?
A Sir?
Q Had you been keeping company with her continuously during that time? A Had been about ten month, I guess.
Q Have you every reason to believe that this chld[sic] was yours? A Yes sir.
Q Have you recognized it as your child since its birth?
A Yes sir.
Q Does it bear your name? A Yes sir.
Q Have you contributed to the support of this child in any way? A No sir
Q Why not? A Just haven't done it.
Q Did you ever go to see it? A No sir.
Q Is its mother living in your neighborhood? A Yes sir.
Q Are you on speaking terms with your wife? A No sir.
Q Have you been since you married her? A Yes sir, I have.
Q Have you held out to the people in your community that you were the father of this child? A Yes sir.
Q Did you live with Lillie Hulsey at all after you married her? A No sir.
Q But you are positive that Henry[sic] Hulsey is your own child? A Yes sir.
Q Did your parents recognize this child as being yours? A Yes.
Q Do they go to see it? A My sister has been to see it.
Q During the time that yu[sic] were keeping company with Lillie Hulsey, did you know of anyone else who was keeping company with her at the same time? A No sir.
Q Was there any misunderstanding between you and the members of her family? A Yes sir.
Q Is that the reason why you have not manifested any more interest in this child than you have? A Yes sir.
Q Are you permitted to go to her home and see this child? A You say what?
Q Are you permitted to go to her home and see this child? A I done[sic] know whether I understand you or not.
Q Is there any objection on the part of her parents to you going there? A Yes sir.
Q That is the reason why you have not been to see it? A Yes sir.
Q Have you offered to support this child? A No sir.
Q You have not offered to? A No sir.
Q The child is living now, is it not? A Yes sir.

(Witness excused)
--o--

Applications for Enrollment of Choctaw Newborn
Act of 1905 Volume XVI

Kate DeBord, stenographer to the Commissioner to the Five Civilized Tribes, being first duly affirmed, states that she correctly reported all proceedings had in the above entitled and numbered cause on the 29th day of January, 1907, and that the above and foregoing is a full, true and correct transcript of her stenographic notes, taken therein on said date.

Kate D^{e}Bord

Subscribed and affirmed to before me this 30th day of January, 1907.

Edward Merrick
Notary Public.

7-N.B.-198
O.L.J./

DEPARTMENT OF THE INTERIOR,
COMMISSIONER TO THE FIVE CIVILIZED TRIBES.

In the matter of the application for the enrollment of Eulah Cordelia Hulsey as a citizen by blood of the Choctaw Nation.

DECISION.

It appears from the record herein that on April 24, 1905, application was made to the Commission to the Five Civilized Tribes for the enrollment of Eulah Cordelia Hulsey as a citizen by blood of the Choctaw Nation, under the provisions of the Act of Congress approved March 3, 1905 (33 Stats., 1060).

It further appears from the record herein that said applicant was born July 20, 1904, and is the daughter of Henry Hulsey whose name appears as No. 8190 upon the final roll of citizens by blood of the Choctaw Nation approved by the Secretary of the Interior January 17, 1904, and Lilly Hulsey, a non-citizen, and that said applicant was living on March 4, 1905.

I am, therefore, of the opinion that Eulah Cordelia Hulsey should be enrolled as a citizen by blood, under the provisions of the Act of Congress approved March 3, 1905 (33 Stats., 1060), and it is so ordered.

Tams Bixby Commissioner.

Muskogee, Indian Territory.
FEB 2 1907

Applications for Enrollment of Choctaw Newborn
Act of 1905   Volume XVI

7-NB-1198

COPY

Muskogee, Indian Territory, February 2, 1907.

Henry Hulsey,
    Stigler, Indian Territory.

Dear Sir:

    Inclosed herewith you will find a copy of the decision of the Commissioner to the Five Civilized Tribes, rendered February 2, 1907, granting the application for the enrollment of Eulah Cordelia Hulsey as a citizen by blood of the Choctaw Nation.

    You are hereby advised that the name of Eulah Cordelia Hulsey will be placed upon the next schedule of citizens by blood of the Choctaw Nation to be submitted to the Secretary of the Interior for his approval.

                                     Respectfully,

                               SIGNED *Tams Bixby*
                                      Commissioner.

Registered.
Incl. 7-NB-1198

7-NB-1198

COPY

Muskogee, Indian Territory, February 2, 1907.

Fowler & Bolger,
    Attorneys at law[sic],
        Poteau, Indian Territory.

Gentleman:

    You are hereby notified that the Commissioner to the Five Civilized Tribes, on February 2, 1907, rendered his decision granting the application for the enrollment of Eulah Cordelia Hulsey as a citizen by blood of the Choctaw Nation.

    You are hereby advised that the name of Eulah Cordelia Hulsey will be placed upon the next schedule of citizens by blood of the Choctaw Nation to be submitted to the Secretary of the Interior for his approval.

                                     Respectfully,

                               SIGNED *Tams Bixby*
Registered.   Commissioner.
Incl. 7-NB-1198

Applications for Enrollment of Choctaw Newborn
Act of 1905 Volume XVI

7-NB-1198

COPY

Muskogee, Indian Territory, February 2, 1907.

Mansfield, McMurray & Cornish,
    Attorneys for the Choctaw and Chickasaw Nations,
        South McAlester, Indian Territory.

Gentlemen:

    Inclosed herewith you will find a copy of the decision of the Commissioner to the Five Civilized Tribes, rendered February 2, 1907, granting the application for the enrollment of Eulah Cordelia Hulsey as a citizen by blood of the Choctaw Nation.

    You are hereby advised that the name of Eulah Cordelia Hulsey will be placed upon the next schedule of citizens by blood of the Choctaw Nation to be submitted to the Secretary of the Interior for his approval.

                        Respectfully,

                      SIGNED *Tams Bixby*
                        Commissioner.

Incl. 7-NB-1198
Registered.

7-2789.

Muskogee, Indian Territory, April 27, 1905.

Henry Hulsey,
    Stigler, Indian Territory.

Dear Sir:

    Receipt is hereby acknowledged of the affidavits of Lilly Hulsey and C. C. Jones, to the birth of Eulah Cordelia Hulsey, child of Henry and Lilly Hulsey, July 20, 1904, and the same have been filed with our records as an application for the enrollment of said child.

    Receipt is also acknowledged of the marriage license and certificate between Henry Hulsey and Lillie McCuslin, which you offer in support of the application for enrollment of your child, and the same has been filed with the records in this case.

                        Respectfully,

                                Chairman.

Applications for Enrollment of Choctaw Newborn
Act of 1905 Volume XVI

7-NB-1198

Muskogee, Indian Territory, September 29, 1905

Fowler & Bolger,
    Attorneys at Law,
        Poteau, Indian Territory.

Gentleman:

    Receipt is hereby acknowledged of your letter of the 20th instant in which you request to be advised as to whether or not the Secretary of the Interior has passed upon and approved the application for the enrollment of Eulah Cordelia Hulsey as a citizen by blood of the Choctaw Nation.

    In reply to your letter you are advised that the rights of said child as a citizen by blood of the Choctaw Nation are derived through her father, her mother being a non-citizen, and that the parents of said child were married April 6, 1904 while said child was born July 20, 1904.

    You are advised that before the rights of Eulah Cordelia Hulsey as a citizen by blood of the Choctaw Nation can be finally determined it will be necessary for both parents of said child to appear in person at this office for the purpose of giving their sworn testimony.

    This appearance should be made as early as possible.

        Respectfully,

                Commissioner.

7-N.B. 1198.

Muskogee, Indian Territory, November 15, 1905.

Henry Hulsey,
    Garland, Indian Territory.

Dear Sir:

    You are hereby notified that before any further action can be taken in the matter of the application for the enrollment of Eulah Cordelia Hulscy as a citizen by blood of the Choctaw Nation, it will be necessary for you to appear at the office of the Commissioner

Applications for Enrollment of Choctaw Newborn
Act of 1905 Volume XVI

to the Five Civilized Tribes at Muskogee, Indian Territory, and give testimony relative to the parentage of said child. This matter should receive your immediate attention.

Respectfully,

Commissioner.

McAlester, Indian Territory, Sept. 19, 1906.

Henry Hulsey,
    Stigler, Indian Territory.

Dear Sir:

    You are hereby notified to appear before this Choctaw Field Party at McAlester, Indian Territory, on Monday September 24, 1906, and give testimony relative to the right of your daughter Eula[sic] Cordelia Hulsey, to enrollment as a New Born citizen by blood of the Choctaw Nation. You will find this party in Room 43, McFarland Hotel, McAlester, Indian Territory.

Very respectfully,

[sic]

---

a. B.

REFER IN REPLY TO THE FOLLOWING:

DEPARTMENT OF THE INTERIOR,
COMMISSIONER TO THE FIVE CIVILIZED TRIBES.

Muskogee, Indian Territory, December 10, 1906.

Lacey P. Bobo,
    Kiowa, Indian Territory.

Dear Sir:

    In the matter of the application for the enrollment of Eulah Cordelia Hulsey as a new born citizen of the Choctaw Nation under the act of March 3, 1905, there is returned herewith a copy of the record and you are requested to secure the testimony of Henry Hulsey, the father of this child.

Respectfully,

EB 2-10.   Tams Bixby Commissioner.

Applications for Enrollment of Choctaw Newborn
Act of 1905 Volume XVI

Boswell, I. T.; Dec. 31, 1906.

Henry Hulsey,
    Garland, I. T.

Dear Sir:

You are advised that all papers in the matter of the application for the enrollment of Eula[sic] Cordelia Hulsey, minor child of Lillie Hulsey (bee[sic] McCaslin), have again been referred to Choctaqw[sic]-Chickasaw Field Party No. 1 for the purpose of procuring testimony as to who the father is. You are advised that under the provisions of the act of Congress approved July 1, 1902, the provisions of the Act approved April 26, 1906, the Secretary of the Interior will have no authority to approve application for the enrollment of any citizen of the Choctaw Nation after March 4, 1907, and it is imperatively necessary that your testimony in the above case be procured. You are requested to advise this party using self-addressed official envelope enclosed, as to whether you are willing to give testimony in this case, and if so what railroad point in the Choctaw Nation will be most convenient for you to appear before this party for the purpose above set forth.

Very respectfully,

[sic]

Hugo, I. T., Jan. 7, 1907.

Henry Hulsey,
    Garland, Indian Territory.

Dear Sir:

Your letter of the 4th inst. advising that you will meet this party at Stigler, Indian Territory, January 15, 1907 for the purpose of giving testimony relative to the application for the enrollment of a minor Choctaw named Eula[sic] Cordelia Hulsey has been received. You are advised that you willingness to give testimony in this case has been noted, and you will be given an additional notice as to when to appear before this party at Stigler, Indian Territory, in this matter, this party not being able to be at Stigler on January 15th, date suggested by you.

It is suggested that in view of the immediate urgency of your testimony in this case being taken that you appear at your earliest convenience before the Commissioner to the Five Civilized Tribes at Muskogee, Indian Territory, with this letter for the purposes above set forth.

Very respectfully,

[sic]

Applications for Enrollment of Choctaw Newborn
Act of 1905   Volume XVI

7 NB - 1198

Muskogee, Indian Territory, January 12, 1907.

Fowler & Bolger,
    Attorneys at Law,
        Poteau, Indian Territory.

Dear Sirs:

    Receipt is hereby acknowledged of your letter of January 5th, asking what has been done with the application of Eulah Hulsey for enrollment as a citizen of the Choctaw Nation. You state you understand that the father of the child, appeared and made a statement of the facts relative to this case.

    In reply you are advised that the testimony of the father, Henry Hulsey, relative to the parentage of this child has not yet been received at this office. The testimony of J. C. Hulsey, grandfather of the child was taken, but before further consideration can be given this application, it will be necessary that the testimony of the father, Henry Hulsey, be furnished. If he has all ready appeared before a representative of the Commissioner in the field and given his testimony, it will not be necessary for him to take further action in the matter, but if he has not, he should appear at this office not later than January 20, 1907, for that purpose.

                Respectfully,

                          Commissioner.

7-NB-1198

Muskogee, Indian Territory, February 15, 1907.

Fowler & Bolger,
    Poteau, Indian Territory.

Gentlemen:

    Receipt is hereby acknowledged of your letter of February 5, 1907, asking if further evidence is necessary in the case of Eulah Hulsey.

    In reply to your letter you are advised that the name of Eulah Cordelia Hulsey has been placed upon a schedule of new born citizens of the Choctaw Nation under the Act of Congress approved March 3, 1905, and you will be notified of Departmental action therein.

                Respectfully,

                          Commissioner.

Applications for Enrollment of Choctaw Newborn
Act of 1905   Volume XVI

7-NB-1198.

Muskogee, Indian Territory, March 6, 1907.

Fowler & Bolger,
    Poteau, Indian Territory.

Gentlemen:

    Receipt is hereby acknowledged of your letter of February 5, asking that you be advised if further evidence is lacking in the matter of the enrollment of Eulah Hulsey.

    In reply you are advised that the name of Eulah Cordelia Hulsey has been placed upon a schedule of new born citizens of the Choctaw Nation under the Act of Congress approved March 3, 1905, and you will be notified of the approval of her enrollment by the Department.

                      Respectfully,

                                            Commissioner.

(The letter below typed as given.)

                                    Garland IT
                                    Jan 4 1906

Sacty BBobo
Dear Sir I will write you in regard to inroling ula Cadiul Hulsey I will *(illegible)* you at Stigler IT Jan 15 for the pupat of in Roling my child
                                    H H Hulsey

<u>Choctaw New Born 1199</u>
    Pearl Brown
    (Born March 14[sic], 1903)

Applications for Enrollment of Choctaw Newborn
Act of 1905   Volume XVI

7- 6740 - 818 7.W.

BIRTH AFFIDAVIT.

DEPARTMENT OF THE INTERIOR.
COMMISSION TO THE FIVE CIVILIZED TRIBES.

IN RE APPLICATION FOR ENROLLMENT, as a citizen of the   Choctaw   Nation, of Pearl Brown   , born on the 14[sic] day of March , 1903

Name of Father: Mat Brown   a citizen of the Choc   Nation.
Name of Mother: Permelia Brown   a citizen of the Choc   Nation.

Postoffice   Wister I.T.

AFFIDAVIT OF MOTHER.

UNITED STATES OF AMERICA, Indian Territory,
Central   DISTRICT.

I, Permelia Brown , on oath state that I am 25 years of age and a citizen by blood , of the Choc Nation; that I am the lawful wife of Mat Brown , who is a citizen, by intermarriage of the Choctaw Nation; that a female child was born to me on 14[sic] day of March , 1903; that said child has been named Pearl Brown , and was living March 4, 1905.

Permelia Brown

Witnesses To Mark:

Subscribed and sworn to before me this 17 day of April , 1905

OL Johnson
Notary Public.

AFFIDAVIT OF ATTENDING PHYSICIAN OR MID-WIFE.

UNITED STATES OF AMERICA, Indian Territory,
                     DISTRICT.

I, William Wallace , a physician , on oath state that I attended on Mrs. Permelia Brown , wife of Mat Brown on the 14[sic] day of March , 1903; that there was born to her on said date a female child; that said child was living March 4, 1905, and is said to have been named Pearl Brown

Wm Wallace M.D.

Applications for Enrollment of Choctaw Newborn
Act of 1905   Volume XVI

Witnesses To Mark:
  Mattie Hart

Subscribed and sworn to before me this 21 day of   April   , 1905

My commission expires   W.E. Larecy
July 9th, 1908.   Notary Public.

NEW BORN AFFIDAVIT

No _____

CHOCTAW ENROLLING COMMISSION

IN THE MATTER OF THE APPLICATION FOR ENROLLMENT as a citizen of the Choctaw Nation, of   Pearl Brown   born on the 13 day of   March   190 3

Name of father   Mat Brown   a citizen of   Choctaw   Nation, final enrollment No. 818
Name of mother   Permelia Brown a citizen of   Choctaw   Nation, final enrollment No. 6740

              Wister I.T   Postoffice.

AFFIDAVIT OF MOTHER

UNITED STATES OF AMERICA
   INDIAN TERRITORY
DISTRICT   Central

   I   Permelia Brown   , on oath state that I am 25 years of age and a citizen by blood of the Choctaw Nation, and as such have been placed upon the final roll of the Choctaw Nation, by the Honorable Secretary of the Interior my final enrollment number being 6740 ; that I am the lawful wife of Mat Brown , who is a citizen of the Choctaw Nation, and as such has been placed upon the final roll of said Nation by the Honorable Secretary of the Interior, his final enrollment number being 818 and that a female child was born to me on the 13 day of March 190 3; that said child has been named Pearl Brown , and is now living.

                    Permelia Brown

184

Applications for Enrollment of Choctaw Newborn
Act of 1905   Volume XVI

WITNESSETH:
Must be two witnesses { *(Name Illegible)*
who are citizens   Lonnie Free

Subscribed and sworn to before me this, the 17 day of February , 190 5

James Bower
Notary Public.

My Commission Expires:
Sept 23-1907

Affidavit of Attending Physician or Midwife

UNITED STATES OF AMERICA,
INDIAN TERRITORY,
Central   DISTRICT

I,   W M Walace[sic]   a   Practicing Physician
on oath state that I attended on Mrs. Permelia Brown   wife of Mat Brown
on the   13   day of   March , 190 3, that there was born to her on said date a   female
child, that said child is now living, and is said to have been named   Pearl Brown

W.M. Wallace   M. D.

Subscribed and sworn to before me this the 20th   day of Feby   1905

WE Larecy
Notary Public.

WITNESSETH:
Must be two witnesses { *(Name Illegible)*
who are citizens and
know the child.   Lonnie Free

We hereby certify that we are well acquainted with   W.M. Walace
a   Practicing Physician   and know   him   to be reputable and of good
standing in the community.

Must be two citizen { Joe Allen
witnesses.   Richard Crowder

185

Applications for Enrollment of Choctaw Newborn
Act of 1905   Volume XVI

BIRTH AFFIDAVIT.

DEPARTMENT OF THE INTERIOR.
COMMISSION TO THE FIVE CIVILIZED TRIBES.

IN RE APPLICATION FOR ENROLLMENT, as a citizen of the   Choctaw   Nation, of   Pearl Brown   , born on the 13   day of   Mch   , 1903

Name of Father: Mat Brown   Roll 7W 818   a citizen of the   Choctaw   Nation.
Name of Mother: Permelia Brown   Roll 6740   a citizen of the   Choctaw   Nation.

Postoffice   Wister I.T.

AFFIDAVIT OF MOTHER.

UNITED STATES OF AMERICA, Indian Territory,
    Central   DISTRICT.

I,   Permelia Brown   , on oath state that I am   25   years of age and a citizen by   blood   , of the   Choc   Nation; that I am the lawful wife of   Mat Brown   , who is a citizen, by   marriage   of the   Choctaw   Nation; that a   female   child was born to me on   13   day of   March   , 1903; that said child has been named   Pearl Brown   , and was living March 4, 1905.

Permelia Brown

Witnesses To Mark:

Subscribed and sworn to before me this   7   day of   June   , 1905

(Name Illegible)
Com Exp Jan 29/1908   Notary Public.

AFFIDAVIT OF ATTENDING PHYSICIAN OR MID-WIFE.

UNITED STATES OF AMERICA, Indian Territory,
    Central   DISTRICT.

I,   William M. Wallace   , a physician   , on oath state that I attended on Mrs.   Permelia Brown   , wife of   Mat Brown   on the   13   day of March   , 1903; that there was born to her on said date a   female   child; that said child was living March 4, 1905, and is said to have been named   Pearl Brown

W M Wallace M.D.

Applications for Enrollment of Choctaw Newborn
Act of 1905   Volume XVI

Witnesses To Mark:

{

    Subscribed and sworn to before me this 24 day of   June   , 1905
    My commission expires
    July 9th, 1908.
                                      W.E. Larecy
                                          Notary Public.

                                                              7-2330.

                          Muskogee, Indian Territory, April 27, 1905.

Mat Brown,
    Wister, Indian Territory.

Dear Sir:

    Receipt is hereby acknowledged of the affidavits of Permelia Brown and W. M. Wallace, to the birth of Pearl Brown, child of Mat and Permelia Brown, March 14, 1903, and the same have been filed with our record as an application for enrollment of said child.

                                Respectfully,

                                                 Chairman.

                                                       7--NB--1199

                          Muskogee, Indian Territory, June 2, 1905.

Mat Brown,
    Wister, Indian Territory.

Dear Sir:

    There is enclosed you herewith for execution application for the enrollment of your infant child, Pearl Brown.

    In the affidavits of February 17, 1905, the date of the applicant's birth is given as March 13, 1903, while in the affidavits of April 21, 1905, this date is given as March 13, 1903. In the enclosed application the date of birth is left blank. Please insert the correct date of birth and when the affidavits have been properly executed return them to this office.

    In having the affidavits executed care should be exercised to see that all names are written in full, as they appear in the body of the affidavits and in the event that either of

Applications for Enrollment of Choctaw Newborn
Act of 1905 Volume XVI

the persons signing same are unable to write, signatures by mark must be attested by two witnesses. Each affidavit must be executed before a Notary Public and the notarial seal and signature of the officer must be attached to each separate affidavit.

This matter should receive your immediate attention as no further action can be taken relative to the enrollment of said child until the Commission has been furnished these affidavits.

Respectfully,

Commissioner in Charge.

FVK-Enc-13

---

7 NB 1199

Muskogee, Indian Territory, June 30, 1905.

Mat Brown,
　　Wister, Indian Territory.

Dear Sir:

Receipt is hereby acknowledged of the affidavits of Permelia Brown and W. M. Wallace to the birth of Pearl Brown, daughter of Mat and Permelia Brown, March 13, 1903, and the same have been filed with our records in the matter of the enrollment of said child.

Respectfully,

Chairman.

Choctaw New Born 1200
　　Leo Daffern
　　(Born Jan. 31, 19040

Applications for Enrollment of Choctaw Newborn
Act of 1905 Volume XVI

BIRTH AFFIDAVIT.

DEPARTMENT OF THE INTERIOR.
COMMISSION TO THE FIVE CIVILIZED TRIBES.

IN RE APPLICATION FOR ENROLLMENT, as a citizen of the Choctaw Nation, of Leo Daffern, born on the 31st day of January, 1904

Name of Father: B. Daffern   a citizen of the United States ~~Nation~~.
Name of Mother: Lorinda Daffern nee James   a citizen of the Choctaw Nation.

Postoffice   Waupanucka[sic], I.T.

AFFIDAVIT OF MOTHER.

UNITED STATES OF AMERICA, Indian Territory,
    Central   DISTRICT.

I, Lorinda Daffern, on oath state that I am 21 years of age and a citizen by blood, of the Choctaw Nation; that I am the lawful wife of B Daffern, who is a citizen, by blood of the Choctaw Nation; that a male child was born to me on 31st day of January, 1904; that said child has been named Leo Daffern, and was living March 4, 1905.

                Lorinda Daffern

Witnesses To Mark:

Subscribed and sworn to before me this 22nd day of April, 1905

                W.H. Angell
                Notary Public.

AFFIDAVIT OF ATTENDING PHYSICIAN OR MID-WIFE.

UNITED STATES OF AMERICA, Indian Territory,
    Central   DISTRICT.

I, B. Daffern, ~~a~~, on oath state that I *am the husband of* ~~attended on~~ Mrs. Lorinda Daffern, ~~wife of~~ *and that* on the 31st day of January, 1904; that there was born to her on said date a male child; that said child was living March 4, 1905, and is said to have been named Leo Daffern *and that the woman who attended on my said wife on the date of the birth of said Leo Daffern is dead*

                B. Daffern

Applications for Enrollment of Choctaw Newborn
Act of 1905   Volume XVI

Witnesses To Mark:

Subscribed and sworn to before me this 22nd day of April , 1905

W.H. Angell
Notary Public.

NEW-BORN AFFIDAVIT.

Number..............

...Choctaw Enrolling Commission...

IN THE MATTER OF THE APPLICATION FOR ENROLLMENT, as a citizen of the Choctaw   Nation, of   Leo Daffern

born on the 31st day of ___January___ 190 4

Name of father B. Daffern   a citizen of   white
Nation final enrollment No. ———   *now Daffern*
Name of mother   Lourinda[sic] James   a citizen of   Choctaw
Nation final enrollment No. 13598

Postoffice   Lehigh I.T.

AFFIDAVIT OF MOTHER.

UNITED STATES OF AMERICA
INDIAN TERRITORY
Central   DISTRICT

I   Lourinda James *now Daffern*   , on oath state that I am 20   years of age and a citizen by blood   of the   Choctaw   Nation, and as such have been placed upon the final roll of the   Choctaw Nation, by the Honorable Secretary of the Interior my final enrollment number being   13598 ; that I am the lawful wife of   B. Daffern   , who is a citizen of the   white   Nation, and as such has been placed upon the final roll of said Nation by the Honorable Secretary of the Interior, his final enrollment number being ——— and that a   male   child was born to me on the 31st day of   January   190 4; that said child has been named   Leo Daffern   , and is now living.

Lourinda James now Daffern

Witnesseth.

Must be two Witnesses who are Citizens.

W C James

Noah Alverson

Applications for Enrollment of Choctaw Newborn
Act of 1905   Volume XVI

Subscribed and sworn to before me this   12th   day of   Jan   190 5

W.A. Shoney
Notary Public.

My commission expires:
Jan 9-1909

Affidavit of Attending Physician or Midwife.

UNITED STATES OF AMERICA ⎫
INDIAN TERRITORY   ⎬
   Central   DISTRICT   ⎭

I,   B Daffern   a   attendant on oath state that I attended on Mrs.   Lourinda Daffern   wife of   B Daffern   on the   31st   day of   January   , 190 4 , that there was born to her on said date a   male   child, that said child is now living, and is said to have been named   Leo Daffern

B. Daffern   ~~M.D.~~

Subscribed and sworn to before me this, the   12th   day of   January   190 5

W.A. Shoney
Notary Public.

WITNESSETH:
Must be two witnesses who are citizens and know the child.
 { W.C. James
   Noah Alverson

We hereby certify that we are well acquainted with   B Daffern   a   attendant   and know   him   to be reputable and of good standing in the community.

{ W.C. James
  Noah Alverson

BIRTH AFFIDAVIT.

DEPARTMENT OF THE INTERIOR.
COMMISSION TO THE FIVE CIVILIZED TRIBES.

IN RE APPLICATION FOR ENROLLMENT, as a citizen of the   Choctaw   Nation, of   Leo Daffern   , born on the   31st   day of   January   , 1904

Name of Father: B. Daffern   a citizen of the United States ~~Nation~~.
Name of Mother: Lorinda Daffern nee James   a citizen of the   Choctaw   Nation.

191

Applications for Enrollment of Choctaw Newborn
Act of 1905   Volume XVI

Postoffice   Waupanucka[sic], I.T.

AFFIDAVIT OF MOTHER.

UNITED STATES OF AMERICA, Indian Territory,
Central   DISTRICT.

I,   Carl Davis   , on oath state that I am   22   years of age and a citizen by blood   , of the   Choctaw   Nation; that I am *personally acquainted with Mrs Lorinda Daffern wife of B. Daffern*   , who is a citizen, by blood   of the Choctaw   Nation; that a   male   child was born to ~~me~~ *her* on   31st day of January   , 1904; that said child has been named   Leo Daffern   , and was living March 4, 1905.

Carl Davis

Witnesses To Mark:

{

Subscribed and sworn to before me this   22   day of   April   , 1905

Dwight Brown
Notary Public.

AFFIDAVIT OF ATTENDING PHYSICIAN OR MID-WIFE.

UNITED STATES OF AMERICA, Indian Territory,
Central   DISTRICT.

am personally acquainted with
I,   John A Kalb   , ~~a~~   , on oath state that I ~~attended on~~ Mrs.   Lorinda Daffern   , wife of   B. Daffern   on the 31st day of January   , 1904; that there was born to her on said date a   male   child; that said child was living March 4, 1905, and is said to have been named   Leo Daffern

John A Kalb

Witnesses To Mark:

{

Subscribed and sworn to before me this   22   day of   April   , 1905

Dwight Brown
Notary Public.

Applications for Enrollment of Choctaw Newborn
Act of 1905 Volume XVI

7-5376.

Muskogee, Indian Territory, April 27, 1905.

B. Daffern,
    Wapanucka, Indian Territory.

Dear Sir:

    Receipt is hereby acknowledged of the affidavits of Carl Davis and John A. Kalb, to the birth of Leo Daffern, child of B. and Lorinda Daffern, January 31, 1904, and the same have been filed with our records as an application for the enrollment of said child.

                   Respectfully,

                                          Chairman.

Choctaw New Born 1201
    Zira Yota
    (Born Aug. 14, 1904)

BIRTH AFFIDAVIT.
DEPARTMENT OF THE INTERIOR.
COMMISSION TO THE FIVE CIVILIZED TRIBES.

IN RE APPLICATION FOR ENROLLMENT, as a citizen of the   Choctaw   Nation, of Zira Yota   , born on the 14   day of August   , 1904

Name of Father: Adam Yota   a citizen of the   Choctaw   Nation.
Name of Mother: Jincy Yota nee Choate   a citizen of the   Choctaw   Nation.

                         Postoffice   Le Flore IT

AFFIDAVIT OF MOTHER.

UNITED STATES OF AMERICA, Indian Territory, }
    Central   DISTRICT. }

    I, Jincy Yota, nee Choate   , on oath state that I am 24   years of age and a citizen by   blood   , of the   Choctaw   Nation; that I am the lawful wife of Adam Yota   , who is a citizen, by blood   of the   Choctaw   Nation; that

Applications for Enrollment of Choctaw Newborn
Act of 1905   Volume XVI

a   female   child was born to me on   14   day of   August   , 1904; that said child has been named   Zira Yota   , and was living March 4, 1905.

                                                  her
                                      Jincy x Yota, nee Choate

Witnesses To Mark: mark
{ Mitchell McCurtain
{ Wally Winloch

Subscribed and sworn to before me this   22   day of   August   , 1905

                                      Robert E Lee
                                      Notary Public.

My Com expires Jan 11 1906

AFFIDAVIT OF ATTENDING PHYSICIAN OR MID-WIFE.

UNITED STATES OF AMERICA, Indian Territory, }
    Central   DISTRICT. }

I,   Sally Lewis   , a   midwife   , on oath state that I attended on Mrs.   Jincy Yota nee Choate   , wife of   Adam Yota   on the   14   day of   August   , 1904; that there was born to her on said date a   female   child; that said child was living March 4, 1905, and is said to have been named   Zira Yota

                                      Sally Lewis

Witnesses To Mark:
{

Subscribed and sworn to before me this   22   day of   August   , 1905

                                      Robert E Lee
                                      Notary Public.

My Com expires Jan 11 1906

BIRTH AFFIDAVIT.
                          DEPARTMENT OF THE INTERIOR.
                 COMMISSION TO THE FIVE CIVILIZED TRIBES.

IN RE APPLICATION FOR ENROLLMENT, as a citizen of the   Choctaw   Nation, of   Zira Yota   , born on the   14   day of August   , 1904

Name of Father: Adam Yota   a citizen of the   Choctaw   Nation.
Name of Mother: Jincy Yota (Choate)   a citizen of the   Choctaw   Nation.

Applications for Enrollment of Choctaw Newborn
Act of 1905   Volume XVI

Postoffice   LeFlore Ind. Ter.

AFFIDAVIT OF MOTHER.

UNITED STATES OF AMERICA, Indian Territory, }
Central   DISTRICT.   }

I,   Jincy Yota, (Choate)   , on oath state that I am   24   years of age and a citizen by   blood   , of the   Choctaw   Nation; that I am the lawful wife of Adam Yota   , who is a citizen, by blood   of the   Choctaw   Nation; that a   female   child was born to me on   14   day of   August   , 1904; that said child has been named   Zira Yota   , and was living March 4, 1905.

            her
          Jincy x Yota
Witnesses To Mark: mark
{ Dennis Wade
{ Adam Yota

Subscribed and sworn to before me this   28   day of   Aug   , 1905

          Robert E Lee
          Notary Public.

Jan 11-1906

AFFIDAVIT OF ATTENDING PHYSICIAN OR MID-WIFE.

UNITED STATES OF AMERICA, Indian Territory, }
Central   DISTRICT.   }

I,   Sally Lewis   , a   midwife   , on oath state that I attended on Mrs.   Jincy Yota   , wife of Adam Yota   on the   14   day of August   , 1904; that there was born to her on said date a   female   child; that said child was living March 4, 1905, and is said to have been named   Zira Yota

          her
         Sally x Lewis
Witnesses To Mark: mark
{ Dennis Wade
{ Adam Yota

Subscribed and sworn to before me this   28   day of   Aug   , 1905

          Robert E Lee
          Notary Public.

Applications for Enrollment of Choctaw Newborn
Act of 1905 Volume XVI

NEW BORN AFFIDAVIT

No _____

CHOCTAW ENROLLING COMMISSION

IN THE MATTER OF THE APPLICATION FOR ENROLLMENT as a citizen of the Choctaw Nation, of **Zira Yota** born on the **14** day of **August** 190 **4**

Name of father **Adam Yota** a citizen of **Choctaw** Nation, final enrollment No. _____

Name of mother **Jincy Yota (nee Choate)** a citizen of **Choctaw** Nation, final enrollment No. **8715**

Leflore I.T. Postoffice.

AFFIDAVIT OF MOTHER

UNITED STATES OF AMERICA
INDIAN TERRITORY
DISTRICT Central

I **Jincy Yota (nee Choate)**, on oath state that I am **23** years of age and a citizen by **blood** of the **Choctaw** Nation, and as such have been placed upon the final roll of the **Choctaw** Nation, by the Honorable Secretary of the Interior my final enrollment number being **8715**; that I am the lawful wife of **Adam Yota**, who is a citizen of the **Choctaw** Nation, and as such has been placed upon the final roll of said Nation by the Honorable Secretary of the Interior, his final enrollment number being _____ and that a **Female** child was born to me on the **14** day of **August** 190 **4**; that said child has been named **Zira Yota**, and is now living.

WITNESSETH: Jincy Yota (nee Choate)
Must be two witnesses who are citizens { Thomas McCurtain
Henry Burns

Subscribed and sworn to before me this, the **20** day of **Feb**, 190 **5**

Robert E Lee
Notary Public.

My Commission Expires: Jan 11-1906

Applications for Enrollment of Choctaw Newborn
Act of 1905   Volume XVI

Affidavit of Attending Physician or Midwife

UNITED STATES OF AMERICA,
INDIAN TERRITORY,
Central   DISTRICT

I,   Sallie Lewis   a   Midwife
on oath state that I attended on Mrs. Jincy Yota (nee Choate)   wife of Adam Lewis[sic] on the   14   day of   August , 190 4, that there was born to her on said date a   female child, that said child is now living, and is said to have been named   Zira Yota

                              Sallie Lewis   M. D.

Subscribed and sworn to before me this the   20   day of February   1905

                        Robert E Lee
                             Notary Public.

WITNESSETH: My com expires Jan 11-1905[sic]
Must be two witnesses { Thomas McCurtain
who are citizens and
know the child.   Henry Burns

We hereby certify that we are well acquainted with   Sallie Lewis
a   midwife   and know   her   to be reputable and of good standing in the community.

                Must be two citizen { Thomas McCurtain
                witnesses.   Henry Burns

7-NB-1201

                Muskogee, Indian Territory, October 10, 1905.

T. V. Sprinkel,
    Wister, Indian Territory.

Dear Sir:

    Receipt is hereby acknowledged of your letter of October 6, 1905, asking if Zira Yota, child of Adam Yota, has been approved so that selection of allotment may now be made for said child.

    In reply to your letter you are advised that the name of Zira Yota, child of Adam Yota, has not yet been placed upon a schedule of citizens by blood of the Choctaw Nation, prepared for forwarding to the Secretary of the Interior. If any further evidence is

Applications for Enrollment of Choctaw Newborn
Act of 1905   Volume XVI

necessary to enable this office to determine her right to enrollment, you will be duly notified.

                    Respectfully,

                                            Commissioner.

                                            7-NB-1201.

                  Muskogee, Indian Territory, June 10, 1905.

Adam Yota,
    Leflore, Indian Territory.

Dear Sir:

    There is enclosed herewith for execution application for the enrollment of your infant child, Zira Yota, born August 14, 1904.

    In the application heretofore filed in this office the date of execution attached to the mother's affidavit is August 22, 1905. This is apparently an error. It will therefore be necessary that you have the enclosed application executed.

    In having these affidavits executed care should be exercised to see that all names are written in full, as they appear in the body of the affidavit, and in the event either of the persons signing the affidavit are unable to write, signatures by mark must be attested by two witnesses. Each affidavit must be executed before a Notary Public and the notarial seal and signature of the officer must be attached to each separate affidavit.

                    Respectfully,

DeB-4/10   Chairman.

7-NB-1201

                  Muskogee, Indian Territory, July 26, 1905.

Adam Yota,
    Leflore, Indian Territory.

Dear Sir:

    Your attention is called to a communication addressed to you by the Commission to the Five Civilized Tribes, under date of June 10, 1905, with which there was inclosed for execution application for the enrollment of your infant child, Zira Yota, born August 14, 1904.

Applications for Enrollment of Choctaw Newborn
Act of 1905   Volume XVI

In said letter you were informed that in the application heretofore filed in this office the date of execution attached to the mother's affidavit is August 22, 1905, an apparent error.

You were requested to have the application re-executed and returned to this office. No reply to this letter has been received.

This matter should receive your immediate attention, as no further action can be taken relative to the enrollment of your said child until the evidence requested is supplied.

Respectfully,

Commissioner.

7-NB-1201.

Muskogee, Indian Territory, September 5, 1905.

Adam Yota,
LeFlore, Indian Territory.

Dear Sir:

Receipt is hereby acknowledged of the affidavits of Jincy Yota, the mother, and Sallie Lewis, midwife, to the birth of your infant child, Zira Yota, born August 14, 1904, offered in support of the application for the enrollment of the said child as a citizen by blood of the Choctaw Nation.

The said affidavits have been filed with the record in this case.

Respectfully,

Acting Commissioner.

7-NB-1201.

Muskogee, Indian Territory, December 11, 1905.

Adam Yota,
Leflore, Indian Territory.

Dear Sir:

Your letter of November 30, 1905, addressed to the United States Indian Agent has been by him referred to this office for consideration and appropriate action. Therein you ask if you can file on land for Zira Yota.

Applications for Enrollment of Choctaw Newborn
Act of 1905   Volume XVI

In reply to your letter you are advised that the name of your daughter Zira Yota has not yet been placed upon a schedule of new born citizens of the Choctaw Nation prepared for forwarding to the Secretary of the Interior, but you will be notified when her enrollment is approved by the Department.

In event further evidence is necessary to enable this office to pass upon the right of your child to enrollment, you will be advised.

        Respectfully,

              Acting Commissioner.

Choctaw New Born 1202
  Louisa Greenwood
  (Born Dec. 12, 1903)

BIRTH AFFIDAVIT.

DEPARTMENT OF THE INTERIOR.
COMMISSION TO THE FIVE CIVILIZED TRIBES.

IN RE APPLICATION FOR ENROLLMENT, as a citizen of the   Choctaw   Nation, of Louisa Greenwood   , born on the 12th day of December , 1903

Name of Father: Hall Greenwood a citizen of the Choctaw   Nation.
Name of Mother: Maggie Greenwood a citizen of the Choctaw   Nation.

      Postoffice   Lenton, Ind. Ter.

AFFIDAVIT OF MOTHER.

UNITED STATES OF AMERICA, Indian Territory, }
 Central   DISTRICT.

I, Maggie Greenwood , on oath state that I am about 25 years of age and a citizen by blood , of the Choctaw Nation; that I am the lawful wife of Hall Greenwood , who is a citizen, by blood of the Choctaw Nation; that a female child was born to me on 12th day of December , 1903; that said child has been named Louisa Greenwood , and was living March 4, 1905.

        Maggie Greenwood

Witnesses To Mark:

Applications for Enrollment of Choctaw Newborn
Act of 1905 Volume XVI

Subscribed and sworn to before me this 20th day of   April   , 1905

Wirt Franklin
Notary Public.

AFFIDAVIT OF ATTENDING PHYSICIAN OR MID-WIFE.

UNITED STATES OF AMERICA, Indian Territory,
 Central   DISTRICT.

I,   Missie Cole   , a mid-wife   , on oath state that I attended on Mrs. Maggie Greenwood   , wife of   Hall Greenwood   on the 12th day of December   , 1903; that there was born to her on said date a   female   child; that said child was living March 4, 1905, and is said to have been named Louisa Greenwood

Missie x Cole

Witnesses To Mark:
 Thos E Oakes
 C.C. Erin

Subscribed and sworn to before me this 21st day of   April   , 1905

My commission expires
July 9th, 1908.   W.E. Larecy
Notary Public.

(The testimony below typed as given.)

Choctaw Nation, Kiamishi Co January 1 - 03.

This day I have join   together Hawl Greenword and Mykey Ward.

Here before me; minister of the Gospel M. E. Church South.

Sim Folsom.

Vester W Rose, stenographer to the Commission to the Five Civilized Tribes, on oath state that the above is a true and correct copy of the marriage certificate on file with the Commission.
Vester W Rose

Subscribed and sworn to before me this 20th day of April, 1905.

Wirt Franklin
Notary Public.

My commission expires January 3, 1909.

Applications for Enrollment of Choctaw Newborn
Act of 1905   Volume XVI

Choctaw New Born 1203
    Ethel O. Evans
    (Born Feb. 2, 1904)

NEW-BORN AFFIDAVIT.

    Number _____

...Choctaw Enrolling Commission...

IN THE MATTER OF THE APPLICATION FOR ENROLLMENT, as a citizen of the Choctaw Nation, of Ethel O. Evans

born on the 2 day of __February__ 190 4

Name of father Lon Evans   a citizen of white
Nation final enrollment No. ——
Name of mother Susan L. Evans   a citizen of Choctaw
Nation final enrollment No. 7404

        Postoffice   Valliant I.T.

AFFIDAVIT OF MOTHER.

UNITED STATES OF AMERICA
INDIAN TERRITORY
  Central DISTRICT

I Susan L Evans , on oath state that I am 22 years of age and a citizen by blood of the Choctaw Nation, and as such have been placed upon the final roll of the Choctaw Nation, by the Honorable Secretary of the Interior my final enrollment number being 7404 ; that I am the lawful wife of Lon Evans , who is a citizen of the —— —— Nation, and as such has been placed upon the final roll of said Nation by the Honorable Secretary of the Interior, his final enrollment number being ——— and that a female child was born to me on the 2 day of February 190 4; that said child has been named Ethel O. Evans , and is now living.

                Susan L Evans

Witnesseth.
  Must be two ⎱ E A Moore
  Witnesses who ⎰
  are Citizens.   *(Name Illegible)*

Applications for Enrollment of Choctaw Newborn
Act of 1905 Volume XVI

Subscribed and sworn to before me this   26   day of   Jan   190 5

                                    James Bower
                                        Notary Public.

My commission expires:
Sept 23, 1907

AFFIDAVIT OF ATTENDING PHYSICIAN OR MIDWIFE

UNITED STATES OF AMERICA
INDIAN TERRITORY
Central   DISTRICT

I,   C.H. Mahar   a   Practicing Physician on oath state that I attended on Mrs. Susan L Evans   wife of   Lon Evans on the 2   day of   February , 190 4 , that there was born to her on said date a   Female child, that said child is now living, and is said to have been named   Ethyl[sic] O. Evans

                              C.H. Mahar   𝓂.𝒟.
       Subscribed and sworn to before me this, the   26   day of
       January   190 5

WITNESSETH: James Bower   Notary Public.
  Must be two witnesses ⎰ E A Moore
  who are citizens   ⎱
                      (Name Illegible)

     We hereby certify that we are well acquainted with   C.H. Mahar
a   Practicing Physician   and know   him   to be reputable and of good standing in the community.

_____   E.A. Moore

_____   *(Name Illegible)*

Department of the Interior,
COMMISSION TO THE FIVE CIVILIZED TRIBES.

   IN RE *Application for Enrollment,* as a citizen of the   Choctaw   Nation,
of   Ethel O. Evans   , born on the 2   day of   Feb   , 1904

Name of Father: Lon Evans   a citizen of the   U.S.   Nation.
Name of Mother: Susan L Evans   a citizen of the   Choctaw   Nation.

Applications for Enrollment of Choctaw Newborn
Act of 1905   Volume XVI

Post-Office: Valliant I.T.

AFFIDAVIT OF MOTHER.

UNITED STATES OF AMERICA, }
INDIAN TERRITORY
Central   District.

I, Susan L Evans, on oath state that I am 23 years of age and a citizen by blood, of the Choctaw Nation; that I am the lawful wife of Lon Evans, who is a citizen, by _____ of the _____ Nation; that a female child was born to me on 2 day of Feb, 1904, that said child has been named Ethel O Evans, and is now living.

Susan L Evans

Subscribed and sworn to before me this 22nd day of April, 1905.

William Swink
Notary Public.

AFFIDAVIT OF ATTENDING PHYSICIAN, OR MID-WIFE.

UNITED STATES OF AMERICA, }
INDIAN TERRITORY
Central   District.

I, Chas H. Mahar, a physician, on oath state that I attended on Mrs. Susan L Evans, wife of Lon Evans on the 2 day of Feb, 1904; that there was born to her on said date a female child; that said child is now living and is said to have been named Ethel O. Evans

Charles H. Mahar M.D.

Subscribed and sworn to before me this 10 day of April, 1905.

Alfred F. Bissell
Notary Public.

Applications for Enrollment of Choctaw Newborn
Act of 1905 Volume XVI

Choctaw 2548.

Muskogee, Indian Territory, April 26, 1905.

Lon Evans,
    Valliant, Indian Territory.

Dear Sir:

    Receipt is hereby acknowledged of the affidavits of Susan L. Evans and Charles H. Mahar to the birth of Ethel O. Evans, daughter of Lon and Susan L. Evans, February 2, 1904, and the same have been filed with our records as an application for the enrollment of said child.

                  Respectfully,

                                  Chairman.

Choctaw New Born 1204
    Anna Ardelia Harrison
    (Born June 3, 1903)

BIRTH AFFIDAVIT.

DEPARTMENT OF THE INTERIOR.
COMMISSION TO THE FIVE CIVILIZED TRIBES.

IN RE APPLICATION FOR ENROLLMENT, as a citizen of the Choctaw Nation, of Anna Ardelia Harrison, born on the 3d day of June, 1903

Name of Father: B W Harrison   a citizen of the _____ Nation.
Name of Mother: Margaret Harrison   a citizen of the Choctaw Nation.

                  Postoffice   Jackson Ind Ter

AFFIDAVIT OF MOTHER.

UNITED STATES OF AMERICA, Indian Territory,
    Central   DISTRICT.

    I, Margaret Harrison, on oath state that I am 29 years of age and a citizen by Blood, of the Choctaw Nation; that I am the lawful wife of B W Harrison, who is a citizen, by marriage of the Choctaw Nation;

Applications for Enrollment of Choctaw Newborn
Act of 1905   Volume XVI

that a   Female   child was born to me on   the 3d   day of   June   , 1903; that said child has been named   Anna Ardelia Harrison   , and was living March 4, 1905.

                              Margaret Harrison

Witnesses To Mark:
{

    Subscribed and sworn to before me this   21st   day of   April   , 1905

                              HW Attaway
                              Notary Public.

AFFIDAVIT OF ATTENDING PHYSICIAN OR MID-WIFE.

UNITED STATES OF AMERICA, Indian Territory,
   Central   DISTRICT.

    I,   Angelina Studdord[sic]   , a   Midwife   , on oath state that I attended on Mrs.   Margaret Harrison   , wife of   B W Harrison   on the Third   day of June   , 1903; that there was born to her on said date a   Female   child; that said child was living March 4, 1905, and is said to have been named   Anna Ardelia Harrison

                              her
                        Angelina x Studdord
Witnesses To Mark: mark
{ TG Abney
  Nannie Watson

    Subscribed and sworn to before me this   14   day of   April   , 1905

                              C C Brannum
                              Notary Public.

                                      Choctaw 3841.

              Muskogee, Indian Territory, April 26, 1905.

B. W. Harrison,
       Jackson, Indian Territory.

Dear Sir:

    Receipt is hereby acknowledged of the affidavits of Margaret Harrison and Angelina Studdord to the birth of Anna Ardelia Harrison, daughter of B. W. and Margaret Harrison, June 3, 1903, and the same have been filed with our records as an application for the enrollment of said child.

Applications for Enrollment of Choctaw Newborn
Act of 1905 Volume XVI

Respectfully,

Chairman.

Choctaw New Born 1205
Howard Jacob Council
(Born Oct. 21, 1904)

NEW-BORN AFFIDAVIT.

Number

...Choctaw Enrolling Commission...

IN THE MATTER OF THE APPLICATION FOR ENROLLMENT, as a citizen of the Choctaw   Nation, of   Howard Jacob Council

born on the   21st day of __October__   190 4

Name of father   James A Council   a citizen of   ———
Nation final enrollment No. ——
Name of mother   Agnes L Folsom now Council   a citizen of   Choctaw
Nation final enrollment No. 10738

Postoffice   Caney I.T.

AFFIDAVIT OF MOTHER.

UNITED STATES OF AMERICA
INDIAN TERRITORY
  Central   DISTRICT

  I   Agnes L Folsom now Council   , on oath state that I am   23   years of age and a citizen by blood   of the   Choctaw   Nation, and as such have been placed upon the final roll of the   Nation[sic]   Nation, by the Honorable Secretary of the Interior my final enrollment number being   10738 ; that I am the lawful wife of   James A Council   , who is a citizen of the — — — —   Nation, and as such has been placed upon the final roll of said Nation by the Honorable Secretary of the Interior, his final enrollment number being — — — and that a   Male   child was born to me on the   21st day of October   190 4; that said child has been named   Howard Jacob Council   , and is now living.

Agnes L Council

Applications for Enrollment of Choctaw Newborn
Act of 1905   Volume XVI

Witnesseth.
   Must be two   } *(Name Illegible)*
   Witnesses who
   are Citizens.   N.J. Tolbert

Subscribed and sworn to before me this 15th day of February 190 5

                    A.E. Folsom
                               Notary Public.

My commission expires:
Jan 9 - 1909

Affidavit of Attending Physician or Midwife

UNITED STATES OF AMERICA,
    INDIAN TERRITORY,
  Central   DISTRICT

    I, J. H. Armstrong a Practicing Physician on oath state that I attended on Mrs. Agnes L Folsom now Council wife of James A Council on the 21st day of October, 190 4, that there was born to her on said date a male child, that said child is now living, and is said to have been named Howard Jacob Council

                    J.H. Armstrong   M. D.

Subscribed and sworn to before me this the 15th day of February 1905

                    A.E. Folsom
                              Notary Public.

WITNESSETH:
   Must be two witnesses { *(Name Illegible)*
   who are citizens and
   know the child.   N.J. Tolbert

    We hereby certify that we are well acquainted with J.H. Armstrong a Practicing Physician and know him to be reputable and of good standing in the community.

                    Must be two citizen { *(Name Illegible)*
                    witnesses.   N.J. Tolbert

Applications for Enrollment of Choctaw Newborn
Act of 1905   Volume XVI

BIRTH AFFIDAVIT.

DEPARTMENT OF THE INTERIOR.
COMMISSION TO THE FIVE CIVILIZED TRIBES.

IN RE APPLICATION FOR ENROLLMENT, as a citizen of the   Choctaw   Nation, of Howard Jacob Council   , born on the   21   day of   October   , 1904

Name of Father: James A Council   a citizen of the   U.S.   Nation.
Name of Mother: Agnes L (Folsom) Council   a citizen of the   Choctaw   Nation.

Postoffice   Caney I.T.

AFFIDAVIT OF MOTHER.

UNITED STATES OF AMERICA, Indian Territory,
Central   DISTRICT.

I,   Agnes L (Folsom) Council   , on oath state that I am   23   years of age and a citizen by   blood   , of the   Choctaw   Nation; that I am the lawful wife of James A Council   , who is a citizen, by — of the   United States   Nation; that a Male   child was born to me on   21   day of   October   , 1904; that said child has been named   Howard Jacob Council   , and was living March 4, 1905.

Agnes L (Folsom) Council

Witnesses To Mark:

Subscribed and sworn to before me this 22 day of   April   , 1905

A Denton Phillips
Notary Public.

AFFIDAVIT OF ATTENDING PHYSICIAN OR MID-WIFE.

UNITED STATES OF AMERICA, Indian Territory,
Central   DISTRICT.

I,   J H Armstrong   , a   M.D.   , on oath state that I attended on Mrs. Agnes L (Folsom) Council   , wife of Jas A Council   on the   21 day of October   , 1904; that there was born to her on said date a .... child; that said child was living March 4, 1905, and is said to have been named ....

J H Armstrong M.D.

Witnesses To Mark:

Applications for Enrollment of Choctaw Newborn
Act of 1905   Volume XVI

Subscribed and sworn to before me this 22 day of   April   , 1905

A Denton Phillips
Notary Public.

Choctaw 3805.

Muskogee, Indian Territory, April 26, 1905.

James A. Council,
    Caney, Indian Territory.

Dear Sir:

    Receipt is hereby acknowledged of the affidavits of Agnes L. (Folsom) Council and J. H. Armstrong to the birth of Howard Jacob Council, son of James A. and Agnes L. Council, October 21, 1904, and the same have been filed with our records as an application for the enrollment of said child.

Respectfully,

Chairman.

Choctaw New Born 1206
    Willie S. Graham
    (Born April 17, 1903)

BIRTH AFFIDAVIT.

DEPARTMENT OF THE INTERIOR.
COMMISSION TO THE FIVE CIVILIZED TRIBES.

IN RE APPLICATION FOR ENROLLMENT, as a citizen of the   Choctaw   Nation, of Willie S. Graham   , born on the 17   day of April   , 1903

Name of Father: Edward L. Graham   a citizen of the non citizen Nation.
Name of Mother: Emma E. Graham   a citizen of the   Choctaw   Nation.

Postoffice   Wapanucka I.T.

Applications for Enrollment of Choctaw Newborn
Act of 1905 Volume XVI

AFFIDAVIT OF MOTHER.

UNITED STATES OF AMERICA, Indian Territory, }
    Central   DISTRICT.

    I, Emma E. Graham, on oath state that I am 23 years of age and a citizen by blood, of the Choctaw Nation; that I am the lawful wife of Edward L Graham, who is a citizen, ~~by~~ of the United States Nation; that a Female child was born to me on 17 day of April, 1903; that said child has been named Willie S. Graham, and was living March 4, 1905.

                                  Emma E. Graham

Witnesses To Mark:
{

    Subscribed and sworn to before me this 23 day of April, 1905

                                  E. J. Ball
                                         Notary Public.

AFFIDAVIT OF ATTENDING PHYSICIAN OR MID-WIFE.

UNITED STATES OF AMERICA, Indian Territory, }
    Central   DISTRICT.

    I, Cicilia Hunter, a midwife, on oath state that I attended on Mrs. Emma E. Graham, wife of Edward L Graham on the 17 day of April, 1903; that there was born to her on said date a female child; that said child was living March 4, 1905, and is said to have been named Willie S. Graham

                                  her
                            Cicilia x Hunter
Witnesses To Mark: mark
{ *(Name Illegible)*
  SE Smith

    Subscribed and sworn to before me this 12 day of April, 1905

                                  J. Poe
                                       Notary Public.

My com expires Jan 23-1908

Applications for Enrollment of Choctaw Newborn
Act of 1905   Volume XVI

Choctaw 3251.

Muskogee, Indian Territory, April 26, 1905.

Edward L. Graham,
    Wapanucka, Indian Territory.

Dear Sir:

    Receipt is hereby acknowledged of the affidavits of Emma E. Franklin[sic] and Cicilia Hunter to the birth of Willie S. Graham, daughter of Edward L. and Emma E. Graham, April 17, 1903, and the same have been filed with our records as an application for the enrollment of said child.

                    Respectfully,

                                      Chairman.

Choctaw New Born 1207
    Lizzie Parrish[sic]
    (Born July 8, 1903)

BIRTH AFFIDAVIT.

DEPARTMENT OF THE INTERIOR.
COMMISSION TO THE FIVE CIVILIZED TRIBES.

    IN RE APPLICATION FOR ENROLLMENT, as a citizen of the   Choctaw   Nation, of Lizzie Parish   , born on the 8th   day of   July   , 1903

Name of Father: Elias Parish   a citizen of the   Choctaw   Nation.
Name of Mother: Eliza Parish   a citizen of the   Choctaw   Nation.

                    Postoffice   Antlers, Ind. Ter.

AFFIDAVIT OF MOTHER.

UNITED STATES OF AMERICA, Indian Territory, ⎫
    Central   DISTRICT. ⎭

    I,   Eliza Parish   , on oath state that I am   about 22   years of age and a citizen by   blood   , of the   Choctaw   Nation; that I am the lawful wife of   Elias Parish   , who is a citizen, by blood   of the   Choctaw   Nation; that a

Applications for Enrollment of Choctaw Newborn
Act of 1905 Volume XVI

female   child was born to me on   8th   day of   July   , 1903; that said child has been named   Lizzie Parish   , and was living March 4, 1905.

                                                her
                                               Eliza x Parish

Witnesses To Mark: mark
{ Robert Anderson
  Vester W Rose

Subscribed and sworn to before me this   24th day of   April   , 1905

                                               Wirt Franklin
                                               Notary Public.

AFFIDAVIT OF ATTENDING PHYSICIAN OR MID-WIFE.

UNITED STATES OF AMERICA, Indian Territory, }
  Central   DISTRICT.

I,   Elias Parish   , a ...., on oath state that I attended on Mrs.   Eliza Parish   , ~~wife of~~ *my wife* on the 8th day of July   , 1903; that there was born to her on said date a   female   child; that said child was living March 4, 1905, and ~~is said to have~~ *has* been named   Lizzie Parish

                                               Elias Parish
Witnesses To Mark:

{

Subscribed and sworn to before me this   24th day of   April   , 1905

                                               Wirt Franklin
                                               Notary Public.

United States of America,   )
)
Indian Territory,   ) ss.
)
Central District.   )

    I, Louisa Thomas, on oath state that I am thirty-two years of age and a citizen by blood of the Choctaw Nation blood; that my post office address is Antlers, Indian Territory; that I am personally acquainted with Eliza Parish, wife of Elias Parish, and have known said parties for about ten years; that since their marriage in 1900 I have lived within two miles of them; that I know of my own knowledge that on or about the 8th day of July, 1903, there was born to said Eliza Parish a female child; that said child is now living and is said to have been named Lizzie Parish.

Applications for Enrollment of Choctaw Newborn
Act of 1905   Volume XVI

her
Louisa x Thomas
mark

Subscribed and sworn to before me this 24th day of April, 1905.

Wirt Franklin
Notary Public.

Witnesses to mark.
   Vester W Rose
   Robert Anderson

United States of America,　)
)
Indian Territory,　　　　　) ss.
)
Central District.　　　　　)

    I, Lizzie Lewis, on oath state that I am about nineteen years of age and a citizen by blood of the Choctaw Nation blood; that my post office address is Antlers, Indian Territory; that I am personally acquainted with Eliza Parish, wife of Elias Parish, and have known them about ten years; that I have lived within three miles of them since their marriage in 1900; that I know of my own knowledge that on or about the 8th day of July, 1903, there was born to said Eliza Parish a female child; that said child is now living and is said to have been named Lizzie Parish.

her
Lizzie x Lewis
mark

Subscribed and sworn to before me this 24th day of April, 1905.

Wirt Franklin
Notary Public.

Witnesses to mark.
   Robert Anderson
   Vester W Rose

Applications for Enrollment of Choctaw Newborn
Act of 1905 Volume XVI

Choctaw New Born 1208
    Floyd Manuel Upton
    (Born Oct. 6, 1903)

NEW-BORN AFFIDAVIT.

    Number............

...Choctaw Enrolling Commission...

    IN THE MATTER OF THE APPLICATION FOR ENROLLMENT, as a citizen of the Choctaw   Nation, of   Floyd Emanuel Upton

born on the 6th day of __October__ 190 3

Name of father James Upton   a citizen of white
Nation final enrollment No. ~~12749~~
Name of mother Martha Upton   a citizen of Choctaw
Nation final enrollment No. 12749

            Postoffice San Bois I.T.

AFFIDAVIT OF MOTHER.

UNITED STATES OF AMERICA
INDIAN TERRITORY
  Western   DISTRICT

    I Martha Upton   , on oath state that I am 20 years of age and a citizen by blood of the Choctaw Nation, and as such have been placed upon the final roll of the Choctaw Nation, by the Honorable Secretary of the Interior my final enrollment number being 12749 ; that I am the lawful wife of James Upton , who is a citizen of the Choctaw Nation, and as such has been placed upon the final roll of said Nation by the Honorable Secretary of the Interior, his final enrollment number being .... and that a Male child was born to me on the 6th day of October 190 3; that said child has been named Floyd Emanuel Upton , and is now living.

                      Martha Upton

Witnesseth.
  Must be two
  Witnesses who   Ridgely Bond
  are Citizens.   J W Rabon

Applications for Enrollment of Choctaw Newborn
Act of 1905 Volume XVI

Subscribed and sworn to before me this 6" day of Jan 190 5

             L.C. Tuey
               Notary Public.

My commission expires: Jan 17-1907

AFFIDAVIT OF ATTENDING PHYSICIAN OR MIDWIFE

UNITED STATES OF AMERICA
INDIAN TERRITORY
 Western   DISTRICT

  I, E Johnson   a practicing physician on oath state that I attended on Mrs. Martha Upton wife of James Upton on the 6th day of October , 190 3 , that there was born to her on said date a male child, that said child is now living, and is said to have been named Floyd Emanuel[sic] Upton

               E. Johnson $\mathcal{M.D.}$

    Subscribed and sworn to before me this, the 6th day of
    Jan 190 5

WITNESSETH: L.C. Tuey   Notary Public.
Must be two witnesses { Ridgely Bond
who are citizens
         J W Rabon

  We hereby certify that we are well acquainted with E Johnson a practicing physician and know him to be reputable and of good standing in the community.

   Ridgely Bond   _____

   J W Rabon   _____

BIRTH AFFIDAVIT.

DEPARTMENT OF THE INTERIOR,
COMMISSION TO THE FIVE CIVILIZED TRIBES.

  In Re Application for Enrollment, as a citizen of the Choctaw Nation, of Floyd Manuel Upton , born on the 6th day of October , 1903

Name of Father: James Upton   a citizen of the United StatesNation.
Name of Mother: Martha Upton   a citizen of the Choctaw Nation.

         Post-office Kinta Ind Ter

Applications for Enrollment of Choctaw Newborn
Act of 1905 Volume XVI

AFFIDAVIT OF MOTHER.

UNITED STATES OF AMERICA, }
INDIAN TERRITORY,
Western   District.

I, Martha Upton , on oath state that I am 20   years of age and a citizen by blood , of the Choctaw   Nation; that I am the lawful wife of James Upton , who is a citizen, by _____ of the   United States   Nation; that a male   child was born to me on 6th day of October , 1903 , that said child has been named Floyd Manuel Upton , and is now living.

                her
              Martha x Upton

WITNESSES TO MARK: mark
{ Edmund Frazier
{ Green McCurtain

Subscribed and sworn to before me this 3rd day of April , 1905.

          (Name Illegible)
            NOTARY PUBLIC.

My commission expires March 4th 1907

AFFIDAVIT OF ATTENDING PHYSICIAN OR MID-WIFE.

UNITED STATES OF AMERICA, }
INDIAN TERRITORY,
Western   District.

I, E Johnson , a physician , on oath state that I attended on Mrs. Martha Upton , wife of James Upton   on the 6th day of October , 1903 ; that there was born to her on said date a   male   child; that said child is now living and is said to have been named Floyd Manuel Upton

          E Johnson MD
WITNESSES TO MARK:
{
{

Subscribed and sworn to before me this 3rd day of April , 1905.

          (Name Illegible)
            NOTARY PUBLIC.

My commission expires March 4th 1907

Applications for Enrollment of Choctaw Newborn
Act of 1905 Volume XVI

Muskogee, Indian Territory, April 7, 1905.

James Upton,
    Kinta, Indian Territory.

Dear Sir:

Receipt is hereby acknowledged of the affidavits of Martha Upton and E. Johnson to the birth of Floyd Upton, son of James and Martha Upton, October 6, 1903.

It is stated in the affidavit of the mother that she is a citizen by blood of the Choctaw Nation and if this is correct you are requested to state her maiden name, the names of her parents, also the name under which she was listed for enrollment, and if she has taken her allotment of the lands of the Choctaw and Chickasaw Nations give her roll number as it appears upon her certificate of allotment.

This matter should receive immediate attention in order that proper disposition may be made of the application for the enrollment of the above named child.

Respectfully,

Commissioner in Charge.

7-4606

Muskogee, Indian Territory, April 28, 1905.

Ridgely Bond,
    Sansbois, Indian Territory.

Dear Sir:

Receipt is hereby acknowledged of your letter of April 18, 1905, stating that your wife, Martha Upton, was enrolled as Martha Trahern.

In reply to your letter you are advised that this information has enabled us to identify her as an enrolled citizen by blood of the Choctaw Nation, and the affidavits heretofore forwarded to the birth of Floyd Manuel Upton have been filed with our records as an application for the enrollment of said child.

Respectfully,

Chairman.

Applications for Enrollment of Choctaw Newborn
Act of 1905   Volume XVI

Choctaw New Born 1209
  Allen Hotubbe[sic]
  Born Nov. 14, 1903

BIRTH AFFIDAVIT.   7-5702

DEPARTMENT OF THE INTERIOR.
COMMISSION TO THE FIVE CIVILIZED TRIBES.

IN RE APPLICATION FOR ENROLLMENT, as a citizen of the   Choctaw   Nation, of Allen Hotubbee   , born on the   14   day of   November   , 1903

Name of Father: Joseph Hotubbee   a citizen of the   Choc   Nation.
Name of Mother: Nellie Hotubbee   a citizen of the   U. States   Nation.

Postoffice   Tuskahoma I.T.

AFFIDAVIT OF MOTHER.

UNITED STATES OF AMERICA, Indian Territory,
  Central   DISTRICT.

I,   Nellie Hotubbee , on oath state that I am   28   years of age and a citizen by   blood   , of the   Choctaw   Nation; that I am the lawful wife of   Joseph Hotubbee , who is a citizen, by   blood   of the   Choctaw   Nation; that a   male   child was born to me on   14   day of   November   , 1903; that said child has been named   Allen Hotubbee , and was living March 4, 1905.

                                  her
                          Nellie x Hotubbee
Witnesses To Mark: mark
  { Chas T. Difendafer
  { OL Johnson

Subscribed and sworn to before me this 11 day of   April   , 1905

                          OL Johnson
                             Notary Public.

Applications for Enrollment of Choctaw Newborn
Act of 1905   Volume XVI

AFFIDAVIT OF ATTENDING PHYSICIAN OR MID-WIFE.

UNITED STATES OF AMERICA, Indian Territory,　}
　Central　　　　　　　　　DISTRICT.

I, Lucy Anderson, a midwife, on oath state that I attended on Mrs. Nellie Hotubbee, wife of Joseph Hotubbee on the 14 day of November, 1903; that there was born to her on said date a male child; that said child was living March 4, 1905, and is said to have been named Allen Hotubbee

　　　　　　　　　　　　　　　　　her
　　　　　　　　　　　　　　Lucy x Anderson
Witnesses To Mark:　　　　　　mark
　{ Chas T. Difendafer
　{ OL Johnson

Subscribed and sworn to before me this 11 day of April, 1905

　　　　　　　　　　　OL Johnson
　　　　　　　　　　　Notary Public.

AFFIDAVIT.

Silas B M°Kinney, being first duly sworn, deposes and say that he is a citizen of the Choctaw Nation and that he is 55 years of age, that his Post Office address is Tuskahoma, I. T. That he is well acquainted with Joe Hotubbee, a citizen of the Choctaw Nation and his wife, Nancy Hotubbee; and that they are the parents of Allen Hotubbee, who has made application to the Commission to the Five Civilized Tribes for enrollment.

Affiant further states that Joe Hotubbee and the said Nancy Hotubbee were married on or about the 27th day of September, 1902 and that he is informed that the marriage certificate of the said Joe Hotubbee shows the name of his said wife as Mary Harriet Moore, that the said Hotubbee married Nancy Moore, sometimes called Nannie Moore, who is now his present wife and that the name inserted in said certificate is clearly a clerical error and that the said Mary Harriet Moore and Nancy Moore are one and the same person.

Affiant further states that he has no interest whatever in the enrollment of Allen Hotubbee aforesaid.

　　　　　　　　　　　Silas B McKinney

Subscribed and sworn to before me this 22 day of July, 1905.

　　　　　　　　　　　Peter W Hudson
　　　　　　　　　　　Notary Public.

My Commission expires　2/24, 1906

Applications for Enrollment of Choctaw Newborn
Act of 1905   Volume XVI

AFFIDAVIT.

George W Bell , being first duly sworn, deposes and say that he is a citizen of the Choctaw   Nation and that he is   46   years of age, that his Post Office address is Tuskahoma, I. T.   .   That he is well acquainted with Joe Hotubbee, a citizen of the Choctaw   Nation and his wife, Nancy Hotubbee; and that they are the parents of Allen Hotubbee, who has made application to the Commission to the Five Civilized Tribes for enrollment.

Affiant further states that Joe Hotubbee and the said Nancy Hotubbee were married on or about the 27th day of September, 1902 and that he is informed that the marriage certificate of the said Joe Hotubbee shows the name of his said wife as Mary Harriet Moore, that the said Hotubbee married Nancy Moore, sometimes called Nannie Moore, who is now his present wife and that the name inserted in said certificate is clearly a clerical error and that the said Mary Harriet Moore and Nancy Moore are one and the same person.

Affiant further states that he has no interest whatever in the enrollment of Allen Hotubbee aforesaid.

George W Bell

Subscribed and sworn to before me this 22 day of   July , 190 5.

Peter W Hudson
Notary Public.

My Commission expires   2/24   , 190 6

UNITED STATES OF AMERICA,)
    Indian Territory,   )
Central Judicial District.   )

Nancy Hotubbee, being first duly sworn deposes and says that she is the wife of Joseph Hotubbee and the mother of Allen Hotubbee, their child. That heretofore on or about the ~~14~~ *11th* day of ~~November~~, *April* ~~1903~~, *1905* in the matter of the enrollment of the said Allen Hotubbee, affiant made an Affidavit and by inadvertence or clerical error it appears by said Affidavit that affiant whose name appears therein as Nellie Hotubbee is a citizen by blood of the Choctaw Nation, however, affiant is informed and believes that a reference to said Affidavit will show that she stated that she was a white woman or a non-citizen; that affiant is a white woman and a non-citizen.

Affiant further states that she is the person who as Nellie Hotubbee made the aforesaid Affidavit and that she goes by the name of Nancy Hotubbee and also by the name of Nannie Hotubbee, the latter being a diminutive for Nancy; that by clerical error

Applications for Enrollment of Choctaw Newborn
Act of 1905 Volume XVI

in the aforesaid Affidavit her appeared as Nellie which probably occurred from the similarity of the sound to her name, Nannie, and she files this her Affidavit aforesaid for the purpose of correcting the aforesaid Clerical errors or statement inadvertently made in the Affidavit aforesaid.

Witnesses to mark
    Peter J. Hudson
    Sam Wall

                    her
Nancy x Hotubbee
      mark

Subscribed and sworn to before me this 6th day of May , 190 5

            RD Francis
            Notary Public.

My Commission expires Jan 8 , 190 8

            Muskogee, Indian Territory, April 15, 1905.

Joseph Hotubbee,
    Tuskahoma, Indian Territory.

Dear Sir:

    Receipt is hereby acknowledged of the affidavits of Nellie Hotubbee and Lucy Anderson to the birth of Allen Hotubbee, son of Joseph and Nellie Hotubbee, November 14, 1903.

    It is stated in the affidavit of the mother that she is a citizen by blood of the Choctaw Nation. If this is correct you are requested to state the name under which she was enrolled, the names of her parents, and if she has selected an allotment of the lands of the Choctaw and Chickasaw Nations please give her roll number as it appears upon her allotment certificate.

            Respectfully,

                Chairman.

(The letter below given without letterhead.)

Applications for Enrollment of Choctaw Newborn
Act of 1905 Volume XVI

Wm O.B.

COMMISSIONERS:
TAMS BIXBY,
THOMAS B. NEEDLES,
C.R. BRECKINRIDGE.
WM. O. BEALL
Secretary

DEPARTMENT OF THE INTERIOR,
COMMISSIONER TO THE FIVE CIVILIZED TRIBES.

REFER IN REPLY TO THE FOLLOWING:

7-NB-1209.

ADDRESS ONLY THE
COMMISSION TO THE FIVE CIVILIZED TRIBES.

Muskogee, Indian Territory, June 1, 1905.

Joseph Hotubbee,
    Tuskahoma, Indian Territory.

Dear Sir:

    Your attention is called to the Commission's letter of April 15, 1905, requesting information by which your wife might be identified.

    If your wife is a Choctaw by blood, as it appears from the affidavits heretofore filed in this office, you are requested to state the names under which she was enrolled, the names of her parents and, if she has selected an allotment, give her roll number as the same appears on her allotment certificate. If she is not a citizen it will be necessary that you furnish either the original or a certified copy of the license and certificate of your marriage to her.

                    Respectfully,
                      T.B. Needles
                      Commissioner in Charge.

7-NB-1209

Muskogee, Indian Territory, July 26, 1905.

Joseph Hotubbee,
    Tuskahoma, Indian Territory.

Dear Sir:

    Referring to the application for the enrollment of our infant child, Allen Hotubbee, born November 14, 1903, it appears that the applicant claims through you.

    In this event it will be necessary that you file in this office, either the original or a certified copy of the license and certificate of your marriage to Nellie Hotubbee, the mother of the applicant.

    Please give this matter your immediate attention as no further action can be taken relative to the enrollment of this child until the evidence requested is supplied.

Applications for Enrollment of Choctaw Newborn
Act of 1905 Volume XVI

Respectfully,

Commissioner.

7-NB-1209

Muskogee, Indian Territory, July 31, 1905.

Martin & Gidney,
    Attorneys at Law,
        Muskogee, Indian Territory.

Gentlemen:

Receipt is hereby acknowledged of your letter of July 27, 1905, enclosing affidavits of Silas B. McKinney and George W. Bell to the marriage of Joe Hotubbee and Nancy Hotubbee which have been filed in support of the application for the enrollment of Allen Hotubbee as a citizen by blood of the Choctaw Nation.

Respectfully,

Commissioner.

Choctaw New Born 1210
    Fannie May Willis
    (Born May 14, 1904)

NEW-BORN AFFIDAVIT.

Number............

...Choctaw Enrolling Commission...

IN THE MATTER OF THE APPLICATION FOR ENROLLMENT, as a citizen of the Choctaw Nation, of Fannie May Willis

born on the 14 day of __May__ 190 4

Applications for Enrollment of Choctaw Newborn
Act of 1905 Volume XVI

Name of father Abner W Willis   a citizen of Choctaw
Nation final enrollment No. 9872
Name of mother Francis Willis   a citizen of Choctaw
Nation final enrollment No. 9873

                         Postoffice   Blue I.T.

AFFIDAVIT OF MOTHER.
UNITED STATES OF AMERICA
INDIAN TERRITORY
Central   DISTRICT

I Francis Willis , on oath state that I am 24 years of age and a citizen by blood of the Choctaw Nation, and as such have been placed upon the final roll of the Choctaw Nation, by the Honorable Secretary of the Interior my final enrollment number being 9873 ; that I am the lawful wife of Abner W Willis , who is a citizen of the Choctaw Nation, and as such has been placed upon the final roll of said Nation by the Honorable Secretary of the Interior, his final enrollment number being 9872 and that a female child was born to me on the 14 day of May 190 4; that said child has been named Fannie May , and is now living.

                                          her
                                   Francis x Willis
Witnesseth.   mark

Must be two Witnesses who are Citizens.   JB Nelson
                    Sidney G Hogan

Subscribed and sworn to before me this 19 day of Jan 190 5

                            JM Routh
                                         Notary Public.
My commission expires:

Affidavit of Attending Physician or Midwife

UNITED STATES OF AMERICA,
INDIAN TERRITORY,
Central   DISTRICT

I, A. B. Strange a Physician on oath state that I attended on Mrs. Francis Willis wife of Abner W Willis on the 14 day of May , 190 4, that there was born to her on said date a female child, that said child is now living, and is said to have been named Fannie May

                            A.B. Strange   M. D.

Applications for Enrollment of Choctaw Newborn
Act of 1905 Volume XVI

Subscribed and sworn to before me this the 19 day of May 1905

JM Routh
Notary Public.

WITNESSETH:
Must be two witnesses who are citizens and know the child. { JB Nelson
Sidney G Hogan

We hereby certify that we are well acquainted with A.B. Strange M.D. a Practicing Physician and know him to be reputable and of good standing in the community.

Must be two citizen witnesses. { JB Nelson
Sidney G Hogan

BIRTH AFFIDAVIT.

DEPARTMENT OF THE INTERIOR.
COMMISSION TO THE FIVE CIVILIZED TRIBES.

IN RE APPLICATION FOR ENROLLMENT, as a citizen of the Choctaw Nation, of Fannie May Willis , born on the 14 day of May , 1904

Name of Father: Abner W Willis   a citizen of the Choctaw Nation.
Name of Mother: Francis Willis   a citizen of the Choctaw Nation.

Postoffice   Blue Ind. Ter.

AFFIDAVIT OF MOTHER.

UNITED STATES OF AMERICA, Indian Territory,
Central DISTRICT.

I, Francis Willis , on oath state that I am 24 years of age and a citizen by Blood , of the Choctaw Nation; that I am the lawful wife of Abner W Willis , who is a citizen, by Blood of the Choctaw Nation; that a Female child was born to me on 14 day of May , 1904; that said child has been named Fannie May , and was living March 4, 1905.

                                       her
                               Francis x Willis
Witnesses To Mark: mark
{ William Puckett Blue I.T.
Sidney Hogan Blue I.T.

Applications for Enrollment of Choctaw Newborn
Act of 1905   Volume XVI

Subscribed and sworn to before me this 12 day of April, 1905

J.M. Routh
Notary Public.

AFFIDAVIT OF ATTENDING PHYSICIAN OR MID-WIFE.

UNITED STATES OF AMERICA, Indian Territory,
Central   DISTRICT.

I, Mrs Annie Gibbs, a midwife, on oath state that I attended on Mrs. Francis Willis, wife of Abner W Willis on the 14 day of May, 1904; that there was born to her on said date a Female child; that said child was living March 4, 1905, and is said to have been named Fannie May

Mrs Annie Gibbs

Witnesses To Mark:

Subscribed and sworn to before me this 12 day of April, 1905

J.M. Routh
Notary Public.

Muskogee, Indian Territory, April 17, 1905.

Abner W. Willis,
Blue, Indian Territory.

Dear Sir:

Receipt is hereby acknowledged of the affidavits of Francis Willis and Mrs. Annie Gibbs to the birth of Fannie May Willis, daughter of Abner and Francis Willis, May 14, 1904.

It is stated in the affidavit of the mother that she is a citizen by blood of the Choctaw Nation. If this is correct you are requested to state the name under which she was enrolled, the names of her parents, and if she has selected an allotment of the lands of the Choctaw or Chickasaw Nations[sic] please give her roll number as it appears upon her allotment certificate.

Respectfully,

Chairman.

Applications for Enrollment of Choctaw Newborn
Act of 1905 Volume XVI

(Copy)

Francis Willis Roll No 9873 certificate No 4136

Yours truly

A. W. Willis
Blue I.T.
4/22

Choctaw New Born 1211
    Fannie P. Folsom
    (Born January 26, 1905)

NEW-BORN AFFIDAVIT.

    Number_____

...Choctaw Enrolling Commission...

    IN THE MATTER OF THE APPLICATION FOR ENROLLMENT, as a citizen of the Choctaw Nation, of Fannie P. Folsom

born on the 26th day of __January__ 190 5

Name of father John N Folsom a citizen of Choctaw
Nation final enrollment No. 10645 *now Folsom*
Name of mother Caroline Jane Johnico a citizen of Choctaw
Nation final enrollment No. 6162

                      Postoffice Caney I.T.

Applications for Enrollment of Choctaw Newborn
Act of 1905 Volume XVI

AFFIDAVIT OF MOTHER.

UNITED STATES OF AMERICA
INDIAN TERRITORY
Central DISTRICT

I Caroline Jane Jonico[sic] *now Folsom* , on oath state that I am 19 years of age and a citizen by blood of the Choctaw Nation, and as such have been placed upon the final roll of the Choctaw Nation, by the Honorable Secretary of the Interior my final enrollment number being 6162 ; that I am the lawful wife of John N. Folsom , who is a citizen of the Choctaw Nation, and as such has been placed upon the final roll of said Nation by the Honorable Secretary of the Interior, his final enrollment number being 10645 and that a Female child was born to me on the 26th day of January 190 5; that said child has been named Fannie P Folsom , and is now living.

Caroline ^Jane^ Johnico now Folsom

Witnesseth.
Must be two Witnesses who are Citizens. } N.J. Tolbert
Ben Byington

Subscribed and sworn to before me this 15th day of February 190 5

A.E. Folsom
Notary Public.

My commission expires:
Jan 9 - 1909

Affidavit of Attending Physician or Midwife

UNITED STATES OF AMERICA,
INDIAN TERRITORY,
Central DISTRICT

I, Pricilla[sic] A Noble a Mid Wife on oath state that I attended on Mrs. Fannie[sic] P.[sic] Folsom wife of John N Folsom on the 26th day of January , 190 5, that there was born to her on said date a Female child, that said child is now living, and is said to have been named Fannie P. Folsom

Priscilla A Noble ~~M. D.~~

Subscribed and sworn to before me this the 15th day of February 1905

A.E. Folsom
Notary Public.

WITNESSETH:
Must be two witnesses who are citizens and know the child. { NJ Tolbert
Ben Byington

229

Applications for Enrollment of Choctaw Newborn
Act of 1905   Volume XVI

We hereby certify that we are well acquainted with   Pricilla[sic] A Noble
a   Mid Wife   and know   her   to be reputable and of good standing in the community.

Must be two citizen witnesses. { N.J. Tolbert
                                  Ben Byington

BIRTH AFFIDAVIT.

DEPARTMENT OF THE INTERIOR.
COMMISSION TO THE FIVE CIVILIZED TRIBES.

IN RE APPLICATION FOR ENROLLMENT, as a citizen of the   Choctaw   Nation, of Fannie P. Folsom   , born on the   26   day of   January   , 1905

Name of Father: John N Folsom   a citizen of the   Choctaw   Nation.
Name of Mother: Caroline Folsom   a citizen of the   Choctaw   Nation.

Postoffice   Caney Ind Ter

AFFIDAVIT OF MOTHER.

UNITED STATES OF AMERICA, Indian Territory,
Central   DISTRICT.

I,   Caroline Folsom   , on oath state that I am   19   years of age and a citizen by   blood   , of the   Choctaw   Nation; that I am the lawful wife of   John N Folsom   , who is a citizen, by blood   of the   Choctaw   Nation; that a   Female   child was born to me on   26   day of   January   , 1905; that said child has been named   Fannie P. Folsom   , and was living March 4, 1905.

Caroline Folsom

Witnesses To Mark:
{

Subscribed and sworn to before me this   15   day of   April   , 1905

A Denton Phillips
Notary Public.

230

Applications for Enrollment of Choctaw Newborn
Act of 1905   Volume XVI

AFFIDAVIT OF ATTENDING PHYSICIAN OR MID-WIFE.

UNITED STATES OF AMERICA, Indian Territory, }
   Central   DISTRICT. }

I,   Priscilla A Noble   , a   Mid wife   , on oath state that I attended on Mrs.   Caroline Folsom   , wife of   John N Folsom   on the 26   day of January, 1905; that there was born to her on said date a   Female   child; that said child was living March 4, 1905, and is said to have been named Fannie P. Folsom

              Priscilla A Noble

Witnesses To Mark:
{

 Subscribed and sworn to before me this 15 day of   April   , 1905

              A Denton Phillips
              Notary Public.

        Muskogee, Indian Territory, April 20, 1905.

John N. Folsom,
 Caney, Indian Territory.

Dear Sir:

 Receipt is hereby acknowledged of the affidavits of Caroline Folsom and Pricilla[sic] A. Noble to the birth of Fannie P. Folsom, daughter of John N. and Caroline Folsom, January 26, 1905.

 It is stated in the affidavit of the mother that she is a citizen by blood of the Choctaw Nation. If this ic correct you are requested to state the name under which she was enrolled, the names of her parents, and if she has selected an allotment of the lands of the Choctaw or Chickasaw Nation please give her roll number as it appears upon her allotment certificate.

           Respectfully,

                 Chairman.

Applications for Enrollment of Choctaw Newborn
Act of 1905   Volume XVI

Caney I. T. April 24, 1905.

Mr. Tams Bixby,

    Dear Sir:

Replying to your letter of 20 this inst, Caroline Johnico. Parent Willie Bohanon and Emmeline selected in Choctaw Nation 159 Roll No. 6162 Certificate 2978.

7-NB-1211

Muskogee, Indian Territory, July 26, 1905.

John N. Folsom,
    Caney, Indian Territory.

Dear Sir:

    Receipt is hereby acknowledged of your letter of July 19, 1905, asking if Fannie Precilla[sic] Folsom has been approved.

    In reply to your letter you are advised that the name of your child Fannie Precilla Folsom has been placed upon a schedule of citizens by blood of the Choctaw Nation which has been forwarded the Secretary of the Interior, but this office has not yet been notified of Departmental action thereon.

                    Respectfully,

                              Commissioner.

Choctaw New Born 1212
    Samuel Webster
    (Born Sept. 20, 1904)

Applications for Enrollment of Choctaw Newborn
Act of 1905 Volume XVI

BIRTH AFFIDAVIT.

DEPARTMENT OF THE INTERIOR.
COMMISSION TO THE FIVE CIVILIZED TRIBES.

IN RE APPLICATION FOR ENROLLMENT, as a citizen of the   Choctaw   Nation, of Samuel Webster   , born on the 20th   day of   Sept   , 1904

Name of Father: Daniel Webster   a citizen of the   Choctaw   Nation.
Name of Mother: Cornelia Webster   a citizen of the   Choctaw   Nation.

Postoffice   Lenton, Ind. Ter.

AFFIDAVIT OF MOTHER.

UNITED STATES OF AMERICA, Indian Territory,
Central   DISTRICT.

I,   Cornelia Webster   , on oath state that I am   17   years of age and a citizen by   blood   , of the   Choctaw   Nation; that I am the lawful wife of Daniel Webster   , who is a citizen, by blood   of the   Choctaw   Nation; that a   male   child was born to me on 20th   day of September   , 1904; that said child has been named   Samuel Webster   , and was living March 4, 1905.

Cornelia Webster

Witnesses To Mark:

Subscribed and sworn to before me this 19th   day of   April   , 1905

Wirt Franklin
Notary Public.

AFFIDAVIT OF ATTENDING PHYSICIAN OR MID-WIFE.

UNITED STATES OF AMERICA, Indian Territory,
Central   DISTRICT.

I,   Nancy Hotema   , a mid-wife   , on oath state that I attended on Mrs.   Cornelia Webster   , wife of   Daniel Webster   on the 20th   day of September   , 1904; that there was born to her on said date a   male   child; that said child was living March 4, 1905, and is said to have been named   Samuel Webster

her
Nancy x Hotema
mark

Applications for Enrollment of Choctaw Newborn
Act of 1905   Volume XVI

Witnesses To Mark:
 { Vester W Rose
   Mrs Fannie Sample

Subscribed and sworn to before me this 19th day of April , 1905

Wirt Franklin
Notary Public.

Choctaw New Born 1213
Ida Jefferson
(Born Jan. 15, 1903)

BIRTH AFFIDAVIT.

DEPARTMENT OF THE INTERIOR.
COMMISSION TO THE FIVE CIVILIZED TRIBES.

IN RE APPLICATION FOR ENROLLMENT, as a citizen of the   Choctaw   Nation, of Ida Jefferson , born on the 15 day of Jan , 1903

Name of Father: Calvin Jefferson   a citizen of the   Choctaw   Nation.
Name of Mother: Betsie Jefferson   a citizen of the   Choctaw   Nation.

Postoffice   Lodi I T

AFFIDAVIT OF MOTHER.

UNITED STATES OF AMERICA, Indian Territory, }
  Central   **DISTRICT.**

I, Betsie Jefferson , on oath state that I am 40 years of age and a citizen by   Blood , of the   Choctaw   Nation; that I am the lawful wife of   Calvin Jefferson , who is a citizen, by Blood   of the   Choctaw   Nation; that a female   child was born to me on 15   day of   Jan , 1903; that said child has been named   Ida Jefferson , and was living March 4, 1905.

 her
Betsie Jefferson x
 mark

Witnesses To Mark:
 { Joel Williams
   E.S. Wolfe

Applications for Enrollment of Choctaw Newborn
Act of 1905   Volume XVI

Subscribed and sworn to before me this   21 day of   April   , 1905

L P Hunt
Notary Public.

My com expires Jan 9th 1908

AFFIDAVIT OF ATTENDING PHYSICIAN OR MID-WIFE.

UNITED STATES OF AMERICA, Indian Territory,
Central   DISTRICT.

I, Phoebe Williams   , a Midwife   , on oath state that I attended on Mrs. Betsie Jefferson   , wife of Calvin Jefferson   on the 15 day of Jan , 1903; that there was born to her on said date a   female   child; that said child was living March 4, 1905, and is said to have been named Ida Jefferson

Phoebe Williams

Witnesses To Mark:

Subscribed and sworn to before me this   21 day of   Jan[sic]   , 1905

L P Hunt
Notary Public.

My com expires Jan 9th 1908

BIRTH AFFIDAVIT.

DEPARTMENT OF THE INTERIOR.
COMMISSION TO THE FIVE CIVILIZED TRIBES.

IN RE APPLICATION FOR ENROLLMENT, as a citizen of the   Choctaw   Nation, of Ida Jefferson   , born on the 15 day of Jan , 1903

Name of Father: Calvin Jefferson   a citizen of the   Choctaw   Nation.
Name of Mother: Betsy[sic] Jefferson   a citizen of the   Choctaw   Nation.

Postoffice   Lodi Ind Ter

Applications for Enrollment of Choctaw Newborn
Act of 1905   Volume XVI

AFFIDAVIT OF MOTHER.

UNITED STATES OF AMERICA, Indian Territory, }
Central   DISTRICT. }

I, Betsie Jefferson , on oath state that I am 40 years of age and a citizen by blood , of the Choctaw Nation; that I am the lawful wife of Calvin Jefferson , who is a citizen, by blood of the Choctaw Nation; that a female child was born to me on 15 day of January , 1903; that said child has been named Ida Jefferson , and was living March 4, 1905.

                  her
             Betsie Jefferson x
Witnesses To Mark: mark
{ J.H. Gallagher
{ *(Name Illegible)*

 Subscribed and sworn to before me this 23 day of June , 1905

           L P Hunt
            Notary Public.
           My com expires Jan 9 - 1908

AFFIDAVIT OF ATTENDING PHYSICIAN OR MID-WIFE.

UNITED STATES OF AMERICA, Indian Territory, }
Central   DISTRICT. }

I, Phoebe Williams , a Midwife , on oath state that I attended on Mrs. Betsie Jefferson , wife of Calvin Jefferson on the 15 day of January, 1903; that there was born to her on said date a female child; that said child was living March 4, 1905, and is said to have been named Ida Jefferson

           Phoebe Williams

Witnesses To Mark:
{

 Subscribed and sworn to before me this 23 day of June , 1905

           L P Hunt
            Notary Public.
My com expires Jan 9 - 1908

Applications for Enrollment of Choctaw Newborn
Act of 1905 Volume XVI

7-3157.

Muskogee, Indian Territory, April 27, 1905.

Calvin Jefferson,
 Lodi, Indian Territory.

Dear Sir:

Receipt is hereby acknowledged of your letter of April 21, 1905 transmitting affidavits of Betsie Jefferson and Phoebe Williams to the birth of Ida Jefferson, daughter of Calvin and Betsie Jefferson, January 15, 1903, and the same have been filed with our records as an application for the enrollment of said child.

Respectfully,

Chairman.

Choctaw N B 1213

Muskogee, Indian Territory, June 28, 1905.

Calvin Jefferson,
 Lodi, Indian Territory.

Dear Sir:

Receipt is hereby acknowledged of the affidavits of Betsie Jefferson and Phoebe Williams to the birth of Ida Jefferson, daughter of Calvin and Betsie Jefferson, January 15, 1903, and the same have been filed with our records in the matter of the enrollment of said child.

Respectfully,

Chairman.

Applications for Enrollment of Choctaw Newborn
Act of 1905   Volume XVI

7-NB-1213.

Muskogee, Indian Territory, June 13, 1905.

Calvin Jefferson,
    Lodi, Indian Territory.

Dear Sir:

    There is enclosed herewith for execution application for the enrollment of your infant child, Ida Jefferson, born January 15, 1903.

    In the midwife's affidavit heretofore filed in this office, she states that the applicant was living on March, 1905, while it appears that her affidavit was executed January 21, 1905. There is evidently an error in the date of execution. It will therefore be necessary that you have the enclosed application executed.

    This matter should receive your immediate attention as no further action can be taken until these affidavits are filed with the Commission.

    Respectfully,

Chairman.

Choctaw New Born 1214
    Wallace H. McMurtry
    (Born May 28, 1903)

BIRTH AFFIDAVIT.

DEPARTMENT OF THE INTERIOR.
COMMISSION TO THE FIVE CIVILIZED TRIBES.

IN RE APPLICATION FOR ENROLLMENT, as a citizen of the Choctaw Nation, of Wallace H. McMurtry, born on the 28 day of May, 1903

Name of Father: John W McMurtry   a citizen of the Choctaw Nation.
    Intermarriage
Name of Mother: Lucy McMurtry   a citizen of the Choctaw Nation.

    Postoffice   Hartshorne I.T.

Applications for Enrollment of Choctaw Newborn
Act of 1905   Volume XVI

AFFIDAVIT OF MOTHER.

UNITED STATES OF AMERICA, Indian Territory, }
Central   DISTRICT.

I, Lucy McMurtry, on oath state that I am 38 years of age and a citizen by Marriage, of the Choctaw Nation; that I am the lawful wife of John W McMurtry, who is a citizen, by Blood of the Choctaw Nation; that a male child was born to me on 28 day of May, 1903; that said child has been named Wallace H McMurtry, and was living March 4, 1905.

Lucy McMurtry

Witnesses To Mark:
{

Subscribed and sworn to before me this 22 day of April, 1905

David A. Bailey
My commission   Notary Public.
Expires Jan 11 - 1909

AFFIDAVIT OF ATTENDING PHYSICIAN OR MID-WIFE.

UNITED STATES OF AMERICA, Indian Territory, }
Central   DISTRICT.

I, W.I. Phillips MD, a M.D., on oath state that I attended on Mrs. Lucy McMurtry, wife of W.[sic] H. McMurtry on the 28 day of May, 1903; that there was born to her on said date a male child; that said child was living March 4, 1905, and is said to have been named Wallace H McMurtry

W.I. Phillips MD

Witnesses To Mark:
{

David A. Bailey
My commission Expires Jan 11 - 1909   Notary Public.

Applications for Enrollment of Choctaw Newborn
Act of 1905   Volume XVI

7-3207.

Muskogee, Indian Territory, April 27, 1905.

John W. McMurtry,
   Hartshorne, Indian Territory.

Dear Sir:

Receipt is hereby acknowledged of the affidavits of Lucy McMurtry and W. I. Phillips to the birth of Wallace H. McMurtry, son of John W. and Lucy McMurtry, May 28, 1903, and the same have been filed with our records as an application for the enrollment of said child.

Respectfully,

Chairman.

Choctaw New Born 1215
   Ella Louise Clark
   (Born Feb. 21, 1905)

BIRTH AFFIDAVIT.

DEPARTMENT OF THE INTERIOR.
COMMISSION TO THE FIVE CIVILIZED TRIBES.

IN RE APPLICATION FOR ENROLLMENT, as a citizen of the   Choctaw   Nation, of Ella Louise Clark   , born on the   21st   day of   February   , 1905

Name of Father: Edwin Clark   a citizen of the   Choctaw   Nation.
Name of Mother: Ina Katharine Clark   a citizen of the   Choctaw   Nation.

Postoffice   Stigler, Indian Territory.

AFFIDAVIT OF MOTHER.

UNITED STATES OF AMERICA, Indian Territory, ⎫
   Central   DISTRICT. ⎭

I,   Ina Katharine Clark   , on oath state that I am   eighteen   years of age and a citizen by   intermarriage   , of the   Choctaw   Nation; that I am the lawful wife of   Edwin Clark   , who is a citizen, by blood   of the   Choctaw   Nation;

240

Applications for Enrollment of Choctaw Newborn
Act of 1905   Volume XVI

that a   female   child was born to me on   twenty-first   day of   February   , 1905; that said child has been named   Ella Louise Clark   , and was living March 4, 1905.

Ina Katharine Clark

Witnesses To Mark:
{

Subscribed and sworn to before me this   15   day of   April   , 1905

E.M. Dalton
Notary Public.
My commission expires Oct. 20, 1908.

AFFIDAVIT OF ATTENDING PHYSICIAN OR MID-WIFE.

UNITED STATES OF AMERICA, Indian Territory, }
   Central   DISTRICT. }

I,   Elum M Russell   , a physician   , on oath state that I attended on Mrs.   Ina Katharine Clark   , wife of   Edwin Clark   on the 21st   day of   February , 1905; that there was born to her on said date a   female   child; that said child was living March 4, 1905, and is said to have been named Ella Louise Clark

Elum M Russell

Witnesses To Mark:
{

Subscribed and sworn to before me this   15   day of   April   , 1905

E.M. Dalton
Notary Public.

My commission expires Oct. 20, 1908.

DEPARTMENT OF THE INTERIOR,
COMMISSION TO THE FIVE CIVILIZED TRIBES.

United States of America,   ◊
                              ◊
Indian Territory,   ◊
                              ◊
Central District.   ◊

I,   Maria Foster   , on oath state that I am   48   years of age and a resident of Stigler, in the Central District of the Indian Territory; that I was present at the home of Edwin Clark in the town of Stigler, in the Central District of the Indian Territory, on the

Applications for Enrollment of Choctaw Newborn
Act of 1905   Volume XVI

21st day of Feb. 1905   ; that there was born to Ina Katharine Clark, wife of the said Edwin Clark on that date a female child; that said child was living on the fourth day of March, 1905, and is said to have been named   Ella Louise Clark

                                    Maria Foster

Subscribed and sworn to before me this   21 day of   April A.D. 1905

                                    E.M. Dalton
                                    Notary Public.

My commission expires Oct 20, 1908

DEPARTMENT OF THE INTERIOR,
COMMISSION TO THE FIVE CIVILIZED TRIBES.

United States of America,   )
)
Indian Territory,   )
)
Central District.   )

I,   Ella Henderson   , on oath state that I am   26   years of age and a resident of Stigler, in the Central District of the Indian Territory; that I was present at the home of Edwin Clark in the town of Stigler, in the Central District of the Indian Territory, on the   21st   day of   Feb. 1905   ; that there was born to Ina Katharine Clark, wife of the said Edwin Clark on that date a female child; that said child was living on the fourth day of March, 1905, and is said to have been named   Ella Louise Clark

                                    Ella Henderson

Subscribed and sworn to before me this. . . . . day of . . . .
                                    E. M. Dalton
                                    ~~Ella Henderson~~
                                    Notary Public.

My commission expires Oct 20, 1908

Applications for Enrollment of Choctaw Newborn
Act of 1905   Volume XVI

7- 4716.

Muskogee, Indian Territory, April 27, 1905.

Edwin Clark,
    Stigler, Indian Territory.

Dear Sir:

    Receipt is hereby acknowledged of your letter of April 22, 1905 transmitting affidavits of Ina Katherina[sic] Clark, Elum M. Russell, Maria Foster and Ella Henderson to the birth of Ella Louise Clark, daughter of Edwin and Ina Katherine Clark, February 21, 1905, and the same have been filed with our records as an application for the enrollment of said child.

Respectfully,

Chairman.

Choctaw New Born 1216
    (Aran Connors)
    (Born April 13, 1904)

BIRTH AFFIDAVIT.

DEPARTMENT OF THE INTERIOR.
COMMISSION TO THE FIVE CIVILIZED TRIBES.

    IN RE APPLICATION FOR ENROLLMENT, as a citizen of the   Choctaw   Nation, of   Aran Connors   , born on the   13" day of   April   , 1904

Name of Father: John P. Connors   a citizen of the   Choctaw   Nation.
Name of Mother: Aran Connors   a citizen of the   Choctaw   Nation.

    Postoffice   Canadian I.T.

AFFIDAVIT OF MOTHER.

UNITED STATES OF AMERICA, Indian Territory, }
    Western   DISTRICT. }

    I,   Aran Connors   , on oath state that I am   33   years of age and a citizen by Blood   , of the   Choctaw   Nation; that I am the lawful wife of   John P. Connors   ,

Applications for Enrollment of Choctaw Newborn
Act of 1905   Volume XVI

who is a citizen, by Intermarriage   of the   Choctaw   Nation; that a   Female child was born to me on   the 13" day of   April   , 1904; that said child has been named   Aran Connors   , and was living March 4, 1905.

Aran Connors

Witnesses To Mark:

{

Subscribed and sworn to before me this 13th   day of   Apr   , 1905

Milton Heistein
Notary Public.

AFFIDAVIT OF ATTENDING PHYSICIAN OR MID-WIFE.

UNITED STATES OF AMERICA, Indian Territory, }
  Western   DISTRICT.

I,   *(Illegible)* R Nowlin   , a   Physician   , on oath state that I attended on Mrs.   Aran Connors   , wife of   John P. Connors   on the 13 day of   April   , 1904; that there was born to her on said date a   Female   child; that said child was living March 4, 1905, and is said to have been named   Aran Connors

N.R. Nowlin
Attending Phy.

Witnesses To Mark:

{

Subscribed and sworn to before me this 20th day of   April   , 1905

(Name Illegible)
Notary Public.

Choctaw New Born 1217
  Thomas Triplett, Jr.
  (Born Feb. 2, 1905)

Applications for Enrollment of Choctaw Newborn
Act of 1905 Volume XVI

NEW BORN AFFIDAVIT

No ....

CHOCTAW ENROLLING COMMISSION

IN THE MATTER OF THE APPLICATION FOR ENROLLMENT as a citizen of the Choctaw Nation, of Thomas Triplett born on the 2nd day of February 190 5

Name of father Thomas Triplett a citizen of United States Nation, final enrollment No. ———
Name of mother Harriet Triplett a citizen of Choctaw Nation, final enrollment No. 7588

Ft Smith Ark RFD#345 Postoffice.

AFFIDAVIT OF MOTHER

UNITED STATES OF AMERICA
INDIAN TERRITORY
DISTRICT Central

I Harriet Triplett , on oath state that I am 27 years of age and a citizen by blood of the Choctaw Nation, and as such have been placed upon the final roll of the Choctaw Nation, by the Honorable Secretary of the Interior my final enrollment number being 7588 ; that I am the lawful wife of Thomas Triplett , who is a citizen of the United States Nation, and as such has been placed upon the final roll of said Nation by the Honorable Secretary of the Interior, his final enrollment number being ——— and that a Male child was born to me on the 2nd day of February 190 5; that said child has been named Thomas Triplett , and is now living.

Harriet Triplett

WITNESSETH:
Must be two witnesses E.L. Hickman
who are citizens Morris Battiest

Subscribed and sworn to before me this, the 25 day of February , 190 5

W.E. Harrell
Notary Public.

My Commission Expires: Aug 6-1908

Applications for Enrollment of Choctaw Newborn
Act of 1905 Volume XVI

Affidavit of Attending Physician or Midwife

UNITED STATES OF AMERICA,
INDIAN TERRITORY,
Central DISTRICT

I, Maggie Johnson a midwife on oath state that I attended on Mrs. Harriet Triplett wife of Thomas Triplett on the 2nd day of February, 190 5, that there was born to her on said date a male child, that said child is now living, and is said to have been named Thomas Triplett

                her
Maggie x Johnson   M. D.
               mark

Subscribed and sworn to before me this the 25 day of February 1905

W.E. Harrell
        Notary Public.

WITNESSETH:
Must be two witnesses who are citizens and know the child.
    E.L. Hickman
    Morris Battiest

We hereby certify that we are well acquainted with Maggie Johnson a midwife and know her to be reputable and of good standing in the community.

Must be two citizen witnesses.
    E.L. Hickman
    Morris Battiest

BIRTH AFFIDAVIT.

DEPARTMENT OF THE INTERIOR.
COMMISSION TO THE FIVE CIVILIZED TRIBES.

IN RE APPLICATION FOR ENROLLMENT, as a citizen of the Choctaw Nation, of Thomas Triplett Jr, born on the 2nd day of February, 1905

Name of Father: Thomas Triplett   a citizen of the United States Nation.
Name of Mother: Harriet Triplett   a citizen of the Choctaw Nation.

Postoffice   Bearden I.T.

Applications for Enrollment of Choctaw Newborn
Act of 1905   Volume XVI

AFFIDAVIT OF ~~MOTHER~~. *father*

UNITED STATES OF AMERICA, Indian Territory, }
Central   DISTRICT.

I, Thomas Triplett, on oath state that I am 41 years of age and a citizen by ———, of the United States ~~Nation~~; that I am the lawful ~~wife~~ *husband* of Harriet Triplett deceased, who is a citizen, by blood of the Choctaw Nation; that a Male child was born to ~~me~~ *her* on 2nd day of February, 1905; that said child has been named Thomas Triplett Jr, and was living March 4, 1905.

Thomas Triplett

Witnesses To Mark:
{

Subscribed and sworn to before me this 21st day of April, 1905

W.E. Harrell
Notary Public.

AFFIDAVIT OF ATTENDING PHYSICIAN OR MID-WIFE.

UNITED STATES OF AMERICA, Indian Territory, }
Central   DISTRICT.

I, Maggie Johnson, a Midwife, on oath state that I attended on Mrs. Harriet Triplett (deceased), wife of Thomas Triplett on the 2nd day of February, 1905; that there was born to her on said date a male child; that said child was living March 4, 1905, and is said to have been named Thomas Triplett Jr

her
Maggie x Johnson
mark

Witnesses To Mark:
{ WE Harrell
  Lewis Johnson

Subscribed and sworn to before me this 21 day of April, 1905

MY COMMISSION EXPIRES AUG. 6, 1908

W.E. Harrell
Notary Public.

Applications for Enrollment of Choctaw Newborn
Act of 1905   Volume XVI

(The affidavit below typed as given.)

AFFIDAVIT OF WITNESS

UNITED STATES OF AMERICA, Indian Territory,
  Central District.

I Edwin L. Hickman a citizen of the Choctaw Nation by bloodstate on oath that I was acquainted with Harriett Triplett deceased (died on the 28th day of March 1905) a citizen by blood of the Choctaw Nation and the lawful wife of Thomas Triplett a citizen of the United States
That a male child was born to her on the 2ond day of February 1905. and was living March 4, 1905. and is said to have been named Thomas Triplett Jr.

                                    Edwin L Hickman
                                         April
Subscribed and sworn to before me this the 21 day of ~~March~~ 1905.

<small>MY COMMISSION EXPIRES AUG. 6, 1908</small>   W.E. Harrell
                                    Notary Public.

(The affidavit below typed as given.)

AFFIDAVIT OF WITNESS

UNITED STATES OF AMERICA, Indian Territory,
  Central District.

  I Morris Battiest a citizen by blood of the Choctaw Nation state on oath that I was acquainted with Harriett Triplett deceased (died on the 28 the of March 1905) a citizen by blood of the Choctaw Nation and the lawful wife of Thomas Triplett a citizen of the United States
That a male child was born to her on the 2ond February 1905. and was living March 4, 1905. and is said to have been named Thomas Triplett Jr.

                                    Morris Battiest

Subscribed and sworn to before me this the 21 day of April 1905.

                                    W.E. Harrell
<small>MY COMMISSION EXPIRES AUG. 6, 1908</small>   Notary Public.

Applications for Enrollment of Choctaw Newborn
Act of 1905   Volume XVI

7-2614

Muskogee, Indian Territory, April 17, 1905.

Thomas Triplett,
    Spiro, Indian Territory.

Dear Sir:

    Receipt is hereby acknowledged of your letter of April 12, 1905, giving names of persons who can make affidavit to the birth of your minor child and stating that your wife Hariett Triplett is dead and you ask that affidavit be filled out using the names of the witnesses as they should appear and the same be forwarded you at Spiro.

    In compliance with your request there is inclosed herewith blank for the enrollment of an infant child upon which you may forward your affidavit as father of the child, and the affidavit of the midwife who was in attendance at the birth of the child. You should also forward the affidavits of two witnesses who know of the birth of this child; that it is still living.

    This matter should receive your immediate attention and when executed the affidavit should be returned to this office within sixty days from March 3, 1905.

                                       Respectfully,

B.C.   Chairman.

7-2614.

Muskogee, Indian Territory, April 27, 1905.

Thomas Triplett,
    R.F.D. #25,
        Ft. Smith, Arkansas.

Dear Sir:

    Receipt is hereby acknowledged of your letter of April 21, 1905 enclosing affidavits of Thomas Triplett and Maggie Johnson to the birth of Thomas Triplett, Jr., son of Thomas and Harriett Triplett, February 2, 1905, and the same have been filed with our records as an application for the enrollment of said child.

                                       Respectfully,

                                                  Chairman.

Applications for Enrollment of Choctaw Newborn
Act of 1905   Volume XVI

Choctaw New Born 1218
   Beulah Pritchard
   (Born Oct. 30, 1904)

BIRTH AFFIDAVIT.

DEPARTMENT OF THE INTERIOR.
COMMISSION TO THE FIVE CIVILIZED TRIBES.

IN RE APPLICATION FOR ENROLLMENT, as a citizen of the   Choctaw   Nation, of Beulah Pritchard   , born on the 30th day of October , 1904

Name of Father: William E Pritchard   a citizen of the   Choctaw   Nation.
Name of Mother: Lizzie Pritchard   a citizen of the   Choctaw   Nation.

Postoffice   Fort Towson Ind Ter

AFFIDAVIT OF MOTHER.

UNITED STATES OF AMERICA, Indian Territory, }
   Central Dis   DISTRICT.

I, Lizzie Pritchard , on oath state that I am 38 years of age and a citizen by Blood , of the Choctaw Nation; that I am the lawful wife of William E. Pritchard , who is a citizen, by Intermarried of the Choctaw Nation; that a Female child was born to me on 30th day of October , 1904; that said child has been named Beulah Pritchard , and was living March 4, 1905.

Lizzie Pritchard
Witnesses To Mark:
{

Subscribed and sworn to before me this 21th[sic] day of April , 1905

Thomas Fennell
Notary Public.

AFFIDAVIT OF ATTENDING PHYSICIAN OR MID-WIFE.

UNITED STATES OF AMERICA, Indian Territory, }
   Central Dis   DISTRICT.

I, Mary Gross , a Midwife , on oath state that I attended on Mrs. Lizzie Pritchard , wife of William E Pritchard   on the 30th day of

Applications for Enrollment of Choctaw Newborn
Act of 1905   Volume XVI

October   , 1904; that there was born to her on said date a   Female   child; that said child was living March 4, 1905, and is said to have been named   Beulah Pritchard

her
Mary x Gross
mark

Witnesses To Mark:
   { William E Pritchard
     Mrs T Fennell

    Subscribed and sworn to before me this 21th[sic] day of   April   , 1905

                                  Thomas Fennell
                                        Notary Public.

                                                                     7-1502.

                            Muskogee, Indian Territory, April 27, 1905.

William E. Pritchard,
    Ft. Towson, Indian Territory.

Dear Sir:

    Receipt is hereby acknowledged of your letter of April 22, 1905 enclosing the affidavits of Lizzie Pritchard and Mary Gross to the birth of Beulah Pritchard, daughter of William E. and Lizzie Pritchard, October 30, 1904, and the same have been filed with our records as an application for the enrollment of said child.

                                    Respectfully,

                                                        Chairman.

Choctaw New Born 1219
    Homer Sockey
    (Born Aug. 2, 1904)

Applications for Enrollment of Choctaw Newborn
Act of 1905   Volume XVI

BIRTH AFFIDAVIT.   7- 8397

DEPARTMENT OF THE INTERIOR.
COMMISSION TO THE FIVE CIVILIZED TRIBES.

IN RE APPLICATION FOR ENROLLMENT, as a citizen of the   Choctaw   Nation, of Homer Sockey   , born on the 2nd   day of August   , 1904

Name of Father: Billie Sockey   a citizen of the   Choctaw   Nation.
Name of Mother: Josephine Sockey   a citizen of the   Choctaw   Nation.

Postoffice   Summerfield Ind. Ter.

AFFIDAVIT OF MOTHER.

UNITED STATES OF AMERICA, Indian Territory, }
Central   DISTRICT.

I,   Josephine Sockey   , on oath state that I am   23   years of age and a citizen by   blood   , of the   Choctaw   Nation; that I am the lawful wife of Billie Sockey   , who is a citizen, by blood   of the   Choctaw   Nation; that a   male   child was born to me on 2nd   day of August   , 1904; that said child has been named   Homer Sockey   , and was living March 4, 1905.

Josephine Sockey

Witnesses To Mark:
{

Subscribed and sworn to before me this   17th   day of   April   , 1905

O.L. Johnson
Notary Public.

AFFIDAVIT OF ATTENDING PHYSICIAN OR MID-WIFE.

UNITED STATES OF AMERICA, Indian Territory, }
Central   DISTRICT.

I,   Emeline Davis   , a   ~~physician~~ *Midwife*   , on oath state that I attended on Mrs. Josephine Sockey   , wife of   Billie Sockey   on the 2nd   day of   August ,1904; that there was born to her on said date a   male   child; that said child was living March 4, 1905, and is said to have been named Homer Sockey

Emeline Davis

252

Applications for Enrollment of Choctaw Newborn
Act of 1905   Volume XVI

Witnesses To Mark:

Subscribed and sworn to before me this 22 day of   April   , 1905

Robert E Lee
Notary Public.
My com expires Jan. 11-1906

NEW BORN AFFIDAVIT

No

CHOCTAW ENROLLING COMMISSION

IN THE MATTER OF THE APPLICATION FOR ENROLLMENT as a citizen of the Choctaw Nation, of   Homer Sockey   born on the 2   day of   August   190 4

Name of father   Billy Sockey   a citizen of   Choctaw   Nation,
final enrollment No...........
Name of mother   Josephine Sockey   a citizen of   Choctaw   Nation,
final enrollment No. 8397

Summerfield I.T   Postoffice.

AFFIDAVIT OF MOTHER

UNITED STATES OF AMERICA
INDIAN TERRITORY
DISTRICT   Central

I   Josephine Sockey   , on oath state that I am   21   years of age and a citizen by   blood   of the   Choctaw   Nation, and as such have been placed upon the final roll of the   Choctaw   Nation, by the Honorable Secretary of the Interior my final enrollment number being 8397   ; that I ~~am was~~ the lawful wife of   Billy Sockey   , who is a citizen of the   Choctaw   Nation, and as such has been placed upon the final roll of said Nation by the Honorable Secretary of the Interior, his final enrollment number being   —   and that a   Male   child was born to me on the   2   day of   August   190 4; that said child has been named Homer Sockey   , and is now living.

Josephine Sockey

253

Applications for Enrollment of Choctaw Newborn
Act of 1905   Volume XVI

WITNESSETH:
Must be two witnesses { Henry J Sexton
who are citizens   Sam Shwinogee

    Subscribed and sworn to before me this, the 17 day of February, 190 5

                                             James Bower
                                                  Notary Public.

My Commission Expires:
Sept 23 - 1907

Affidavit of Attending Physician or Midwife

UNITED STATES OF AMERICA,
   INDIAN TERRITORY,
   Central   DISTRICT

    I, Dr A. R. Sick   a   Practicing Physician
on oath state that I attended on Mrs. **Josephine Sockey** *divorced* wife of Billy Sockey
on the 2 day of August , 1904, that there was born to her on said date a male child,
that said child is now living, and is said to have been named Homer Sockey

                                     A. R. Sisk   M. D.

    Subscribed and sworn to before me this the 20 day of Feb   1905

                                    John W Dunlap
             My commission   Notary Public.
WITNESSETH: expires Jan the 28 - 1909
Must be two witnesses { Henry J Sexton
who are citizens and
know the child.   Sam Shwinogee

    We hereby certify that we are well acquainted with   A. R. Sisk
a   Practicing Physician   and know   him   to be reputable and of good
standing in the community.

                              Must be two citizen { Henry J Sexton
                              witnesses.   Sam Shwinogee

Applications for Enrollment of Choctaw Newborn
Act of 1905   Volume XVI

7-2856.

Muskogee, Indian Territory, April 326, 1905.

Billie Sockey,
    Summerfield, Indian Territory.

Dear Sir:

    Receipt is hereby acknowledged of the affidavits of Josephine Sockey and Emeline Davis to the birth of Homer Sockey, son of Billie and Josephine Sockey, August 2, 1904, and the same have been filed with our records as an application for the enrollment of said child.

                      Respectfully,

                                              Chairman.

Choctaw New Born 1220
    Loise Louisa Dodson
    (Born Feb. 9, 1904)

BIRTH AFFIDAVIT.
DEPARTMENT OF THE INTERIOR.
COMMISSION TO THE FIVE CIVILIZED TRIBES.

    IN RE APPLICATION FOR ENROLLMENT, as a citizen of the   Choctaw   Nation, of Loise Louisa Dodson   , born on the 9th day of February   , 1904

Name of Father: John W. Dodson *Intermarried* a citizen of the   Choctaw   Nation.
Name of Mother: Emma Dodson   a citizen of the   Choctaw   Nation.

                      Postoffice   Bennington I.T.

AFFIDAVIT OF MOTHER.

UNITED STATES OF AMERICA, Indian Territory,
    Central   DISTRICT.

    I,   Emma Dodson   , on oath state that I am   about 37   years of age and a citizen by   Blood   , of the   Choctaw   Nation; that I am the lawful wife of

Applications for Enrollment of Choctaw Newborn
Act of 1905   Volume XVI

John W. Dodson , who is a citizen, by marriage of the Choctaw Nation; that a female child was born to me on the 9th day of February , 1904; that said child has been named Loise Louisa Dodson , and was living March 4, 1905.

                 Emma Dodson

Witnesses To Mark:
{

  Subscribed and sworn to before me this 22nd day of April , 1905

             C.C. McClard
             Notary Public.

AFFIDAVIT OF ATTENDING PHYSICIAN OR MID-WIFE.

UNITED STATES OF AMERICA, Indian Territory,
 Central   DISTRICT.

  I, M. J. Spence , as midwife , on oath state that I attended on Mrs. Emma Dodson , wife of John W. Dodson on the 9th day of February , 1904; that there was born to her on said date a Female child; that said child was living March 4, 1905, and is said to have been named Loise Louisa Dodson

             M. J. Spence

Witnesses To Mark:
{

  Subscribed and sworn to before me this 22nd day of April , 1905

             C.C. McClard
             Notary Public.

                 7-2717.

       Muskogee, Indian Territory, April 26, 1905.

John W. Dodson,
  Bennington, Indian Territory.

Dear Sir:

  Receipt is hereby acknowledged of the affidavits of Emma Dodson and M. J. Spence to the birth of Lois Louisa Dodson, daughter of John W. and Emma Dodson, February 9, 1904, and the same have been filed with our records as an application for the enrollment of said child.

Applications for Enrollment of Choctaw Newborn
Act of 1905 Volume XVI

Respectfully,

Chairman.

Choctaw New Born 1221
    Lester Naylor
    (Born April 25, 1903)

NEW-BORN AFFIDAVIT.

Number..................

...Choctaw Enrolling Commission...

IN THE MATTER OF THE APPLICATION FOR ENROLLMENT, as a citizen of the Choctaw Nation, of Lester Naylor

born on the 25 day of __April__ 190 3

Name of father Newton Naylor   a citizen of United States
Nation final enrollment No...................
Name of mother Ida Naylor   a citizen of Choctaw
Nation final enrollment No. 7677

         Postoffice   Conser I.T.

AFFIDAVIT OF MOTHER.

UNITED STATES OF AMERICA
INDIAN TERRITORY
    Central   DISTRICT

I Ida Naylor , on oath state that I am 32 years of age and a citizen by Blood of the Choctaw Nation, and as such have been placed upon the final roll of the Choctaw Nation, by the Honorable Secretary of the Interior my final enrollment number being 7677 ; that I am the lawful wife of Newton Naylor , who is a citizen of the United States ~~Nation~~, and as such has been placed upon the final roll of said Nation by the Honorable Secretary of the Interior, his final enrollment number being .... and that a Female child was born to me on the 25 day of April 190 3; that said child has been named Lester Naylor , and is now living.

                 Ida Naylor

Applications for Enrollment of Choctaw Newborn
Act of 1905 Volume XVI

Witnesseth.

Must be two Witnesses who are Citizens. } John Folsom

S.C. Carshall

Subscribed and sworn to before me this 16 day of Feb 190 5

James Bower
        Notary Public.

My commission expires:
Sept 23 - 1907

AFFIDAVIT OF ATTENDING PHYSICIAN OR MIDWIFE

UNITED STATES OF AMERICA
INDIAN TERRITORY
  Central   DISTRICT

I, Sarah Naylor a midwife on oath state that I attended on Mrs. Ida Naylor wife of Newton Naylor on the 25 day of April , 190 3 , that there was born to her on said date a Female child, that said child is now living, and is said to have been named Lester Naylor

            her
Sarah x Naylor

Subscribed and sworn to before me this, the mark 17 day of Feb 190 5

WITNESSETH:
Must be two witnesses who are citizens { John Folsom
S.C. Carshall

E.W. Moore   Notary Public.

We hereby certify that we are well acquainted with Sarah Naylor a midwife and know her to be reputable and of good standing in the community.

    John Folsom

    S.C. Carshall

Applications for Enrollment of Choctaw Newborn
Act of 1905   Volume XVI

BIRTH AFFIDAVIT.

DEPARTMENT OF THE INTERIOR.
COMMISSION TO THE FIVE CIVILIZED TRIBES.

IN RE APPLICATION FOR ENROLLMENT, as a citizen of the   Choctaw   Nation, of Lester Naylor   , born on the   25" day of   April   , 1903

Name of Father: Newton Naylor   a citizen of the   U.S.   Nation.
Name of Mother: Ida Naylor   a citizen of the   Choctaw   Nation.

Postoffice   Conser Ind. Ter

AFFIDAVIT OF MOTHER.

UNITED STATES OF AMERICA, Indian Territory,
Central   DISTRICT.

I, Ida Naylor   , on oath state that I am 33   years of age and a citizen by Blood   , of the   Choctaw   Nation; that I am the lawful wife of   Newton Naylor , who is a citizen, by .... of the   United States   Nation; that a   Female   child was born to me on   25"   day of   April   , 1903; that said child has been named Lester Naylor   , and was living March 4, 1905.

Ida Naylor

Witnesses To Mark:
{

Subscribed and sworn to before me this 22"   day of   April   , 1905

E.W. Moore
Notary Public.

AFFIDAVIT OF ATTENDING PHYSICIAN OR MID-WIFE.

UNITED STATES OF AMERICA, Indian Territory,
Central   DISTRICT.

I,   Sarah Naylor   , a   midwife   , on oath state that I attended on Mrs. Ida Naylor   , wife of   Newton Naylor   on the 25" day of April , 1903; that there was born to her on said date a   Female   child; that said child was living March 4, 1905, and is said to have been named   Lester Naylor

her
Sarah x Naylor
mark

Applications for Enrollment of Choctaw Newborn
Act of 1905   Volume XVI

Witnesses To Mark:
  { S.J. Folsom
    Carnolie Runton

    Subscribed and sworn to before me this 22   day of   April   , 1905

                                        E.W. Moore
                                              Notary Public.

                                                        7-2643.

                    Muskogee, Indian Territory, April 26, 1905.

Newton Naylor,
    Conser, Indian Territory.

Dear Sir:

    Receipt is hereby acknowledged of the affidavits of Ida Naylor and Sarah Naylor, to the birth of Lester Naylor, daughter of Newton and Ida Naylor, April 25, 1903, and the same have been filed with our records as an application for the enrollment of said child.

                                        Respectfully,

                                                 Chairman.

Choctaw New Born 1222
    Luke Jackson
    (Born Feb. 17, 1904)

Applications for Enrollment of Choctaw Newborn
Act of 1905 Volume XVI

NEW-BORN AFFIDAVIT.

Number..............

...Choctaw Enrolling Commission...

IN THE MATTER OF THE APPLICATION FOR ENROLLMENT, as a citizen of the Choctaw Nation, of Luke Jackson

born on the 7th[sic] day of __February__ 190 4

Name of father Joseph Jackson   a citizen of   Choctaw
Nation final enrollment No. 6821
Name of mother Rosie Jackson   a citizen of   Choctaw
Nation final enrollment No. 6822

Postoffice   Heavener I.T.

AFFIDAVIT OF MOTHER.

UNITED STATES OF AMERICA
INDIAN TERRITORY
Central   DISTRICT

I   Rosie Jackson   , on oath state that I am 39 years of age and a citizen by blood of the Choctaw Nation, and as such have been placed upon the final roll of the Choctaw Nation, by the Honorable Secretary of the Interior my final enrollment number being 6822 ; that I am the lawful wife of Joseph Jackson , who is a citizen of the Choctaw Nation, and as such has been placed upon the final roll of said Nation by the Honorable Secretary of the Interior, his final enrollment number being 6821 and that a Male child was born to me on the 7"[sic] day of February 190 4; that said child has been named Luke Jackson , and is now living.

Rosie Jackson

Witnesseth.
Must be two ⎫ *(Name Illegible)*
Witnesses who ⎬
are Citizens. ⎭ Lillie A Blake

Subscribed and sworn to before me this 7th day of Feb   190 5

J.M. Young
Notary Public.

My commission expires:
         March 6, 1905

Applications for Enrollment of Choctaw Newborn
Act of 1905   Volume XVI

AFFIDAVIT OF ATTENDING PHYSICIAN OR MIDWIFE

UNITED STATES OF AMERICA
INDIAN TERRITORY
Central   DISTRICT

I, Mollie McCurtain a Midwife on oath state that I attended on Mrs. Rosie Jackson wife of Joseph Jackson on the 7th day of February, 1904, that there was born to her on said date a male child, that said child is now living, and is said to have been named Luke Jackson

her
Mollie x McCurtain
mark

Subscribed and sworn to before me this, the 30" day of January 1905

WITNESSETH: J.M. Young   Notary Public.

Must be two witnesses who are citizens   *(Name Illegible)*
Eveline Benton
Also attest to mark.

We hereby certify that we are well acquainted with Mollie McCurtain a Midwife and know her to be reputable and of good standing in the community.

S J Folsom   Heavener I.T.

C. Runton   Heavener I.T.

7na 6822
BIRTH AFFIDAVIT.

DEPARTMENT OF THE INTERIOR.
COMMISSION TO THE FIVE CIVILIZED TRIBES.

IN RE APPLICATION FOR ENROLLMENT, as a citizen of the Choctaw Nation, of Luke Jackson, born on the 17th day of February, 1904

Name of Father: Joseph Jackson   a citizen of the Choc Nation.
Name of Mother: Rosie Jackson   a citizen of the Choc Nation.

Postoffice   Heavener I.T.

Applications for Enrollment of Choctaw Newborn
Act of 1905   Volume XVI

AFFIDAVIT OF MOTHER.

UNITED STATES OF AMERICA, Indian Territory, }
Central   DISTRICT.

I, Rosie Jackson, on oath state that I am 39 years of age and a citizen by blood, of the Choc Nation; that I am the lawful wife of Joseph Jackson, who is a citizen, by blood of the Choctaw Nation; that a male child was born to me on 17th day of February, 1904; that said child has been named Luke Jackson, and was living March 4, 1905.

Rosie Jackson

Witnesses To Mark:

Subscribed and sworn to before me this 22ond day of April, 1905.

W.N. Estes
Notary Public.

AFFIDAVIT OF ATTENDING PHYSICIAN OR MID-WIFE.

UNITED STATES OF AMERICA, Indian Territory, }
Central   DISTRICT.

I, Mollie McCurtain, a midwife, on oath state that I attended on Mrs. Rosie Jackson, wife of Joseph Jackson on the 17th day of February, 1904; that there was born to her on said date a male child; that said child was living March 4, 1905, and is said to have been named Luke Jackson

her
Mollie x McCurtain
mark

Witnesses To Mark:
  { *(Name Illegible)*
  { *(Name Illegible)*

Subscribed and sworn to before me this 22ond day of April, 1905

W.N. Estes
Notary Public.

Applications for Enrollment of Choctaw Newborn
Act of 1905   Volume XVI

BIRTH AFFIDAVIT.

DEPARTMENT OF THE INTERIOR.
COMMISSION TO THE FIVE CIVILIZED TRIBES.

IN RE APPLICATION FOR ENROLLMENT, as a citizen of the Choctaw Nation, of Luke Jackson, born on the 17th day of Feb, 1904

Name of Father: Joseph Jackson   Roll 6821   a citizen of the Choctaw Nation.
Name of Mother: Rosie Jackson   " 6822   a citizen of the Choctaw Nation.

Postoffice   Heavener Ind. Ter.

AFFIDAVIT OF MOTHER.

UNITED STATES OF AMERICA, Indian Territory,
Central DISTRICT.

I, Rosie Jackson, on oath state that I am 39 years of age and a citizen by blood, of the Choctaw Nation; that I am the lawful wife of Joseph Jackson, who is a citizen, by blood of the Choctaw Nation; that a male child was born to me on 17 th day of Feb, 1904; that said child has been named Luke Jackson, and was living March 4, 1905.

Rosie Jackson

Witnesses To Mark:

Subscribed and sworn to before me this 3d day of July, 1905

W.N. Estes
Notary Public.

AFFIDAVIT OF ATTENDING PHYSICIAN OR MID-WIFE.

UNITED STATES OF AMERICA, Indian Territory,
DISTRICT.

I, Mollie McCurtain, a midwife, on oath state that I attended on Mrs. Rosie Jackson, wife of Joseph Jackson on the 17th day of Feb, 1904; that there was born to her on said date a male child; that said child was living March 4, 1905, and is said to have been named Luke Jackson

Applications for Enrollment of Choctaw Newborn
Act of 1905   Volume XVI

Witnesses To Mark:
{ BH Cagle
  G W Barlow

her
Mollie x McCurtain
mark

Subscribed and sworn to before me this 3d   day of   July   , 1905

W.N. Estes
Notary Public.

7-2357.

Muskogee, Indian Territory, April 26, 1905.

Joseph Jackson,
    Heavener, Indian Territory.

Dear Sir:

Receipt is hereby acknowledged of the affidavits of Rosie Jackson and Mollie McCurtain to the birth of Luke Jackson, son of Joseph and Rosie Jackson, February 17, 1904, and the same have been filed with our records as an application for the enrollment of said child.

Respectfully,

Chairman.

7--NB--1222

Muskogee, Indian Territory, June 2, 1905.

Joseph Jackson,
    Heavener, Indian Territory.

Dear Sir:

There is enclosed you herewith for execution application for the enrollment of your infant child, Luke Jackson.

In the affidavits of February 7, 1905, the date of the applicant's birth is given as February 7, 1904, while in the affidavits under date of April 22, 1905, this date of birth is left blank. Please insert the correct date and when the affidavits have been properly executed return them to this office.

Applications for Enrollment of Choctaw Newborn
Act of 1905 Volume XVI

In having these affidavits executed care should be exercised to see that all names are written in full, as they appear in the body of the affidavit, and in the event that either of the persons signing the affidavit are unable to write, signatures by mark must be attested by two witnesses. Each affidavit must be executed before a Notary Public and the notarial seal and signature of the officer must be attached to each separate affidavit.

This matter should receive your immediate attention as no further action can be taken relative to the enrollment of said child until the Commission has been furnished these affidavits.

Respectfully,

Commissioner in Charge.

Enc-FVK-12

---

7 NB-1222.

Muskogee, Indian Territory, July 10, 1905.

Joseph Jackson,
Heavener, Indian Territory.

Dear Sir:

Receipt is hereby acknowledged of the affidavits of Rosie Jackson and Mollie McCurtain to the birth of Lake[sic] Jackson, son of Joseph Jackson and Rosie Jackson, February 17, 1904, and the same have been filed with the records of this office in the matter of the enrollment of said child.

Respectfully,

Commissioner.

7-NB 1222

Muskogee, Indian Territory, September 9, 1905.

Joseph R. Jackson,
Heavener, Indian Territory.

Dear Sir:

Replying to your recent inquiry, you are advised that on August 22, 1905, the Secretary of the Interior approved the enrollment of your minor child, Luke Jackson as a citizen of the Choctaw Nation and the name of said child appears upon the final roll of new-born citizens by blood of the Choctaw Nation opposite number 1434.

Applications for Enrollment of Choctaw Newborn
Act of 1905   Volume XVI

The child is now entitled to an allotment and selection thereof should be made without delay at the land office for the nation in which the prospective allotment is located.

Respectfully,

Acting Commissioner.

Choctaw New Born 1223
    Clifford Anderson Bennett
    (Born Sept. 30, 1902)
    Crecia Ann Bennett
    (Born Sept 30, 1902)

BIRTH AFFIDAVIT.

DEPARTMENT OF THE INTERIOR.
COMMISSION TO THE FIVE CIVILIZED TRIBES.

IN RE APPLICATION FOR ENROLLMENT, as a citizen of the   Choctaw   Nation, of Clifford Anderson Bennett   , born on the 30 day of September , 1902

Name of Father: Thomas Bennett   a ~~citizen~~ of the   U S   Nation.
Name of Mother: Lucy E Bennett   a citizen of the   Choctaw   Nation.

Postoffice   Healdton Ind. Ter.

AFFIDAVIT OF MOTHER.

UNITED STATES OF AMERICA, Indian Territory,
   Southern   DISTRICT.

I, Lucy E Bennett , on oath state that I am 34 years of age and a citizen by Blood , of the Choctaw Nation; that I am the lawful wife of Thomas Bennett , who is a citizen, ~~by of U~~ of the U. S. Nation; that a Male child was born to me on 30 day of September , 1902; that said child has been named Clifford Anderson Bennett , and was living March 4, 1905.

Lucy E Bennett

Witnesses To Mark:

Applications for Enrollment of Choctaw Newborn
Act of 1905   Volume XVI

Subscribed and sworn to before me this 24 day of   April   , 1905

                         U.T. Rexroat
                         Notary Public.

AFFIDAVIT OF ATTENDING PHYSICIAN OR MID-WIFE.

UNITED STATES OF AMERICA, Indian Territory,
  Southern   DISTRICT.

I,   Dr. A. C. Strange   , a physician   , on oath state that I attended on Mrs.   Lucy E Bennett   , wife of   Thomas Bennett   on the   30   day of September   , 1902; that there was born to her on said date a   Male   child; that said child was living March 4, 1905, and is said to have been named Clifford Anderson Bennett

                         A E Strange MD
Witnesses To Mark:

Subscribed and sworn to before me this 18 day of   April   , 1905

                         U.T. Rexroat
                         Notary Public.

BIRTH AFFIDAVIT.
DEPARTMENT OF THE INTERIOR.
COMMISSION TO THE FIVE CIVILIZED TRIBES.

IN RE APPLICATION FOR ENROLLMENT, as a citizen of the   Choctaw   Nation, of Crecia Ann Bennett   , born on the   30   day of   September   , 1902

Name of Father: Thomas Bennett   a citizen of the   U S   Nation.
Name of Mother: Lucy E Bennett   a citizen of the   Choctaw   Nation.

                   Postoffice   Healdton Ind. Ter.

AFFIDAVIT OF MOTHER.

UNITED STATES OF AMERICA, Indian Territory,
  Southern   DISTRICT.

I,   Lucy E Bennett   , on oath state that I am   34   years of age and a citizen by   Blood   , of the   Choctaw   Nation; that I am the lawful wife of   Thomas Bennett   , who is a citizen, by   of the   U. S.   Nation; that a

Applications for Enrollment of Choctaw Newborn
Act of 1905   Volume XVI

Female   child was born to me on 30   day of   September , 1902; that said child has been named   Crecia Ann Bennett   , and was living March 4, 1905.

                                                      Lucy E Bennett

Witnesses To Mark:
{

    Subscribed and sworn to before me this   24   day of   April   , 1905

                                                      U.T. Rexroat
                                                      Notary Public.

AFFIDAVIT OF ATTENDING PHYSICIAN OR MID-WIFE.

UNITED STATES OF AMERICA, Indian Territory, }
  Southern   DISTRICT.

    I,   Dr. A. C. Strange   , a physician   , on oath state that I attended on Mrs.   Lucy E Bennett   , wife of   Thomas Bennett   on the 30   day of September   , 1902; that there was born to her on said date a   Female   child; that said child was living March 4, 1905, and is said to have been named Crecia Ann Bennett

                                                        A E Strange MD

Witnesses To Mark:
{

    Subscribed and sworn to before me this   18   day of   April   , 1905

                                                      U.T. Rexroat
                                                      Notary Public.

Choctaw New Born 1224
    Ella Jones
    (Born July 28, 1904)

Applications for Enrollment of Choctaw Newborn
Act of 1905 Volume XVI

7-9235.

DEPARTMENT OF THE INTERIOR,
COMMISSION TO THE FIVE CIVILIZED TRIBES.
SOUTH McALESTER, I. T.		APRIL 24, 1905.

In the matter of the application for the enrollment of Ella Jones as a citizen by blood of the Choctaw Nation.

Robert Jones being first duly sworn testifies as follows:

EXAMINATION BY THE COMMISSION:

Q What is your name? A Robert Jones.
Q What is your age? A Twenty-two.
Q What is your post office address? A Vireton.
Q You have this day made application for the enrollment of your child Ella Jones as a citizen of the Choctaw Nation; when was this child born? A July 28, 1904.
Q Who is the mother of Ella Jones? A Rena Jones.
Q What was her name before you married her? A McLish.
Q Is she living at the present time? A No, sir.
Q When did she die? A February last February.
Q This year? A Yes, sir.
Q What day? A I don't know what day.
Q February 1905? A Yes, sir.

Witness excused.

Lewis Carnes being first duly sworn testifies as follows:

EXAMINATION BY THE COMMISSION:

Q What is your name? A Lewis Carnes.
Q What is your age? A Twenty-three.
Q What is your post office address? A Featherston.
Q Are you a citizen by blood of the Choctaw Nation? A Yes, sir.
Q Are you acquainted with Robert Jones who has this day made application for his child Ella Jones? A Yes, sir.
Q How far from Robert Jones do you live? A About five miles.
Q Do you know when his child Ella Jones was born? A July 28, 1904.
Q Is this child living today? A Yes, sir.

Witness excused.

Chas. T. Difendafer being first duly sworn states that the above and foregoing, is a full, true and correct transcript of his stenographic notes taken in said cause on said date.

Chas. T. Difendafer

Applications for Enrollment of Choctaw Newborn
Act of 1905   Volume XVI

Subscribed and sworn to before me this 24th day of April 1905.

OL Johnson
Notary Public.

7- 9235
BIRTH AFFIDAVIT.

DEPARTMENT OF THE INTERIOR.
COMMISSION TO THE FIVE CIVILIZED TRIBES.

IN RE APPLICATION FOR ENROLLMENT, as a citizen of the   Choctaw   Nation, of Ella Jones   , born on the   28   day of   July   , 1904

Name of Father: Robert Jones   a citizen of the   Choc   Nation.
Name of Mother: Rena Jones nee McLish   a citizen of the   Choc   Nation.

Postoffice   Vireton I.T.

AFFIDAVIT OF ATTENDING PHYSICIAN OR MID-WIFE.

UNITED STATES OF AMERICA, Indian Territory,
   Central   DISTRICT.

I,   Ellen Kate   , a   midwife   , on oath state that I attended on Mrs.   Rena Jones   , wife of   Robert Jones   on the   28   day of   July   , 1904; that there was born to her on said date a   female   child; that said child was living March 4, 1905, and is said to have been named   Ella Jones

                                                   her
                                           Ellen x Kate
Witnesses To Mark: mark
   { Chas T Difendafer
   { OL Johnson

Subscribed and sworn to before me this   24   day of   April   , 1905

OL Johnson
Notary Public.

Applications for Enrollment of Choctaw Newborn
Act of 1905   Volume XVI

NEW BORN AFFIDAVIT

No _____

CHOCTAW ENROLLING COMMISSION

IN THE MATTER OF THE APPLICATION FOR ENROLLMENT as a citizen of the Choctaw Nation, of   Ella Jones   born on the   28th day of   July   190 4

Name of father   Robert Jones   a citizen of   Choctaw   Nation, final enrollment No. _____   dec^d

Name of mother   Rena Jones, nee McClish   a citizen of   Choctaw   Nation, final enrollment No.   9235

Carbon   Postoffice.

AFFIDAVIT OF MOTHER

UNITED STATES OF AMERICA
    INDIAN TERRITORY
DISTRICT _____

I   Rena Jones, nee McClish dec^d , on oath state that I am   22   years of age and a citizen by   blood   of the   Choctaw   Nation, and as such have been placed upon the final roll of the   Choctaw   Nation, by the Honorable Secretary of the Interior my final enrollment number being   9235   ; that I am the lawful wife of   Robert Jones   , who is a citizen of the   Choctaw   Nation, and as such has been placed upon the final roll of said Nation by the Honorable Secretary of the Interior, his final enrollment number being _____ and that a   Female   child was born to me on the   28th day of   July   190 4; that said child has been named   Ella Jones   , and is now living.

WITNESSETH: Rena Jones
  Must be two witnesses { N.B. Ainsworth   by *Robert Jones*
  who are citizens   Lee Silmon

Subscribed and sworn to before me this, the   15   day of   March   , 190 5

James Bower
Notary Public.

My Commission Expires:
    Sept 23 - 1907

Applications for Enrollment of Choctaw Newborn
Act of 1905 Volume XVI

Affidavit of Attending Physician or Midwife

UNITED STATES OF AMERICA,
INDIAN TERRITORY,
Central   DISTRICT

I, Ellen Cate   a   Midwife on oath state that I attended on Mrs. Rena Jones *(nee McClish (deceased)* wife of Robert Jones on the 28 day of July , 190 4, that there was born to her on said date a Female child, that said child is now living, and is said to have been named Ella Jones

                      her
                 Ellen x Cate   M. D.
                    mark

Subscribed and sworn to before me this the 15 day of March 1905

                  James Bower
                           Notary Public.

WITNESSETH:
Must be two witnesses who are citizens and know the child.
{ Lee Silmon
{ N. B. Ainsworth

We hereby certify that we are well acquainted with Ellen Cate a Midwife and know her to be reputable and of good standing in the community.

               Must be two citizen { Lee Silmon
               witnesses.   { N.B. Ainsworth

7--NB--1224

Muskogee, Indian Territory, June 3, 1905.

Robert Jones,
    Vireton, Indian Territory.

Dear Sir:

    Referring to the application for the enrollment of your infant child, Ella Jones, born July 28, 1904, it is noted from the affidavits heretofore filed in this office that the mother of the applicant is dead.

    In this event it will be necessary that the affidavits of two persons, who are disinterested and not related to the applicant, who have actual knowledge of the facts that the child was born, the date of her birth; that she was living on March 4, 1905, and that Rena Jones, formerly Rena McClish, was her mother be filed in this office.

Applications for Enrollment of Choctaw Newborn
Act of 1905   Volume XVI

The evidence of Lewis Carnes to these facts has been filed. It will, therefore, be necessary that you secure the affidavit of another person. For this purpose there is inclosed herewith blank application.

In having the affidavit executed care should be exercised to see that all names are written in full, as they appear in the body of the affidavit, and in the event the person signing the same is unable to write, signature by mark must be attested by two witnesses. The affidavit must be executed before a Notary Public and the notarial seal and signature of the officer must be attached thereto.

You are advised that the Commission has been unable to identify you as a citizen of the Choctaw Nation. If you are a citizen of the Choctaw Nation and have selected lands in allotment you are requested to furnish the Commission with your roll number as the same appears upon your certificate of allotment.

This matter should receive your immediate attention as no further action can be taken relative to the enrollment of said child until the Commission is in receipt of this information.

        Respectfully,

Enc-FVK-26

7-NB-1224

        Muskogee, Indian Territory, July 26. 1905.

Robert Jones,
  Vireton, Indian Territory.

Dear Sir:

Your attention is called to a communication addressed to you by the Commission to the Five Civilized Tribes, under date of June 3, 1905, requesting additional evidence in the matter of the enrollment of your child, Ella Jones, born July 28, 1904.

In said letter you were requested that as your wife is dead you supply the affidavits of two persons who are not related to the applicant, and who have actual knowledge of the facts, that the child was born, the date of her birth, that she was living March 4, 1905, and that Rena Jones, formerly Rena McClish, was her mother.

You were informed that the evidence of Lewis Carnes to these facts has been filed in this office and that it would be necessary that you secure the affidavit of one other person; you were further requested to furnish this office with information to identify you as a citizen of the Choctaw Nation. No reply to this letter has been received.

Applications for Enrollment of Choctaw Newborn
Act of 1905   Volume XVI

This matter should receive your immediate attention as no further action can be taken relative to the enrollment of your said child until the evidence requested has been supplied.

Respectfully,

Commissioner.

Choctaw New Born 1225
    Daniel Hailey Walcott
    (Born May 17, 1903)

BIRTH AFFIDAVIT.

DEPARTMENT OF THE INTERIOR.
COMMISSION TO THE FIVE CIVILIZED TRIBES.

IN RE APPLICATION FOR ENROLLMENT, as a citizen of the   Choctaw   Nation, of Daniel Hailey Walcott , born on the 7th   day of May , 1903

Name of Father: Arthur Walcott   a citizen of the   Choctaw   Nation.
Name of Mother: Lutie Mary Walcott   a citizen of the   Choctaw   Nation.

Postoffice   Ardmore, Ind. Ter.

AFFIDAVIT OF MOTHER.

UNITED STATES OF AMERICA, Indian Territory,
    Southern   DISTRICT.

I, Lutie Mary Walcott , on oath state that I am 32 years of age and a citizen by blood , of the Choctaw Nation; that I am the lawful wife of Arthur Walcott , who is a citizen, by Intermarriage of the Choctaw Nation; that a male child was born to me on 7th day of May , 1903; that said child has been named Daniel Hailey Walcott , and was living March 4, 1905.

Lutie Mary Walcott

Witnesses To Mark:

275

Applications for Enrollment of Choctaw Newborn
Act of 1905 Volume XVI

Subscribed and sworn to before me this 24th day of April , 1905

H.C. Miller
Notary Public.

AFFIDAVIT OF ATTENDING PHYSICIAN OR MID-WIFE.

UNITED STATES OF AMERICA, Indian Territory,　}
Southern　　　　　　　　DISTRICT.

I, Harriet Frisbie , a Mid wife , on oath state that I attended on Mrs. Lutie Mary Walcott , wife of Arthur Walcott on the 7th day of May , 1903; that there was born to her on said date a male child; that said child was living March 4, 1905, and is said to have been named Daniel Hailey Walcott

Mrs Harriet Frisbie

Witnesses To Mark:
{

Subscribed and sworn to before me this 24th day of April , 1905

H.C. Miller
Notary Public.

Choctaw New Born 1226
　　Abbie Roebuck
　　(Born Dec. 9, 1902)

BIRTH AFFIDAVIT.
DEPARTMENT OF THE INTERIOR.
COMMISSION TO THE FIVE CIVILIZED TRIBES.

IN RE APPLICATION FOR ENROLLMENT, as a citizen of the Choctaw Nation, of Abbie Roebuck , born on the 9th day of December , 1902

Name of Father: William Roebuck　　　a citizen of the Choctaw Nation.
Name of Mother: Isabella Roebuck　　　a citizen of the Choctaw Nation.

Postoffice　　Nelson, Ind. Ter.

276

Applications for Enrollment of Choctaw Newborn
Act of 1905   Volume XVI

AFFIDAVIT OF MOTHER.

UNITED STATES OF AMERICA, Indian Territory, }
Central   DISTRICT.

I, Isabella Roebuck, on oath state that I am 38 years of age and a citizen by blood, of the Choctaw Nation; that I am the lawful wife of William Roebuck, who is a citizen, by blood of the Choctaw Nation; that a female child was born to me on 9th day of December, 1902; that said child has been named Abbie Roebuck, and was living March 4, 1905.

                      her
               Isabella x Roebuck

Witnesses To Mark: mark
{ Robert Anderson
  Vester W Rose

Subscribed and sworn to before me this 24th day of April, 1905

                  Wirt Franklin
                  Notary Public.

AFFIDAVIT OF ATTENDING PHYSICIAN OR MID-WIFE.

UNITED STATES OF AMERICA, Indian Territory, }
Central   DISTRICT.

I, W N John, a physician, on oath state that I attended on Mrs. Isabella Roebuck, wife of William Roebuck on the 9th day of December, 1902; that there was born to her on said date a female child; that said child was living March 4, 1905, and is said to have been named Abbie Roebuck

                  W.N. John

Witnesses To Mark:
{

Subscribed and sworn to before me this 24th day of April, 1905

                  Wirt Franklin
                  Notary Public.

Applications for Enrollment of Choctaw Newborn
Act of 1905 Volume XVI

Choctaw New Born 1227
    Abner Battiest
    (Born July 3, 1904)

BIRTH AFFIDAVIT.

DEPARTMENT OF THE INTERIOR.
COMMISSION TO THE FIVE CIVILIZED TRIBES.

IN RE APPLICATION FOR ENROLLMENT, as a citizen of the Choctaw Nation, of Abner Battiest, born on the 3rd day of July, 1904

Name of Father: Stephen Battiest   a citizen of the Choctaw Nation.
Name of Mother: Frances Battiest   a citizen of the Choctaw Nation.

    Postoffice   Finley, Ind. Ter.

AFFIDAVIT OF MOTHER.

UNITED STATES OF AMERICA, Indian Territory, ⎱
    Central   DISTRICT. ⎰

    I, Frances Battiest, on oath state that I am 21 years of age and a citizen by blood, of the Choctaw Nation; that I am the lawful wife of Stephen Battiest, who is a citizen, by blood of the Choctaw Nation; that a male child was born to me on 3rd day of July, 1904; that said child has been named Abner Battiest, and was living March 4, 1905. *and that no one but my said husband was present when said child was born.* her
                              Frances x Battiest
Witnesses To Mark: mark
  ⎰ Robert Anderson
  ⎱ Vester W Rose

    Subscribed and sworn to before me this 24th day of April, 1905

                      Wirt Franklin
                          Notary Public.

Applications for Enrollment of Choctaw Newborn
Act of 1905 Volume XVI

AFFIDAVIT OF ATTENDING PHYSICIAN OR MID-WIFE.

UNITED STATES OF AMERICA, Indian Territory,
Central DISTRICT.

I, Stephen Battiest , ~~a~~ _____ , on oath state that I attended on Mrs. Frances Battiest , ~~wife of~~ *my wife* on the 3rd day of July , 1904; that there was born to her on said date a male child; that said child was living March 4, 1905, and ~~is said to have~~ *has* been named Abner Battiest; *and that no one else was present when said child was born*

Stephen Battiest

Witnesses To Mark:
{

Subscribed and sworn to before me this 24th day of April , 1905

Wirt Franklin
Notary Public.

NEW-BORN AFFIDAVIT.

Number _____

Choctaw Enrolling Commission.

IN THE MATTER OF THE APPLICATION FOR ENROLLMENT, as a citizen of the Choctaw Nation, of Abner Battiest

born on the 3rd day of July 190 4

Name of father Stephen Battiest   a citizen of   Choctaw
Nation final enrollment No 5710
Name of mother Francis[sic] Battiest   a citizen of   Choctaw
Nation final enrollment No 5413

Postoffice Finley Ind Ter

AFFIDAVIT OF MOTHER.

UNITED STATES OF AMERICA,
INDIAN TERRITORY,
Central DISTRICT

I Francis Battiest on oath state that I am 21 years of age and a citizen by Blood of the Choctaw Nation, and as such have been placed upon the final roll of the Choctaw Nation, by the Honorable Secretary of the Interior my final enrollment number being 5413 ; that I am the lawful

Applications for Enrollment of Choctaw Newborn
Act of 1905 Volume XVI

wife of   Stephen Battiest   , who is a citizen of the   Choctaw   Nation, and as such has been placed upon the final roll of said Nation by the Honorable Secretary of the Interior, his final enrollment number being   5710   and that a   male   child was born to me on the   3rd day of   July 190 4 ; that said child has been named   Abner Battiest , and is now living.

                                                                                             her
                                                          Francis x Battiest

WITNESSETH: mark

Must be two   Wesly[sic] Edward
Witnesses who
are Citizens.   Mack McKenzie

         Subscribed and sworn to before me this   20th day of   Jan   190 5

                                               Su Finley
                                                                                        Notary Public.
My commission expires   May 1908

Affidavit of Attending Physician or Midwife

UNITED STATES OF AMERICA,
    INDIAN TERRITORY,
  Central   DISTRICT

       I,   Stephen Battiest   a
on oath state that I attended on Mrs.   Francis Battiest   wife of   Stephen Battiest on the   3rd day of   July   , 190 4, that there was born to her on said date a   male   child, that said child is now living, and is said to have been named   Abner Battiest

                                                               Stephen Battiest   M. D.

         Subscribed and sworn to before me this the   20th day of   Jan   1905

                                                 Su Finley
                                                                       Notary Public.

WITNESSETH:

Must be two witnesses   Wesley Sherred
who are citizens and
know the child.   Wesly[sic] Edward

       We hereby certify that we are well acquainted with   Wesley Sherred
a   Wesley Edward   and know   them   to be reputable and of good standing in the community.

                                        Must be two citizen   Goodman McKenzie
                                        witnesses.   Mack McKenzie

Applications for Enrollment of Choctaw Newborn
Act of 1905   Volume XVI

United States of America,)
)
Indian Territory,   ) ss.
)
Central District.   )

    I, Mack McKenzie, on oath state that I am twenty-three years of age and a citizen by blood of the Choctaw Nation; that my post office address is Finley, Indian Territory; that I am personally acquainted with Frances Battiest, wife of Stephen Battiest, and have known said parties about ten years; that since their marriage in 1900, I have lived within five miles of where they have lived, near Finley, Indian Territory, and have often visited them at their home; that I know of my own knowledge that on or about the 3rd day of July, 1904, there was born to the said Frances Battiest a male child; that said child is now living and has been named Abner Battiest.

                                                                                                                   Mack McKenzie

Subscribed and sworn to before me this 24th day of April, 1905.

                                                                              Wirt Franklin
                                                                              Notary Public.

United States of America,)
)
Indian Territory,   ) ss.
)
Central District.   )

    I, Josephus M. Sherred, on oath state that I am thirty-three years of age and a citizen by blood of the Choctaw Nation; that my post office address is Finley, Indian Territory; that I am personally acquainted with Frances Battiest, wife of Stephen Battiest, and have known both of said parties nearly all their lives; that since their marriage in 1900, I have lived within four miles of where they have lived, near Finley, Indian Territory, and have often visited them at their home; that I know of my own knowledge that on or about the 3rd day of July, 1904, there was born to the said Frances Battiest a male child; that said child is now living and has been named Abner Battiest.

                                                                                                        Josephus Sherred

Subscribed and sworn to before me this 24th day of April, 1905.

                                                                              Wirt Franklin
                                                                             Notary Public.

Applications for Enrollment of Choctaw Newborn
Act of 1905   Volume XVI

Choctaw New Born 1228
    John Winship
    (Born Feb. 18, 1905)

BIRTH AFFIDAVIT.

DEPARTMENT OF THE INTERIOR.
COMMISSION TO THE FIVE CIVILIZED TRIBES.

IN RE APPLICATION FOR ENROLLMENT, as a citizen of the Choctaw Nation, of John Winship, born on the 18 day of February, 1905

Name of Father: Sampson Winship   a citizen of the Choc Nation.
Name of Mother: Seyan Winship   a citizen of the Choc Nation.

Postoffice   Wilburton I.T.

AFFIDAVIT OF MOTHER.

UNITED STATES OF AMERICA, Indian Territory,
    Central   **DISTRICT.**

I, Seyan Winship, on oath state that I am 22 years of age and a citizen by blood, of the Choctaw Nation; that I am the lawful wife of Sampson Winship, who is a citizen, by blood of the Choctaw Nation; that a male child was born to me on 18 day of February, 1905; that said child has been named John Winship, and was living March 4, 1905.

                                  her
                          Seyan x Winship
Witnesses To Mark: mark
    Chas. T. Difendafer
    OL Johnson

Subscribed and sworn to before me this 24 day of April, 1905

                            OL Johnson
                            Notary Public.

Applications for Enrollment of Choctaw Newborn
Act of 1905   Volume XVI

AFFIDAVIT OF ATTENDING PHYSICIAN OR MID-WIFE.

UNITED STATES OF AMERICA, Indian Territory,
Central   DISTRICT.

I, Sarah Wade, a midwife, on oath state that I attended on Mrs. Seyan Winship, wife of Sampson Winship on the 18 day of February, 1905; that there was born to her on said date a male child; that said child was living March 4, 1905, and is said to have been named John Winship

                                          her
                                Sarah x Wade
Witnesses To Mark: mark
  { Chas. T. Difendafer
    OL Johnson

Subscribed and sworn to before me this 24 day of April, 1905

                              OL Johnson
                              Notary Public.

Choctaw New Born 1229
    Henry Simpson
    (Born Sept. 30, 1904)

BIRTH AFFIDAVIT.

DEPARTMENT OF THE INTERIOR.
COMMISSION TO THE FIVE CIVILIZED TRIBES.

IN RE APPLICATION FOR ENROLLMENT, as a citizen of the Choctaw Nation, of Henry Simpson, born on the 30 day of September, 1904

Name of Father: Robert Simpson   a citizen of the United States Nation.
Name of Mother: Lucinda Simpson *nee Newton*   a citizen of the Choctaw Nation.

                        Postoffice   Stuart I.T.

Applications for Enrollment of Choctaw Newborn
Act of 1905   Volume XVI

AFFIDAVIT OF MOTHER.

UNITED STATES OF AMERICA, Indian Territory, }
Central   DISTRICT.

  I, Lucinda Simpson nee Newton , on oath state that I am 20 years of age and a citizen by blood , of the Choctaw Nation; that I am the lawful wife of Robert Simpson , who is a citizen, by —— of the United States Nation; that a male child was born to me on 30 day of September , 1904; that said child has been named Henry Simpson , and was living March 4, 1905.

            Lucinda Simpson

Witnesses To Mark:
{

  Subscribed and sworn to before me this 24 day of April , 1905

            OL Johnson
              Notary Public.

AFFIDAVIT OF ATTENDING PHYSICIAN OR MID-WIFE.

UNITED STATES OF AMERICA, Indian Territory, }
Central   DISTRICT.

  I, Katie Newton , a midwife , on oath state that I attended on Mrs. Lucinda Simpson , wife of Robert Simpson on the 30 day of September , 1904; that there was born to her on said date a male child; that said child was living March 4, 1905, and is said to have been named Henry Simpson

            Katie Newton

Witnesses To Mark:
{

  Subscribed and sworn to before me this 24 day of April , 1905

            OL Johnson
              Notary Public.

Applications for Enrollment of Choctaw Newborn
Act of 1905   Volume XVI

NEW-BORN AFFIDAVIT.

Number...............

...Choctaw Enrolling Commission...

IN THE MATTER OF THE APPLICATION FOR ENROLLMENT, as a citizen of the Choctaw   Nation, of   Henry Simpson

born on the   30   day of   September   190 5[sic]

Choctaw

Name of father   Robt C Simpson   a citizen of   United States
Nation final enrollment No.   15218[sic]
Name of mother   Lucinda Simpson   a citizen of   Choctaw
Nation final enrollment No.   13218

Postoffice   Stuart IT

AFFIDAVIT OF MOTHER.

UNITED STATES OF AMERICA
INDIAN TERRITORY
Central   DISTRICT

I   Lucinda Simpson   , on oath state that I am   20   years of age and a citizen by   Birth   of the   Choctaw   Nation, and as such have been placed upon the final roll of the   Choctaw   Nation, by the Honorable Secretary of the Interior my final enrollment number being   13218 ; that I am the lawful wife of   Robt C Simpson   , who is a citizen of the   United States   Nation, and as such has been placed upon the final roll of said Nation by the Honorable Secretary of the Interior, his final enrollment number being   13218   and that a   Male   child was born to me on the   30"   day of   September   190 4; that said child has been named   Henry , and is now living.

Lue Simpson

Witnesseth.
Must be two ⎤   Samuel L Wooley
Witnesses who ⎥
are Citizens. ⎦   Mrs JH Bruce

Subscribed and sworn to before me this   16   day of   Jan   190 5

JH Elliott
Notary Public.

My commission expires: July 8 1908

Applications for Enrollment of Choctaw Newborn
Act of 1905   Volume XVI

AFFIDAVIT OF ATTENDING PHYSICIAN OR MIDWIFE

UNITED STATES OF AMERICA
INDIAN TERRITORY
Central   DISTRICT

I,   Katie Newton   a   Midwife on oath state that I attended on Mrs.   Lucinda Simpson   wife of   Robt C Simpson on the   30   day of   Sept   , 190 4 , that there was born to her on said date a   male   child, that said child is now living, and is said to have been named   Henry

                                            Katie Newton   *midwife*
            Subscribed and sworn to before me this, the   16"   day of
                Jan   190 5

WITNESSETH: JH Elliott   Notary Public.
Must be two witnesses   { Samuel L Wooley
who are citizens   { Mrs JH Bruce

We hereby certify that we are well acquainted with   Katie Newton a   Midwife   and know   her   to be reputable and of good standing in the community.

    Mrs JH Bruce   Stuart I.T.

    Samuel L Wooley   Stuart I.T

Choctaw New Born 1230
    Reno Cecil Wright
    (Born May 20, 1903)

BIRTH AFFIDAVIT.
DEPARTMENT OF THE INTERIOR.
COMMISSION TO THE FIVE CIVILIZED TRIBES.

IN RE APPLICATION FOR ENROLLMENT, as a citizen of the   Choctaw   Nation, of Reno Cecil Wright   , born on the   20   day of   May   , 1903

Name of Father: John Wright   a citizen of the United States Nation.
Name of Mother: Sarah Ann Margaret Wright   a citizen of the   Choctaw   Nation.

Applications for Enrollment of Choctaw Newborn
Act of 1905   Volume XVI

Postoffice   Atlee I.T.

AFFIDAVIT OF MOTHER.

UNITED STATES OF AMERICA, Indian Territory,
Southern   DISTRICT.

I, Sarah Ann Margaret Wright , on oath state that I am   22   years of age and a citizen by   blood   , of the   Choctaw   Nation; that I am the lawful wife of   John Wright   , who is a citizen, by .... of the   United States   Nation; that a male   child was born to me on   20   day of   May   , 1903; that said child has been named   Reno Cecil Wright   , and was living March 4, 1905.

Sarah Ann Margaret Wright

Witnesses To Mark:

Subscribed and sworn to before me this   31st day of   March   , 1905

W.A. Wilson
Notary Public.

AFFIDAVIT OF ATTENDING PHYSICIAN OR MID-WIFE.

UNITED STATES OF AMERICA, Indian Territory,
Southern   DISTRICT.

I,   John W. Moore   , a practicing physician   , on oath state that I attended on Mrs.   Sarah Ann Margaret Wright   , wife of   John Wright   on the 20   day of   May   , 1903; that there was born to her on said date a   male   child; that said child was living March 4, 1905, and is said to have been named   Reno Cecil Wright

John W Moore

Witnesses To Mark:

Subscribed and sworn to before me this   4th day of   April 4th [sic]   , 1905

W.A. Wilson
Notary Public.

Applications for Enrollment of Choctaw Newborn
Act of 1905   Volume XVI

Muskogee, Indian Territory, April 15, 1905.

John Wright,
 Atlee, Indian Territory.

Dear Sir:

Receipt is hereby acknowledged of the affidavits of Sarah Ann Margaret Wright and John W. Moore to the birth of Reno Acie[sic] Wright, son of John and Sarah Ann Margaret Wright, May 20, 1903.

It is stated in the affidavit of the mother that she is a citizen by blood of the Choctaw Nation. If this is correct you are requested to state under what name she was enrolled, the names of her parents, and if she has selected an allotment of the lands of the Choctaw or Chickasaw Nation to give her roll number as it appears on her allotment certificate.

Respectfully,

Chairman.

Choctaw New Born 1231
 Edward Carney
 (Born Feb. 1, 1905)

7-N.B.-1231.

DEPARTMENT OF THE INTERIOR,
COMMISSIONER TO THE FIVE CIVILIZED TRIBES.
Muskogee, Indian Territory, November 8, 1905.

In the matter of the application the application for the enrollment of Edward Carney as a citizen by blood of the Choctaw Nation.
 S. G. Smith, South McAlester, Indian Territory, appearing as attorney for the applicant.

Artemissa Carney being first duly sworn testified as follows:
Examination by the Commissioner.
Q What is your name? A Artemissa Carney.
Q How old are you? A Twenty-nine.
Q What is your postoffice address? A Quinton, Indian Ter.
Q Did you make application on May 2, 1905, for the enrollment of your child, Edward Carney? A Yes sir.

Applications for Enrollment of Choctaw Newborn
Act of 1905   Volume XVI

Q What was your maiden name? A Artemissa Lewis.
Q Did you afterwards marry Jonas Carney? A Yes sir.
Q Are you the mother of Edward Carney? A Yes sir.
Q Is Jonas Carney the father of Edward Carney? A Yes sir.
Q When were you married to Jonas Carney? A 1898 I thnk.

The mother of Edward Carney is identified as Artemissa Lewis upon Choctaw Care No. 3019, opposite No. 8851 upon the final roll as approved by the Secretary of the Interior.

----o----

Frances R. Lane upon oath states that as stenographer to the Commissioner to the Five Civilized Tribes she correctly reported the testimony in the above case and that the foregoing is an accurate transcript of her stenographic notes thereof.

Frances R Lane

Subscribed and sworn to before me this November 10, 1905.

Edward Merrick
Notary Public.

BIRTH AFFIDAVIT.

DEPARTMENT OF THE INTERIOR.
COMMISSION TO THE FIVE CIVILIZED TRIBES.

IN RE APPLICATION FOR ENROLLMENT, as a citizen of the Choctaw Nation, of Edward Carney, born on the 1st day of February, 1905

Name of Father: Jonas Carney   a citizen of the Choctaw Nation.
Name of Mother: Artemissa Carney   a citizen of the Choctaw Nation.

Postoffice   Quinton, Ind. Ter

AFFIDAVIT OF MOTHER.

UNITED STATES OF AMERICA, Indian Territory,
Western   DISTRICT.

I, Artemissa Carney, on oath state that I am about 29 years of age and a citizen by blood, of the Choctaw Nation; that I am the lawful wife of Jonas Carney, who is a citizen, by blood of the Choctaw Nation; that a male child was born to me on 1st day of February, 1905; that said child has been named Edward Carney, and was living March 4, 1905.

Applications for Enrollment of Choctaw Newborn
Act of 1905   Volume XVI

                                    her
                              Artemissa x Carney
Witnesses To Mark: mark
{ R W Shaw
{ Harrie Blake

    Subscribed and sworn to before me this 3 day of   February   , 1906

                                J.M. White
                                      Notary Public.

AFFIDAVIT OF ATTENDING PHYSICIAN OR MID-WIFE.

UNITED STATES OF AMERICA, Indian Territory, }
   Western   DISTRICT. }

    I,   Serena Carney   , a   midwife   , on oath state that I attended on Mrs. Artemissa Carney , wife of   Jonas Carney   on the 1st day of February , 1905; that there was born to her on said date a   male   child; that said child was living March 4, 1905, and is said to have been named Edward Carney

                                   her
                            Serena x Carney
Witnesses To Mark: mark
{ R W Shaw
{ Harrie Blake

    Subscribed and sworn to before me this 3 day of   February   , 1906

                                J.M. White
                                    Notary Public.

BIRTH AFFIDAVIT.
                        DEPARTMENT OF THE INTERIOR.
              COMMISSION TO THE FIVE CIVILIZED TRIBES.

    IN RE APPLICATION FOR ENROLLMENT, as a citizen of the   Choctaw   Nation, of Edward Carney   , born on the 1 day of February , 1905

Name of Father: Jonas Carney   a citizen of the   Choctaw   Nation.
Name of Mother: Artemissa Carney   a citizen of the   Choctaw   Nation.

                       Postoffice   Quinton, Ind. T.

Applications for Enrollment of Choctaw Newborn
Act of 1905 Volume XVI

AFFIDAVIT OF MOTHER.

UNITED STATES OF AMERICA, Indian Territory,
Western DISTRICT.

I, Artemissa Carney, on oath state that I am 28 years of age and a citizen by In=termarriage, of the Choctaw Nation; that I am the lawful wife of Jonas Carney, who is a citizen, by blood of the Choctaw Nation; that a Male child was born to me on 1st day of February, 1905; that said child has been named Edward Carney, and was living March 4, 1905.

                                        her
Witnesses To Mark: Artemissa x Carney
  { Allen Carney   mark
  { Ellar Carney

Subscribed and sworn to before me this 22 day of April, 1905

                                 J.M. White
                                 Notary Public.

AFFIDAVIT OF ATTENDING PHYSICIAN OR MID-WIFE.

UNITED STATES OF AMERICA, Indian Territory,
Western DISTRICT.

I, Serena Carney, a Midwife, on oath state that I attended on Mrs. Artemissa Carney, wife of Jonas Carney on the 1st day of February, 1905; that there was born to her on said date a Male child; that said child was living March 4, 1905, and is said to have been named Edward Carney

                                        her
Witnesses To Mark: Serena x Carney
  { Allen Carney   mark
  { Serena Carney

Subscribed and sworn to before me this 22 day of April, 1905

                                 J.M. White
                                 Notary Public.

Applications for Enrollment of Choctaw Newborn
Act of 1905 Volume XVI

BIRTH AFFIDAVIT.

DEPARTMENT OF THE INTERIOR.
COMMISSION TO THE FIVE CIVILIZED TRIBES.

IN RE APPLICATION FOR ENROLLMENT, as a citizen of the Choctaw Nation, of Edward Carney, born on the 1st day of February, 1905

Name of Father: Jonas Carney   a citizen of the Choctaw Nation.
Name of Mother: Artimissa Carney nee Lewis   a citizen of the Choctaw Nation.

Postoffice   Quinton, I. T.

AFFIDAVIT OF MOTHER.

UNITED STATES OF AMERICA, Indian Territory,
Western DISTRICT.

I, Artimissa Carney, nee Lewis, on oath state that I am 28 years years of age and a citizen by blood, of the Choctaw Nation; that I am the lawful wife of Jonas Carney, who is a citizen, by blood of the Choctaw Nation; that a Male child was born to me on 1st day of February, 1905, that said child has been named Edward Carney, and is now living.

           her
         Artimissa x Carney
Witnesses To Mark: mark
  (Name Illegible)
  A. V. Stewart

Subscribed and sworn to before me this 23rd day of September, 1905.

         (Name Illegible)
         Notary Public.

AFFIDAVIT OF ATTENDING PHYSICIAN OR MID-WIFE.

UNITED STATES OF AMERICA, Indian Territory,
Western DISTRICT.

I, Serena Carney, a midwife, on oath state that I attended on Mrs. Artimissa Carney, nee Lewis, wife of Jonas Carney on the 1st day of February, 1905; that there was born to her on said date a Male child; that said child is now living and is said to have been named Edward Carney

          her
        Serena x Carney
          mark

Applications for Enrollment of Choctaw Newborn
Act of 1905 Volume XVI

Witnesses To Mark:
{ *(Name Illegible)*
  A.V. Stewart

Subscribed and sworn to before me this 23rd day of September , 1905.

(Name Illegible)
Notary Public.

In the matter of the application of Edward Carney for enrollment as a citizen by blood of the Choctaw Nation.

United States of America   *

Indian Territory   SS

Western Judicial District   *

On this the 4th. day of October, 1905, before me, J.M. White , a Notary Public in and for the Western District of the Indian Territory appeared in person Jonas Carney and Artimissa Carney nee Lewis, who being first duly sworn on oath depose and say; that affiants are husband and wife and that they were united in the bonds of matrimony at the Middle Sansbois church, about 3 miles southeast of the present site of the town of Quinton, Indian Territory, on about the 20th. day of November, 1898, by one, L. W. Cobb, a Choctaw minister of the gospel; that affiants do not remember the exact date of said marriage, other than that said marriage was consumated[sic] in the year 1898 and in the month of November of said year; that there were present as witnesses to said marriage on said date, among others, the following named persons, to wit: Sim Colbert, Joe Moore, Morton Carney, Coleman Riddle and Ishem Perry.

That the above named applicant is the lawful child of affiants.

That affiants were married according to the laws of the Choctaw Nation and have at all times since said date lived together as husband and wife.

That affiants are unable to produce any certificate by way of evidence to marriage.

Executed in presence of .
ON Nelson
W.A. King

her
Artimissa x Carney
mark
Jonas Carney

Subscribed and sworn to before me this 4th. day of November, 1905.

J.M. White

Applications for Enrollment of Choctaw Newborn
Act of 1905   Volume XVI

Notary Public.

In the Matter of the Application of Edward Carney for enrollment as a citizen by blood of the Choctaw Nation.

United States of America   *
Indian Territory   *   SS
   Central   Judicial District   *

On this the 7th day of November, 1905 [Oct.] before me   A.J. Arnote , a Notary Public in and for the said District and Territory appeared L.W. Cobb who being first duly sworn on oath deposes and says; that he is of the age of 57 years and that his place of residence is   Antlers , Indian Territory; affiant further states that he is a stenographer to the Commission to the Five Civilized Tribes, and that the above and foregoing is a true transcript of his stenographic notes taken in said case on said date. Choctaw minister of the gospel and that one or about the 20th. day of November, 1898, at the Middle Sansbois church about 3 miles southeast of the present site of the town of Quinton, Indian Territory, he united in the bonds of matrimony one Jonas Carney and one, Artimissa Lewis; that said parties were lawfully married according to the laws of the Choctaw Nation.

L.W. Cobb

Subscribed and sworn to before me this 7th day of November [Oct.] 1905.

A.J. Arnote
Notary Public.

In the matter of the application of Edward Carney for enrollment as a citizen by blood of the Choctaw Nation.

United States of America   *
Indian Territory   *   SS
Western Judicial District.   *

On   this   10th   day of   October   1906 [January] before me_____, a Notary Public in and for the said District and Territory appeared   Joe Moore   , who being first duly sworn on oath deposes and says; that he is of the age of 46 years; that his place of residence is near Quinton Indian Territory. Affiant further states that he is a Choctaw citizen by blood of the Choctaw Nation, and in no ways interested in the results of the application of the said Edward Carney. Affiant further states that on or about the 20th, day of Nov. 1898, at the middle San Bois' Church about three miles southeast of the present site of Quinton Indian Territory, he attended as a witness at the marriage of Jonas Carnes and Artimissa Lewis, by one L. W. Cobb a

Applications for Enrollment of Choctaw Newborn
Act of 1905   Volume XVI

Choctaw Minister of the Gospel, and among others present who witnessed said marriage ceremony were the following:

Sim Colbert, Chas Bascom, Morton Carney and Isham Perry

Attest
Guy A. Curry
Robert Carney *sworn*

Joe x Moore

Subscribed and ^ to before me this   10 day of January, 1906

J.M. White
Notary Public.

In the matter of the application of Edward Carney for enrollment as a citizen by blood of the Choctaw Nation.

United States of America   *
Indian Territory   *   SS
Western Judicial District. *

On this   16th   day of October 1906 *January* before me *(Name Illegible)*, a Notary Public in and for the said District and Territory appeared Charles Bascom, who being first duly sworn on oath deposes and says; that he is of the age of   31   years; that his place of residence is near Quinton Indian Territory. Affiant further states that he is a Choctaw citizen by blood of the Choctaw Nation, and in no ways interested in the results of the application of the said Edward Carney. Affiant further states that on or about the 20th, day of Nov. 1898, at the middle San Bois' Church about three miles southeast of the present site of Quinton Indian Territory, he attended as a witness at the marriage of Jonas Carnes and Artimissa Lewis, by one L. W. Cobb a Choctaw Minister of the Gospel, and among others present who witnessed said marriage ceremony were the following:

Charles Bascom

sworn
Subscribed and ^ to before me this 16th day of January, 1906

(Name Illegible)
Notary Public.

Applications for Enrollment of Choctaw Newborn
Act of 1905 Volume XVI

7-NB-1231

Muskogee, Indian Territory, June 1, 1905.

Jonas Carney,
    Quinton, Indian Territory.

Dear Sir:

    Referring to your application for the enrollment of your infant child, Edward Carney, born February 1, 1905, it is noted from the affidavits heretofore filed in this office that the applicant claims through you.

    In this event it will be necessary that you file in this office, either the original, or a certified copy of the license and certificate of your marriage to the applicant's mother, Artemissa Carney.

                        Respectfully,

                                  Chairman.

Muskogee, Indian Territory, July 26, 1905.

James Carney,
    Quinton, Indian Territory.

Dear Sir:

    Your attention is called to a communication addressed to you by the Commission to the Five Civilized Tribes under date of June 1, 1905, in which you were requested to furnish either the original or a certified copy of the license and certificate of your marriage to your wife Artimissa Carney, for filing in support of the application for enrollment of your infant child, Edward Carney, born February 1, 1905. No reply to this letter has been received.

    The matter should receive your immediate attention as no further action can be taken relative to the enrollment of your said child until this evidence is supplied.

                        Respectfully,

                                  Commissioner.

Applications for Enrollment of Choctaw Newborn
Act of 1905 Volume XVI

7-NB-1231.

Muskogee, Indian Territory, September 18, 1905

Guy A. Curry,
    Attorney at Law,
        Quinton, Indian Territory.

Dear Sir:

    Receipt is hereby acknowledged of your letter of the 9th instant in which you state that you have been retained by the applicant as attorney in the matter of the application for the enrollment of Edward Carney, son of Jonas and Artemissa Carney, for enrollment as a citizen by blood of the Choctaw Nation and you request to be advised of the status of this case and what evidence is necessary to be supplied.

    In reply to your letter you are advised that this office has twice requested Jonas Carney, Quinton, Indian Territory, evidence of the marriage between himself and Artemissa Carney, the mother of said Edward Carney, and to such request no response has been made.

    From a careful examination of the proof of birth on file in this case it appears that the signatures, with the exception of one, Eller Carney, to the marks of affiants Artemissa Carney and Serena Carney, are all in one handwriting and appear to have been written by the notary public before whom the affidavits were sworn to.

    You are therefore advised that in addition to the evidence of marriage, above referred to, it will be necessary for you to furnish this office with proper proof of the birth of said Edward Carney and if the mother of the child and the attending midwife at his birth are unable to write and their signatures are by mark such signatures must be attested by two disinterested persons who can write.

                    Respectfully,

                            Acting Commissioner.

B C
Env.

Applications for Enrollment of Choctaw Newborn
Act of 1905   Volume XVI

7-NB-1231

Muskogee, Indian Territory, January 19, 1906.

Jonas Carney,
 Quinton, Indian Territory.

Dear Sir:

There is inclosed herewith for execution affidavit partially filled out to the birth of your child Edward Carney February 1, 1905.

You are advised that in the affidavits executed April 22, 1905, before J. M. White, Notary Public, the signature by mark of Serena Carney is witnessed by Allen Carney and Serena Carney. Please give this matter your immediate attention and see that signatures by mark are attested by two witnesses who can sign their own names.

Respectfully,

Commissioner.

EB 1-18.

7-NB-1231

Muskogee, Indian Territory, January 24, 1906.

Seymour G. Smith,
 South McAlester, Indian Territory.

Dear Sir:

Receipt is hereby acknowledged of your letter of January 14, 1906, asking if Edward Carney, son of Jonas and Artemissia[sic] Carney has been approved and can make selection of allotment.

In reply to your letter you are advised that it appears from the affidavits heretofore filed in this case that Serena Carney has witnessed her own signature by mark must be attested by two witnesses. to the affidavit of the midwife and new affidavits partially filled out were forwarded Jonas Carney on January 19, 1906 at Quinton and he was requested to have the same executed being careful to see that the signatures by mark were attested by disinterested witnesses who could sign their own names. Upon receipt of the additional evidence requested the enrollment of this child will receive further consideration.

Respectfully,

Acting Commissioner.

Applications for Enrollment of Choctaw Newborn
Act of 1905   Volume XVI

7-NB-1231

Muskogee, Indian Territory, February 3, 1906.

Guy A. Curry,
    Quinton, Indian Territory.

Dear Sir:

    Receipt is hereby acknowledged of your letter of January 30, 1906, inclosing affidavits of Artimissa Carney and Serena Carney to the birth of Edward Carney, February 1, 1905; also affidavits of Artimissa Carney, L. W. Dobb, Charles Bascom and Joe Moore to the marriage of Jonas Carney and Artimissa Lewis about November 20, 1898 and the same have been filed with the record in the matter of the application for the enrollment of Edward Carney as a new born citizen of the Choctaw Nation.

                      Respectfully,

                                Acting Commissioner.

7-NB-1231

Muskogee, Indian Territory, February 8, 1906.

Jonas Carney,
    Quinton, Indian Territory.

Dear Sir:

    Receipt is hereby acknowledged of the affidavits of ArtiMissa[sic] Carney and Serena Carney to the birth of Edward Carney, son of yourself and Artimissa Carney, February 1, 1905, and the same have been filed with the records in the matter of the enrollment of said child.

                      Respectfully,

                                Acting Commissioner.

Applications for Enrollment of Choctaw Newborn
Act of 1905 Volume XVI

7-4596.

Muskogee, Indian Territory, April 28, 1905.

Jonas Carney,
 Quinton, Indian Territory.

Dear Sir:

Receipt is hereby acknowledged of the affidavits of Artemissa Carney and Serena Carney to the birth of Edward Carney, son of Jonas and Artemissa Carney, February 1, 1905, and the same have been filed with our records as an application for the enrollment of said child.

Respectfully,

Chairman.

7-NB-1231

Muskogee, Indian Territory, June 12, 1906.

Guy A. Curry,
 Quinton, Indian Territory.

Dear Sir:

Receipt is hereby acknowledged of your letter of May 24, 1906, asking the status of the application for the enrollment of Edward Carney, child of Jonas and Artemissa Carney.

In reply to your letter you are advised that the name of Edward Carney, child of Jonas and Artemissa Carney will be placed upon the next schedule of new born citizens of the Choctaw Nation under the act of March 3, 1905, which is prepared for forwarding to the Secretary of the Interior, and you will be notified when his enrollment is approved by the Department.

Respectfully,

Commissioner.

Applications for Enrollment of Choctaw Newborn
Act of 1905   Volume XVI

Choctaw New Born 1232
   Burnnie Lee Lloyd
   (Born March 15, 1903)

BIRTH AFFIDAVIT.
                               DEPARTMENT OF THE INTERIOR.
                        COMMISSION TO THE FIVE CIVILIZED TRIBES.

IN RE APPLICATION FOR ENROLLMENT, as a citizen of the   Choctaw   Nation, of Burnnie Lee Lloyd   , born on the   15   day of   March   , 1903

Name of Father: John M. Lloyd   a citizen of the   Choctaw   Nation.
Name of Mother: Ida Lloyd   a citizen of the   Choctaw   Nation.

                        Postoffice   Bennington I.T.

                        AFFIDAVIT OF MOTHER.

UNITED STATES OF AMERICA, Indian Territory,
   Central   DISTRICT.

I,   Ida Lloyd   , on oath state that I am   29   years of age and a citizen by Blood   , of the   Choctaw   Nation; that I am the lawful wife of   John M. Lloyd   , who is a citizen, by Marriage   of the   Choctaw   Nation; that a   male child was born to me on   15th day of   March   , 1903; that said child has been named   Burnnie Lee Lloyd   , and was living March 4, 1905.

                        Ida Lloyd
Witnesses To Mark:

   Subscribed and sworn to before me this 8th day of   Apr   , 1905

                        JW Lloyd
                                Notary Public.

                        AFFIDAVIT OF ATTENDING PHYSICIAN OR MID-WIFE.

UNITED STATES OF AMERICA, Indian Territory,
   Central   DISTRICT.

I,   B.C. Rutherford   , a Physician   , on oath state that I attended on Mrs.   Ida Lloyd   , wife of   John M Lloyd   on the   15th day of   March   ,

Applications for Enrollment of Choctaw Newborn
Act of 1905   Volume XVI

1903; that there was born to her on said date a   male   child; that said child was living March 4, 1905, and is said to have been named   Burnnie Lee Lloyd

B.C. Rutherford M.D.

Witnesses To Mark:
{

Subscribed and sworn to before me this 8th day of   Apr   , 1905

JW Lloyd
Notary Public.

7-5443.

Muskogee, Indian Territory, April 28, 1905.

John M. Lloyd,
    Bennington, Indian Territory.

Dear Sir:

    Receipt is hereby acknowledged of your letter of April 15, 1905 enclosing affidavits of Ida Lloyd and B. C. Rutherford to the birth of Burnnie Lee Lloyd, son of John M. and Ida Lloyd, Indian Territory March 15, 1903, and the same have been filed with our records as an application for the enrollment of said child.

Respectfully,

Chairman.

<u>Choctaw New Born 1233</u>
    Fannie Putman
    (Born January 21, 1903)

Applications for Enrollment of Choctaw Newborn
Act of 1905 Volume XVI

BIRTH AFFIDAVIT.

Department of the Interior,
COMMISSION TO THE FIVE CIVILIZED TRIBES.

IN RE APPLICATION FOR ENROLLMENT, as a citizen of the Choctaw Nation, of Fannie Putman , born on the 21st day of Jan. , 190 3

Name of Father: S.G. Putman   a citizen of the Choctaw Nation.
Name of Mother: Susan Putman   a citizen of the Choctaw Nation.

Post-Office: Midland, Chicasaw Nationan,I.T.[sic]

AFFIDAVIT OF MOTHER.

UNITED STATES OF AMERICA,
   INDIAN TERRITORY,
  Southern   District.

I, Susan Putman -*11089* , on oath state that I am Twenty years of age and a citizen by blood , of the Choctaw Nation; that I am the lawful wife of S.G. Putman , who is a citizen, by Inter-married of the Choctaw Nation; that a female child was born to me on 21st day of Jan. , 190 3, that said child has been named Fannie Putman , and is now living.

                                                 Susan Putman

WITNESSES TO MARK:
  Mattie Hart

Subscribed and sworn to before me this 21 *day of* April , 190 5

                                                 John Casteel
                                                  Notary Public.

AFFIDAVIT OF ATTENDING PHYSICIAN OR MID-WIFE.

UNITED STATES OF AMERICA,
   Central TERRITORY,
  ~~Southern~~   District.

I, Dr.------Wallace , a Phycian[sic] , on oath state that I attended on Mrs. Susan Putman , wife of S.G. Putman on the 21st day of Jan. ,190 3; that there was born to her on said date a female child; that said child is now living and is said to have been named Fannie Putman

                                                 W.M. Wallace M.D.

Applications for Enrollment of Choctaw Newborn
Act of 1905 Volume XVI

WITNESSES TO MARK:

{

Subscribed and sworn to before me this 19 day of   April   , 190 5

My com expires
July 9th 1908

W.E. Larecy
Notary Public.

~~7-5906.~~

Muskogee, Indian Territory, April 27, 1905.

S. G. Putman,
    Midland, Indian Territory.

Dear Sir:

    Receipt is hereby acknowledged of the affidavits of Susan Putman and W. M. Wallace to the birth of Fannie Putman, daughter of S. G. Putman and Susan Putman, January 21, 1903, and the same have been filed with our records as an application for the enrollment of said child.

                Respectfully,

                                      Chairman.

7-NB-1233

Muskogee, Indian Territory, August 2, 1905.

S. G. Putman,
    Midland, Indian Territory.

Dear Sir:

    Receipt is hereby acknowledged of your letter of July 25, 1905, asking if Fannie Putman has been approved.

    In reply to your letter you are advised that on July 22, 1905, the Secretary of the Interior approved the enrollment of your child Fannie Putman as a citizen by blood of the Choctaw Nation and selection of allotment may now be made in her behalf in accordance with the rules and regulations governing the selection of allotments and the designation of homesteads in the Choctaw and Chickasaw Nations.

                Respectfully,

                                      Commissioner.

Applications for Enrollment of Choctaw Newborn
Act of 1905 Volume XVI

Choctaw New Born 1234
    Ruby Grace Woods
    (Born Feb. 26[sic], 1903)

BIRTH AFFIDAVIT.

DEPARTMENT OF THE INTERIOR.
COMMISSION TO THE FIVE CIVILIZED TRIBES.

IN RE APPLICATION FOR ENROLLMENT, as a citizen of the   Choctaw   Nation, of Ruby Grace Woods   , born on the 23   day of February, 1903

Name of Father: Simon H Woods   a citizen of the Choctaw Nation.
Name of Mother: Nancy A Woods   a citizen of the Choctaw Nation.

                     Postoffice   Talihina I.T.

AFFIDAVIT OF MOTHER.

UNITED STATES OF AMERICA, Indian Territory, }
    Central   DISTRICT.

    I, Nancy A Woods   , on oath state that I am 24   years of age and a citizen by Blood   , of the Choctaw   Nation; that I am the lawful wife of   Simon H Woods   , who is a citizen, by Blood   of the   Choctaw   Nation; that a female   child was born to me on 23   day of February   , 1903; that said child has been named Ruby Grace Woods   , and was living March 4, 1905.

                     Nancy A Woods

Witnesses To Mark:
{

    Subscribed and sworn to before me this 22 day of April   , 1905

                     Sam T. Roberts Jr
                     Notary Public.

AFFIDAVIT OF ATTENDING PHYSICIAN OR MID-WIFE.

UNITED STATES OF AMERICA, Indian Territory, }
    Central   DISTRICT.

    I, Parlean Green   , a Midwife   , on oath state that I attended on Mrs. Nancy A Woods   , wife of Simon H Woods   on the 23   day of

Applications for Enrollment of Choctaw Newborn
Act of 1905 Volume XVI

February   , 1903; that there was born to her on said date a   female   child; that said child was living March 4, 1905, and is said to have been named Ruby Grace Woods

               her
            Parlean x Green
Witnesses To Mark: mark
 { T.G. Hendricks
 { *(Name Illegible)*

  Subscribed and sworn to before me this 22 day of   April   , 1905

            Sam T. Roberts Jr
            Notary Public.

              7-2130.

      Muskogee, Indian Territory, April 27, 1905.

Simon H. Woods,
  Talihina, Indian Territory.

Dear Sir:

  Receipt is hereby acknowledged of the affidavits of Nancy A. Woods and Parlean Green to the birth of Ruby Grace Woods, daughter of Simon H. and Nancy A. Woods, February 23, 1903 and the same have been filed with our records as an application for the enrollment of said child.
        Respectfully,

              Chairman.

Choctaw New Born 1235
  Wyneter Wyers
  (Born July 28, 1904)

Applications for Enrollment of Choctaw Newborn
Act of 1905   Volume XVI

7-7908 7-121 PW

BIRTH AFFIDAVIT.

DEPARTMENT OF THE INTERIOR.
COMMISSION TO THE FIVE CIVILIZED TRIBES.

IN RE APPLICATION FOR ENROLLMENT, as a citizen of the   Choctaw   Nation, of Wyneter Wyers   , born on the 28 day of   July , 1904

Name of Father: John Wyers   a citizen of the Choctaw   Nation.
Name of Mother: Irene Wyers   a citizen of the Choctaw   Nation.

Postoffice   McCurtain Ind Ter

AFFIDAVIT OF MOTHER.

UNITED STATES OF AMERICA, Indian Territory, }
     Central   DISTRICT.

I,   Irene Wyers   , on oath state that I am 35 years of age and a citizen by blood , of the Choctaw   Nation; that I am the lawful wife of   John W Wyers , who is a citizen, by intermarriage of the   Choctaw   Nation; that a   female child was born to me on 28 day of July   , 1904; that said child has been named Wyneter Wyers , and was living March 4, 1905.

                               Irene Wyers
Witnesses To Mark:
{

Subscribed and sworn to before me this 4th day of   April   , 1905

                               OL Johnson
                                 Notary Public.

AFFIDAVIT OF ATTENDING PHYSICIAN OR MID-WIFE.

UNITED STATES OF AMERICA, Indian Territory, }
     Central   DISTRICT.

I,   Sarah J Gammel   , a midwife   , on oath state that I attended on Mrs. Irene Wyers   , wife of John W Wyers   on the 28 day of July , 1904; that there was born to her on said date a   female   child; that said child was living March 4, 1905, and is said to have been named Wyneter Wyers
                                  her
                          Sarah J x Gammel
                                  mark

Applications for Enrollment of Choctaw Newborn
Act of 1905   Volume XVI

Witnesses To Mark:
{ Floyd Nivens
{ G.W. McKibben

Subscribed and sworn to before me this 24   day of   April   , 1905

My commission   Frank E. Parke
Expires Feb. 2, 1908   Notary Public.

7-2711.

Muskogee, Indian Territory, April 27, 1905.

John W. Wyers,
   McCurtain, Indian Territory.

Dear Sir:

   Receipt is hereby acknowledged of the affidavits of Irene Wyers and Sarah J. Gammel to the birth of Wyneter Wyers, daughter of John W. and Irene Wyers, July 28, 1904, and the same have been filed with our records as an application for the enrollment of said child.

                      Respectfully,

                                Chairman.

<u>Choctaw New Born 1236</u>
   Mattie Williams
   (Born Jan. 16, 1903)

BIRTH AFFIDAVIT.
DEPARTMENT OF THE INTERIOR.
COMMISSION TO THE FIVE CIVILIZED TRIBES.

   IN RE APPLICATION FOR ENROLLMENT, as a citizen of the   Choctaw   Nation, of   Mattie Williams   , born on the 16   day of   January   , 1903

Name of Father: Thomas Williams   a citizen of the   Choctaw   Nation.
Name of Mother: Lucy Williams   a citizen of the   Choctaw   Nation.

                      Postoffice   Noah I.T.

Applications for Enrollment of Choctaw Newborn
Act of 1905   Volume XVI

AFFIDAVIT OF MOTHER.

UNITED STATES OF AMERICA, Indian Territory, }
  Central   DISTRICT.

I, Lucy Williams, on oath state that I am 29 years of age and a citizen by blood, of the Choctaw Nation; that I am the lawful wife of Thomas Williams, who is a citizen, by blood of the Choctaw Nation; that a Female child was born to me on 16th day of January, 1903; that said child has been named Mattie Williams, and was living March 4, 1905.

                                                    her
                                      Lucy x Williams

Witnesses To Mark: mark
{ J.M. Campbell
{ Paul Stephens   Noah I.T.

Subscribed and sworn to before me this 17th day of April, 1905

my commission   Jeff Gardner
expires 23rd Dec 1905   Notary Public.

AFFIDAVIT OF ATTENDING PHYSICIAN OR MID-WIFE.

UNITED STATES OF AMERICA, Indian Territory, }
  Central   DISTRICT.

                                                                                    was present

I, Newman Noah, a ...., on oath state that I ~~attended on~~ Mrs. Lucy Williams, wife of Thomas Williams on the 16th day of January, 1903; that there was born to her on said date a Female child; that said child was living March 4, 1905, and is said to have been named Mattie Williams

                                                 his
                                      Newman x Noah

Witnesses To Mark: mark
{ J.M. Campbell
{ Paul Stephens   Noah I.T.

Subscribed and sworn to before me this 17th day of April, 1905

my commission   Jeff Gardner
expires 23rd Dec 1905   Notary Public.

Applications for Enrollment of Choctaw Newborn
Act of 1905   Volume XVI

Choctaw New Born 1237
   Author C. Moran
   (Born April 20, 1904)

BIRTH AFFIDAVIT.

DEPARTMENT OF THE INTERIOR.
COMMISSION TO THE FIVE CIVILIZED TRIBES.

IN RE APPLICATION FOR ENROLLMENT, as a citizen of the   Choctaw   Nation, of Author C Moran   , born on the 20th day of   April , 1904

Name of Father: John W. Moran   a citizen of the   Choctaw   Nation.
Name of Mother: Emma Moran   a citizen of the   Choctaw   Nation.

Postoffice   Valliant I.T.

AFFIDAVIT OF MOTHER.

UNITED STATES OF AMERICA, Indian Territory,
   Central   DISTRICT.

I, Emma Moran   , on oath state that I am 26   years of age and a citizen by intermarriage   , of the   Choctaw   Nation; that I am the lawful wife of   John W. Moran   , who is a citizen, by Blood   of the   Choctaw   Nation; that a male   child was born to me on 20th day of   April   , 1904; that said child has been named Author C Moran   , and was living March 4, 1905.

Emma Moran

Witnesses To Mark:

Subscribed and sworn to before me this 15th day of April   , 1905

E.J. Gardner
   Notary Public.

AFFIDAVIT OF ATTENDING PHYSICIAN OR MID-WIFE.

UNITED STATES OF AMERICA, Indian Territory,
   Central   DISTRICT.

I, Lydia L. Felker   , a midwife   , on oath state that I attended on Mrs.   Emma Moran   , wife of   John W. Moran   on the 20th day of April ,

Applications for Enrollment of Choctaw Newborn
Act of 1905   Volume XVI

1904; that there was born to her on said date a male child; that said child was living March 4, 1905, and is said to have been named Author C. Moran

Lydia L. Felker

Witnesses To Mark:
{

Subscribed and sworn to before me this 22nd day of April , 1905

E.J. Gardner
Notary Public.

7-4010.

Muskogee, Indian Territory, April 27, 1905.

John W. Moran,
   Valliant, Indian Territory.

Dear Sir:

Receipt is hereby acknowledged of the affidavits of Emma Moran and Lydia L. Felker to the birth of Arthor[sic] C. Moran, son of John W. and Emma Moran, April 20, 1904, and the same have been filed with our records as an application for the enrollment of said child.

Respectfully,

Chairman.

Choctaw New Born 1238
   Zelpha Johnson
   (Born June 6, 1903)

Applications for Enrollment of Choctaw Newborn
Act of 1905   Volume XVI

BIRTH AFFIDAVIT.

DEPARTMENT OF THE INTERIOR.
COMMISSION TO THE FIVE CIVILIZED TRIBES.

IN RE APPLICATION FOR ENROLLMENT, as a citizen of the   Choctaw   Nation, of Zelpha Johnson   , born on the   6 day of   June   , 1903

Name of Father: J.P. Johnson   a citizen of the   U.S.   ~~Nation~~.
Name of Mother: Maud Johnson   a citizen of the   Choctaw   Nation.

Postoffice   Non Ind. Ter.

AFFIDAVIT OF MOTHER.

UNITED STATES OF AMERICA, Indian Territory, }
   Central   DISTRICT. }

I,   Mrs. Maud Johnson   , on oath state that I am   24   years of age and a citizen by   Blood   , of the   Choctaw   Nation; that I am the lawful wife of   J. P. Johnson   , who is a citizen, by   Blood   of the   U.S.   Nation; that a   Female   child was born to me on   6 day of June   , 1903; that said child has been named   Zelpha Johnson   , and was living March 4, 1905.

Maud Johnson

Witnesses To Mark:
{

Subscribed and sworn to before me this   22   day of   Apr   , 1905

C.E. McCain
Notary Public.

AFFIDAVIT OF ATTENDING PHYSICIAN OR MID-WIFE.

UNITED STATES OF AMERICA, Indian Territory, }
   Central   DISTRICT. }

I,   Mrs. H. E. Cartwright   , a   midwife   , on oath state that I attended on Mrs.   Maud Johnson   , wife of   J. P. Johnson   on the   6 day of June   , 1903; that there was born to her on said date a   Female   child; that said child was living March 4, 1905, and is said to have been named   Zelpha Johnson

H E Cartwright

Witnesses To Mark:
{

Applications for Enrollment of Choctaw Newborn
Act of 1905 Volume XVI

Subscribed and sworn to before me this 22 day of Apr   , 1905

C.E. McCain
Notary Public.

7-2744.

Muskogee, Indian Territory, April 27, 1905.

J. P. Johnson,
    Non, Indian Territory.

Dear Sir:

Receipt is hereby acknowledged of the affidavits of Maud Johnson and H.E. Cartwright to the birth of Zelpha Johnson, daughter of J. P. and Maud Johnson, June 6, 1903, and the same have been filed with our records as an application for the enrollment of said child.

Respectfully,

Chairman.

Choctaw New Born 1239
    Theodore R. Robinson
    (Born Aug. 1, 1904)

BIRTH AFFIDAVIT.
DEPARTMENT OF THE INTERIOR.
COMMISSION TO THE FIVE CIVILIZED TRIBES.

IN RE APPLICATION FOR ENROLLMENT, as a citizen of the   Choctaw   Nation, of Theodore Roosevelt Robinson   , born on the 1st   day of August   , 1904

Name of Father: John W. Robinson   a citizen of the Choctaw   Nation.
Name of Mother: Jane Robinson   a citizen of the Choctaw   Nation.

Postoffice   Hartshorne, Ind. Ter.

Applications for Enrollment of Choctaw Newborn
Act of 1905   Volume XVI

AFFIDAVIT OF MOTHER.

UNITED STATES OF AMERICA, Indian Territory,
Central   DISTRICT.

    I,   Jane Robinson   , on oath state that I am   41   years of age and a citizen by   blood   , of the   Choctaw   Nation; that I am the lawful wife of   John W. Robinson , who is a citizen, by intermarriage   of the   Choctaw   Nation; that a   male   child was born to me on   1st day of   August   , 1904; that said child has been named   Theodore Roosevelt Robinson   , and was living March 4, 1905.

                                  Jane Robinson

Witnesses To Mark:

    Subscribed and sworn to before me this 1st day of   May   , 1905

                                Wm J. Hulsey
                                Notary Public.

AFFIDAVIT OF ATTENDING PHYSICIAN OR MID-WIFE.

UNITED STATES OF AMERICA, Indian Territory,
Central   DISTRICT.

    I,   C. C. Savage   , a   Physician   , on oath state that I attended on Mrs.   Jane Robinson   , wife of   John W. Robinson   on the 1st day of May[sic] , 1905[sic]; that there was born to her on said date a   male   child; that said child was living March 4, 1905, and is said to have been named Theodore Roosevelt Robinson

                                  C C Savage

Witnesses To Mark:

    Subscribed and sworn to before me this 1st day of   May   , 1905

                                Wm J. Hulsey
                                Notary Public.

Applications for Enrollment of Choctaw Newborn
Act of 1905 Volume XVI

BIRTH AFFIDAVIT.

DEPARTMENT OF THE INTERIOR.
COMMISSION TO THE FIVE CIVILIZED TRIBES.

IN RE APPLICATION FOR ENROLLMENT, as a citizen of the Choctaw Nation, of Theodore R Robinson , born on the 1st day of August , 1904

Name of Father: John W. Robinson a citizen of the Choctaw Nation.
Name of Mother: Jane Robinson a citizen of the Choctaw Nation.

Postoffice Hartshorne, Ind. Terry.

AFFIDAVIT OF MOTHER.

UNITED STATES OF AMERICA, Indian Territory, }
 Central DISTRICT.

I, Jane Robinson , on oath state that I am 41 years of age and a citizen by Blood , of the Choctaw Nation; that I am the lawful wife of John W. Robinson , who is a citizen, by Marriage of the Choctaw Nation; that a male child was born to me on 1st day of August , 1904; that said child has been named Theodore R Robinson , and was living March 4, 1905.

Jane Robinson

Witnesses To Mark:
{

Subscribed and sworn to before me this 22$^{\underline{d}}$ day of April , 1905

WR Patterson
Notary Public.

AFFIDAVIT OF ATTENDING PHYSICIAN OR MID-WIFE.

UNITED STATES OF AMERICA, Indian Territory, }
 Central DISTRICT.

I, C. C. Savage , a Physician , on oath state that I attended on Mrs. Jane Robinson , wife of John W. Robinson on the 1st day of August , 1904; that there was born to her on said date a male child; that said child was living March 4, 1905, and is said to have been named Theodore Roosevelt Robinson

Christopher C Savage M.C.

Applications for Enrollment of Choctaw Newborn
Act of 1905   Volume XVI

Witnesses To Mark:
{

Subscribed and sworn to before me this 22ᵈ day of   April   , 1905

WR Patterson
Notary Public.

BIRTH AFFIDAVIT.

DEPARTMENT OF THE INTERIOR.
COMMISSION TO THE FIVE CIVILIZED TRIBES.

IN RE APPLICATION FOR ENROLLMENT, as a citizen of the   Choctaw   Nation, of Theodore R Robinson   , born on the √ day of _____, 1 ____

Name of Father: John W. Robinson   a citizen of the   Choctaw   Nation.
Name of Mother: Jane Robinson   a citizen of the   Choctaw   Nation.

Postoffice   Hartshorne, Ind. Ter.

AFFIDAVIT OF MOTHER.

UNITED STATES OF AMERICA, Indian Territory,}
   Central   DISTRICT.}

I,   Jane Robinson   , on oath state that I am   41   years of age and a citizen by   blood   , of the   Choctaw   Nation; that I am the lawful wife of   John W. Robinson   , who is a citizen, by intermarriage   of the   Choctaw   Nation; that a   male   child was born to me on   1ˢᵗ   day of   August 1 , 1904; that said child has been named Theodore R Robinson   , and was living March 4, 1905.

Jane Robinson

Witnesses To Mark:
{

Subscribed and sworn to before me this 20ᵗʰ   day of   June   , 1905

Wm J. Hulsey
Notary Public.

Applications for Enrollment of Choctaw Newborn
Act of 1905   Volume XVI

AFFIDAVIT OF ATTENDING PHYSICIAN OR MID-WIFE.

UNITED STATES OF AMERICA, Indian Territory, }
    Central   DISTRICT. }

    I, C. C. Savage , a Physician , on oath state that I attended on Mrs. Jane Robinson , wife of John W. Robinson on the 1st day of May[sic] , 1905[sic]; that there was born to her on said date a male child; that said child was living March 4, 1905, and is said to have been named Theodore R Robinson

                                  C C Savage M.D.

Witnesses To Mark:

    Subscribed and sworn to before me this 20th day of June , 1905

                                  Wm J. Hulsey
                                        Notary Public.

                                                7-3163.

                    Muskogee, Indian Territory, April 27, 1905.

John W. Robinson,
    Hartshorne, Indian Territory.

Dear Sir:

    Receipt is hereby acknowledged of the affidavits of Jane Robinson and Christopher C. Savage to the birth of Theodore R. Robinson, son of John W. and Jane Robinson, August 1, 1904, and the same have been filed with our records as an application for the enrollment of said child.

                                Respectfully,

                                                   Chairman.

Applications for Enrollment of Choctaw Newborn
Act of 1905   Volume XVI

7 N.B. 1239.

Muskogee, Indian Territory, June 1, 1905.

John W. Robinson,
    Hartshorne, Indian Territory.

Dear Sir:

    Receipt is hereby acknowledged of the affidavits of Jane Robinson and C. C. Savage to the birth of Theodore Roosevelt Robinson, son of John W. and Jane Robinson, August 1, 1904, and the same have been filed with our records in the matter of the enrollment of said child.

                  Respectfully,

                  Commissioner in Charge.

7-NB-1239.

Muskogee, Indian Territory, June 13, 1905.

John W. Robinson,
    Hartshorne, Indian Territory.

Dear Sir:

    There is enclosed herewith for execution application for the enrollment of your infant child, Theodore R. Robinson.

    In the affidavits of May 1, 1905, heretofore filed in this office, the mother gives the date of the applicant's birth as August 1, 1904, while the attending physician gives it gives it[sic] as May 1, 1905. Both of the affidavits filed April 22, 1905, give it as August 1, 1904.

    In the enclosed application the date of birth is left blank. Please insert the correct date, and when the affidavits are properly executed return them to this office.

    In having these affidavits executed care should be exercised to see that all names are written in full, as they appear in the body of the affidavit, and in the event either of the persons signing the affidavit are unable to write, signatures by mark must be attested by two witnesses. Each affidavit must be executed before a Notary Public and the notarial seal and signature of the officer must be attached to each separate affidavit.

                  Respectfully,

                            Chairman.

Index

Anna Ardelia 205,206
B W 205,206
Margaret 205,206
HART, Mattie 184
HATFIELD, J G 165
HEISTEIN, Milton 244
HELTING, C 92
HENDERSON
   Ella 242,243
   Jos B 93
HENDRICKS, T G 306
HENSHAW, George A 35
HICKMAN
   E L 245,246
   Edwin L 248
HICKS, Holton J 159
HILL, Frank 157,158
HOGAN
   Sidney 226
   Sidney G 225,226
HOLCOMB, C L 50
HOLLAND, L B 73
HOMER, Sol J 58
HOOVER, J T 119,120,121
HOTEMA, Nancy 233
HOTUBBE, Allen 219
HOTUBBEE
   Allen 219,220,221,222,223,224
   Joe 220,221,224
   Joseph 219,220,221,222,223
   Nancy 220,221,222,224
   Nannie 222
   Nellie 219,220,221,222,223
HOWZE
   Jessie Myrtle 150,151,153
   Morris L 150,151,152,153
   Sophronia 150,151,152,153
   William Lee 152
   Willie Lee 150,152,153
HUDSON
   Peter J 222
   Peter W 220,221
HULSEY
   Cadiul 182
   Eula Cordelia 179,180
   Eulah 181,182
   Eulah Cordelia 166,167,169,171,
172,173,175,176,177,178,179,181,182
   H H 182
   Henry 166,167,168,169,170,171,
172,173,174,175,176,177,178,179,180
,181
   Henry H 170
   J C 171
   Lillie 172,173,174,180
   Lilly 166,169,175,177
   Lovicey 172
   Wm J 314,316,317
HUNT, L P 235,236
HUNTER
   Cicilia 211,212
   Juma 321
   Thos W 322
IRETON
   David R 24,25,26,27,28,29
   Frederick Henry 23,26,27,28,29
   Minnie A 25,26,28
   Minnie Ann 24,25,26,27,29
   Rufus Claude 23,24,25,26,29
IVEY, Mrs J N 30
IZARD, John C 119,120
JACK
   Allen 112,113,114,115,116
   Lauina 112,113,114
   Louina 114,115
   Louvina 116
   Martin 112,113,114,115,116
JACKSON
   Joseph 261,262,263,264,265,266
   Joseph R 266
   Lake 266
   Luke 260,261,262,263,264,265,266
   Rosie 261,262,263,264,265,266
JAMES
   Lorinda 189,191
   Lourinda 190
   W C 190,191
JEFFERSON
   Betsie 234,235,236,237
   Betsy 235
   Calvin 234,235,236,237,238
   Daniel 131
   Ida 234,235,236,237,238
JETER, J T 137

333

Applications for Enrollment of Choctaw Newborn
Act of 1905   Volume XVI

7 NB 1239

Muskogee, Indian Territory, June 24, 1905.

John W. Robinson,
    Hartshorne, Indian Territory.

Dear Sir:

    Receipt is hereby acknowledged of the affidavits of Jane Robinson and C. C. Savage to the birth of Theodore R. Robinson, son of John W. and Jane Robinson, August 1, 1904, and the same have been filed with our records in the matter of the enrollment of said child.

                      Respectfully,

                                    Chairman.

Choctaw New Born 1240
    Nalio Turley
    (Born Sept. 24, 1904)

7-3652.

Muskogee, Indian Territory, April 27, 1905.

J. D. Turley,
    Boswell, Indian Territory.

Dear Sir:

    Receipt is hereby acknowledged of the affidavits of Sissie Turley and Chas. Lynch to the birth of Nolia[sic] Turley, daughter of J. D. and Sissie Turley, September 24, 1904, and the same have been filed with our records as an application for the enrollment of said child.

                      Respectfully,

                                    Chairman.

Applications for Enrollment of Choctaw Newborn
Act of 1905 Volume XVI

Choctaw N B 1240

Muskogee, Indian Territory, June 26, 1905.

J. D. Turley,
    Boswell, Indian Territory.

Dear Sir:

    Receipt is hereby acknowledged of the affidavits of Sissie B. Turley and Charles S. Lynch to the birth of Nalia Turley, daughter of J. T[sic]. and Sissie B. Turley, September 24, 1904, and the same have been filed with in the matter of the enrollment of said child.

                  Respectfully,

                                  Chairman.

7-NB-1240.

Muskogee, Indian Territory, June 19, 1905.

J. D. Turley,
    Boswell, Indian Territory.

Dear Sir:

    There is enclosed herewith application for the enrollment of your infant child, Nalio[sic] Turley, born September 24, 1904.

    In the affidavits heretofore filed in this office the mother signs her name as Sissie Turley. In the enclosed affidavits it is inserted as Sissie B. Turley in compliance with the records of the Commission, in which manner you will please have her to sign.

    In having these affidavits executed care should be exercised to see that all names are written in full, as they appear in the body of the affidavit, and if either of the persons signing the affidavits is unable to write, signature by mark must be attested by two witnesses. Each affidavit must be executed before a Notary Public and the notarial seal and signature of the officer must be attached to each separate affidavit.

    You are requested to give this matter your immediate attention as no further action can be taken until these affidavits are filed with the Commission.

                  Respectfully,

                                  Chairman.

DeB--4/19.

Applications for Enrollment of Choctaw Newborn
Act of 1905   Volume XVI

BIRTH AFFIDAVIT.

DEPARTMENT OF THE INTERIOR.
COMMISSION TO THE FIVE CIVILIZED TRIBES.

IN RE APPLICATION FOR ENROLLMENT, as a citizen of the   Choctaw   Nation, of Nalia Turley   , born on the 24th day of September , 1904

Name of Father: J.D. Turley   a citizen of the   U.S.   ~~Nation~~.
Name of Mother: Sissie B. Turley   a citizen of the   Choctaw   Nation.

Postoffice   Boswell, I.T.

AFFIDAVIT OF MOTHER.

UNITED STATES OF AMERICA, Indian Territory, }
   Central   DISTRICT.

I, Sissie B. Turley , on oath state that I am 23 years of age and a citizen by blood , of the Choctaw Nation; that I am the lawful wife of J.D. Turley, who is a citizen, by .... of the U.S. Nation; that a female child was born to me on 24th day of September , 1904; that said child has been named Nalia Turley , and was living March 4, 1905.

                                  her
                            Sissie x Turley
Witnesses To Mark: mark
{ Juma Hunter
  Jas R Armstrong

Subscribed and sworn to before me this 8th day of April , 1905

                            JR Armstrong
                              Notary Public.

AFFIDAVIT OF ATTENDING PHYSICIAN OR MID-WIFE.

UNITED STATES OF AMERICA, Indian Territory, }
   Central   DISTRICT.

I, Chas S. Lynch , a M.D. , on oath state that I attended on Mrs. Sissie Turley , wife of JD Turley on the 24th day of September , 1904; that there was born to her on said date a female child; that said child was living March 4, 1905, and is said to have been named Nalia Turley

Applications for Enrollment of Choctaw Newborn
Act of 1905   Volume XVI

                           Chas Lynch MD

Witnesses To Mark:
{

    Subscribed and sworn to before me this   15   day of   April   , 1905

                          Thos W Hunter
                             Notary Public.

BIRTH AFFIDAVIT.

DEPARTMENT OF THE INTERIOR.
COMMISSION TO THE FIVE CIVILIZED TRIBES.

    IN RE APPLICATION FOR ENROLLMENT, as a citizen of the   Choctaw   Nation, of   Nalio Turley   , born on the   24   day of   Sept   , 1904

Name of Father: J.D. Turley   a citizen of the   U.S.   Nation.
Name of Mother: Sissie B. Turley   a citizen of the   Choctaw   Nation.

                  Postoffice   Boswell, I.T.

AFFIDAVIT OF MOTHER.

UNITED STATES OF AMERICA, Indian Territory,
    Central   DISTRICT.

    I,   Sissie B. Turley   , on oath state that I am   23   years of age and a citizen by   blood   , of the   Choctaw   Nation; that I am the lawful wife of   J.D. Turley, who is a citizen, by ———— of the   United States   Nation; that a   female   child was born to me on   24   day of   September   , 1904; that said child has been named   Nalio Turley   , and was living March 4, 1905.

                             her
                    Sissie B x Turley
Witnesses To Mark: mark
{ J M Harris
  G.T. Cox

    Subscribed and sworn to before me this   21st   day of   June   , 1905

                          Perry M Clark
                          Notary Public.

Applications for Enrollment of Choctaw Newborn
Act of 1905   Volume XVI

AFFIDAVIT OF ATTENDING PHYSICIAN OR MID-WIFE.

UNITED STATES OF AMERICA, Indian Territory,
Central DISTRICT.

I, Charles S. Lynch, a Physician, on oath state that I attended on Mrs. Sissie B. Turley, wife of J.D. Turley on the 24 day of September, 1904; that there was born to her on said date a female child; that said child was living March 4, 1905, and is said to have been named Nalio Turley

Charles S Lynch MD

Witnesses To Mark:
{ J M Harris

Subscribed and sworn to before me this 21st day of June, 1905

Perry M Clark
Notary Public.

Choctaw New Born 1241
    Max Leo Booker
    (Born Oct. 9, 1902)

BIRTH AFFIDAVIT.
DEPARTMENT OF THE INTERIOR.
COMMISSION TO THE FIVE CIVILIZED TRIBES.

IN RE APPLICATION FOR ENROLLMENT, as a citizen of the Choctaw Nation, of Max Leo Booker, born on the 9th day of October, 1902

Name of Father: John Booker   a citizen of the Choctaw Nation.
Name of Mother: Lourena L. Booker   a citizen of the Choctaw Nation.
              (nee Robinson)
                          Postoffice   Caddo, Indian Territory.

Applications for Enrollment of Choctaw Newborn
Act of 1905   Volume XVI

AFFIDAVIT OF MOTHER.

UNITED STATES OF AMERICA, Indian Territory, }
Central   DISTRICT.

I, Lourena L. Booker (nee Robinson), on oath state that I am 40 years of age and a citizen by blood, of the Choctaw Nation; that I ~~am~~ was the lawful wife of John Booker, when this child was born, who is a citizen, by marraige[sic] of the Choctaw Nation; that a male child was born to me on 9th day of October, 1902; that said child has been named Max Leo Booker, and was living March 4, 1905.

Lourena L Booker

Witnesses To Mark:
{

Subscribed and sworn to before me this 20th day of April, 1905

JL Rappolee
Notary Public.

AFFIDAVIT OF ATTENDING PHYSICIAN OR MID-WIFE.

UNITED STATES OF AMERICA, Indian Territory, }
Central   DISTRICT.

I, LeRoy Long, a Physician, on oath state that I attended on Mrs. Lourena L. Booker, wife of John Booker on the 9th day of October, 1902; that there was born to her on said date a male child; that said child was living March 4, 1905, and is said to have been named Max Leo Booker

LeRoy Long

Witnesses To Mark:
{

Subscribed and sworn to before me this 24th day of April, 1905

Brooks Fort
Notary Public.

Com Ex 3/6/07.

Applications for Enrollment of Choctaw Newborn
Act of 1905 Volume XVI

NEW-BORN AFFIDAVIT.

Number............

...Choctaw Enrolling Commission...

IN THE MATTER OF THE APPLICATION FOR ENROLLMENT, as a citizen of the Choctaw Nation, of Max Leo Booker

born on the 9th day of __October__ 190 2

Name of father John Booker   a citizen of   white
Nation final enrollment No. ~~13149~~
Name of mother Rena Booker *known as Robinson*   a citizen of   Choctaw
Nation final enrollment No. 13149

Postoffice   Caddo I.T.

AFFIDAVIT OF MOTHER.

UNITED STATES OF AMERICA
INDIAN TERRITORY
   Central   DISTRICT

     I   Rena Booker *known as Robinson*   , on oath state that I am 41 years of age and a citizen by blood of the Choctaw Nation, and as such have been placed upon the final roll of the Choctaw Nation, by the Honorable Secretary of the Interior my final enrollment number being 13149 ; that I am the lawful wife of John Booker , who is a citizen of the White Nation, and as such has been placed upon the final roll of said Nation by the Honorable Secretary of the Interior, his final enrollment number being ~~13149~~ and that a ~~female~~ child was born to me on the 9th day of October 190 2; that said child has been named Max Leo Booker , and is now living.

                              Rena Booker-Robison

Witnesseth.
   Must be two   }   J.J. Gardner
   Witnesses who
   are Citizens.   R.L. Gardner

Subscribed and sworn to before me this 16 day of Jan 190 5

                         W.A. Shoney
                               Notary Public.

My commission expires:
Jan 10, 1909

Applications for Enrollment of Choctaw Newborn
Act of 1905   Volume XVI

Affidavit of Attending Physician or Midwife

UNITED STATES OF AMERICA,
INDIAN TERRITORY,
Central   DISTRICT

I, Leroy Long   a   Physician on oath state that I attended on Mrs. Rena Booker   wife of   John Booker on the 9th day of   October   , 190 2, that there was born to her on said date a   male child, that said child is now living, and is said to have been named   Max Leo Booker

LeRoy Long   M. D.

Subscribed and sworn to before me this the   9th day of   February   1905

Brooks Fort
Notary Public.

WITNESSETH:
Must be two witnesses who are citizens and know the child.
J.J. Gardner
RL Gardner

We hereby certify that we are well acquainted with   Leroy Long a   Physician   and know   him   to be reputable and of good standing in the community.

Must be two citizen witnesses.
J.J. Gardner
R L Gardner

(The affidavit below typed as given.)

Commission to the Five Civilized Tribes:

In the matter of the application for the enrollment of Max Leo Booker.

Comes now Mrs Lourena L. Booker, who after first being duly sworn states on her other, that she is the identical person , whoes name appears upon the rolls of the Commission as Lourena L. Robinson, and that she was married to John Booker on the 20th day of October 1901,and that since the birth of the child Max Leo Booker, that John Booker and myself have seperated and that I have the child in my possession.

I have not our marriage certificate and do not know where it was recorded.

Lourena L. Booker

Applications for Enrollment of Choctaw Newborn
Act of 1905   Volume XVI

Subscribed and sworn to before me on this the 20th day of April 1905.

JL Rappolee
Notary Public.

COMMISSIONERS:
TAMS BIXBY,
THOMAS B. NEEDLES,
C.R. BRECKINBRIDGE.

WM. O. BEALL
Secretary

ADDRESS ONLY THE
COMMISSION TO THE FIVE CIVILIZED TRIBES.

DEPARTMENT OF THE INTERIOR,
COMMISSIONER TO THE FIVE CIVILIZED TRIBES.

$W^m O.B.$

REFER IN REPLY TO THE FOLLOWING:

7-4765.

Muskogee, Indian Territory, April 27, 1905.

John Booker,
    Caddo, Indian Territory.

Dear Sir:

    Receipt is hereby acknowledged of the affidavits of Lourena L. Booker and LeRoy Long to the birth of Max Leo Booker, son of John and Lourena L. Booker, October 9, 1902, and the same have been filed with our records as an application for the enrollment of said child.

Respectfully,

Tams Bixby   Chairman.

Index

AARON, John 78
ABNEY, T G 206
ADAIR, Anna 26,29
ADAMS
   Anna 79,80,81
   Elena 80
   Lauina 112,113
   Lillie 114,116
   Lilly 114
   Reuben 79,80,81
   Selena 79,81
AHEKATUBBY
   Emma 146,147,148,149,150
   John 146,147,148,149,150
   Willie 146,147,148,149,150
AINSWORTH, N B 272,273
ALLEN, Joe 185
ALVERSON, Noah 190,191
AMOS, Sidney 112
ANDERSON
   Lucy 220,222
   Robert 117,134,135,140,148,149, 154,213,214,277,278
   Sarah 53,54
   Wright 36,37
ANGELL, W H 63,69,189,190
ARMSTRONG
   J D 26,28
   J H 208,209
   J H, MD 208,209
   J R 16,19,20,22,321
   Jas R 321
   Jos R 16,20
ARNOTE, A J 82,294
ASHFORD, Thomas 101
ATOKO
   Betsey 80,81
   Sarphim 80
ATTAWAY, H W 206
AUTRY
   N A 95
   Nancie A 98
   Nancy A 95,97,98
BAILEY, David A 239
BALL, E J 211
BARLOW, G W 265
BASCOM
   Charles 295,299
   Chas 295
BATTIEST
   Abner 278,279,280,281
   Annie 153,154,155
   Frances 278,279,281
   Francis 279,280
   L L 131
   Louisa 153,154
   Morris 245,246,248
   Osborne 153,154
   Stephen 278,279,280,281
BEARDEN, Chas E 13,14
BEEMAN, T L 33,35
BEGLEY, John 109
BELL, George W 221,224
BENNETT
   Clifford Anderson 267,268
   Crecia Ann 267,268,269
   Lucy E 267,268,269
   Thomas 267,268,269
BENTON, Eveline 262
BISSELL, Alfred F 204
BIXBY, Tams 4,17,23,44,64,65,70,167, 169,175,176,177,179,232,327
BLAKE
   Harrie 290
   Lillie A 261
BLUE
   Levenia 47,49,50,51
   Levina 47,48
   Melvina 47,48,49,50
   Willie 48,50,51
   Willy 47,48,49,50
BOBO
   Lacey P 171,173,179
   Sacty B 182
BOGLER, Mr 170
BOHANAN
   Harmon J 138,139,140,141
   Harmon J, Jr 138,140
   Josie 156
   Lula 138,139,140,141
   Mrs Harmon J 139
BOHANON
   Emmeline 232
   Thomas B 146,147

Index

Willie 232
BOLGER, Mr 170
BOND, Ridgely 215,216,218
BOOKER
   John 323,324,325,326,327
   Lourena L 323,324,326,327
   Max Leo 323,324,325,326,327
   Rena 325,326
BOWER, James 41,48,89,185,203,254, 258,272,273
BOWERS, James 84
BOYD, C H 74
BOZARTH, C G 151,152,153
BRANNUM, C C 206
BRISTOW, J H 93,94
BROWN
   Dwight 192
   John T 15,20,21
   Mat 183,184,185,186,187,188
   Pearl 182,183,184,185,186,187,188
   Permalia 185
   Permelia 183,184,186,187,188
   Wm O 17
BRUCE, Mrs J H 285,286
BURNS
   Henry 112,196,197
   Jackson 164,165
   Laura 164,165
   Lona 28,29
   William 164,165
BUTLER
   J F 125,126,127,128,129,130
   J L 127
   Lizzie 125,126,127,128,129
   Mary 148
   Prince 147,148
   Rosey 124,125,126,127,128,129,130
BUTTLER
   J F 126,128
   Lizzie 126,127,128
   Rasey 128
   Rosey 126
BYBEE
   Ellis 132,133
   Nora 132,133
   Will D 132
BYINGTON

Ben 229,230
Cyrus 89,90
CAGLE, B H 265
CAMPBELL, J M 309
CARNES, Lewis 270,274
CARNEY
   Allen 291,298
   Artemissa 288,289,290,291,296, 297,300
   Artemissia 298
   ArtiMissa 299
   Artimissa 292,293,296,299
   Edward 288,289,290,291,292,293, 294,295,296,297,298,299,300
   Ellar 291
   Eller 297
   James 296
   Jonas 289,290,291,292,293,294,295, 296,297,298,299,300
   Morton 293,295
   Robert 295
   Serena ... 290,291,292,297,298,299,300
CARROLL
   Birdie 42,43,45,46,47,161,162
   Ernest 161,162,163,164
   Laura 43,161,162
   Laura L 162,163,164
   Mary E 160,162,163,164
   Mary Ernestine 161,162
   Miss B M 44,45
CARSHALL, S C 258
CARTER, Elizabeth 82,83,84
CARTWRIGHT
   H E 313
   Mrs H E 312
CASSELL
   J F 93
   J T 92,93,94
   Myrtle Parks 92,93,94
   Serena 92,93,94
CASTEEL, John 303
CATE, Ellen 273
CHOATE, Jincy 193,194,195,196,197
CLARK
   Edwin 240,241,242,243
   Edwin O 166,167
   Ella Louise 240,241,242

330

Ina Katharine 240,241,242
Ina Katherina 243
Perry M 322,323
COBB, L W 293,294,295,299
COCKE, John 83,84
COLBERT
   Selena 79,80,81
   Sim 293,295
COLE, Missie 201
COLLINS
   Joseph 11,12,13
   Lemuel Henry 11,12,13
   Mattie 11,12,13
CONNORS
   Aran 243,244
   John P 243,244
COSTELOW, N S 108,109
COUNCIL
   Agnes L 207,208,209,210
   Howard Jacob 207,208,209,210
   James 209,210
   James A 207,208,210
COVINGTON, W P 173
COX, G T 322
CROWDER
   George T 21
   George W 22,23
   Paralee 16,18,20,21
   Richard 185
CULBERSON, James 61
CULLAR
   Birdie 42,43,45,46,47,161,162
   Georgia E 42,45,47
   Georgia Eugene 42,43
   Georgie E 46
   J C 42,43,44,45,46,47
CURRY, Guy A 295,297,299,300
DAFFERN
   B 189,190,191,192,193
   Leo 188,189,190,191,192,193
   Lorinda 189,191,192,193
   Lourinda 190,191
DALTON, E M 241,242
DAVIS
   Carl 192,193
   Cassie 145
   Emeline 252,255

Hugh 145
S P 96,97
Sterling P 98
DAY, Nannie 141
DEAN, W J 109
DEBORD, Kate 175
DIFENDAFER, Chas T 107,219,220,
270,271,282,283
DODD, E W 155
DODSON
   Emma 255,256
   John W 255,256
   Lois Louisa 256
   Loise Louisa 255,256
DOWLAND
   Frank 14,15,16,18,19,20,21,23
   Luther Lee 14,15,16,17,21,22,23
   Mattie 14,15,16,17,18,19,20
   Myrtle Lee 14,15,18,19,20
DUDLEY, Nancy 106,107,108,109,111
DUNLAP, John W 254
DURANT
   Rina J 9
   Wallace 75
DYER
   E E 41,42,89
   T D 85,86,95
   Wm 109
EDWARD, Wesly 280
ELLIOTT, J H 285,286
ERIN, C C 201
ERVIN
   Bin F 142,143
   Emm May 144
   Emma May 144,145
   Nellie 144,145
   W J 144,145
ESTES, W N 109,263,264,265
EVANS
   Ethel O 202,203,204,205
   Ethyl O 203
   Lon 202,203,204,205
   Susan L 202,203,204,205
EVERIDGE
   Edgar 141,143,144
   Edward M 141,142,143,144
   Egar 141,142

Index

J H 139,140
   Lula 141,142,143,144
EWING, C H 89,90,91
FANNIN, E J 44,45,167,168,169
FELKER, Lydia L 310,311
FENNELL
   Mrs T 251
   Thomas 77,79,250,251
FINLEY, Su 280
FINNS, Vincenta W 76
FLING
   Perry 13,14,136,137,142,143
   Perry E A 12,138,144
   Perry, MD 13,136,142
FOLSOM
   Agnes L 207,208,209,210
   Caroline 230,231
   Caroline Jane 228,229
   A E 43,57,161,162,208,229
   Fannie P 228,229,230,231
   Fannie Precilla 232
   Finis Ewing 57
   John 106,231,258
   John N 228,229,230,231,232
   S J 260,262
   Sim 201
FORT, Brooks 324,326
FOSTER, Maria 241,242,243
FOWLER
   C D 74
   Clark C 87
   H L 132
   J L 133
   Josephine 132,133
FOWLER & BOLGER 169,176,178,
181,182
FRANCIS, R D 222
FRANKLIN
   Emma E 212
   Wirt 12,117,118,134,135,137,
   138,140,143,144,148,149,150,154,156
   ,201,213,214,233,234,277,278,279
   ,281
FRAZIER, Edmund 217
FREE, Lonnie 185
FRISBIE, Harriet 276
FULLER, W E 145

GALLAGHER, J H 236
GAMMEL, Sarah J 307,308
GARDNER
   E J 310,311
   J J 325,326
   Jeff 309
   R L 325,326
GIBBS, Annie 227
GLENN, W T 136,139,141,147
GOING
   Ellen 130
   Simeon 36,37,38
GRAHAM
   Edward L 210,211,212
   Emma E 210,211,212
   Hardy 53
   Mary Ann 51,52,53,54,55
   Motsey 51,52,53,54,55
   Motsy 55
   Thomas 51,52,53,54,55
   Willie S 210,211,212
GRANT
   Alice 30,31,32
   Charley M 30,31,32
   Charleyne 30,31,32
GREEN, Parlean 305,306
GREENWOOD
   Hall 200,201
   Hawl 201
   Louisa 200,201
   Maggie 200,201
GRIGGS
   Mary 101,102,104
   Willy 100,101,102,104
GROSS, Mary 250,251
GRUBBS, M E 139,140
GUESS, Bettie 57,58,59
HALL, Susie 136
HARGRAVES, J H 127
HARGROVE, J H 127
HARKIN, William M 41,42
HARRELL, W E 245,246,247,248
HARRIS
   J M 322
   W L 49,50
   W S 50
HARRISON

Index

JOHN, W N 277
JOHNICO
   Caroline 232
   Caroline Jane 228,229
JOHNSON
   E 216,217,218
   E, MD 216,217
   J P 312,313
   Lewis 247
   Maggie 246,247,249
   Maud 312,313
   O L 107,183,219,220,252,271,
   282,283,284,307
   Zelpha 311,312,313
JONES
   C C 166,167,177
   Ella 269,270,271,272,273,274
   Rena 270,271,272,273,274
   Robert 270,271,272,273,274
JONICO, Caroline Jane 229
KALB, John A 192,193
KANIUBBE
   Betsy 134,135
   Lizzie 134,135
   Moses 134,135
KANUEBBE, Lizzie 134
KATE, Ellen 271
KEMP
   Elima 131
   Ellen 130,131
   Israel 130,131
   Nelson 130,131
KING
   J A 20
   John A 15,21
   W A 293
KREBBS, O M 7
LANE, Frances R 171,289
LARECY, W E 100,101,102,103,104,
184,185,187,201,304
LAUFTER, Tim 35
LEE, Robert E 80,112,113,114,194,
195,196,197,253
LEFLORE
   Bee 1,2,3
   Ben 1,2,3,4
   Forbis 2,3,6

   Joseph 48,49
   Manda 5,8
   Mandy 1,2,3,6,7
   Selina 48,49,50
   Tandy 1,5,6,7,8
   W L 1,2,6
   William 3,4,5,7,8,9
   William L 2
LENTZ, John M 95
LEWIS
   Adam 197
   Artemissa 289
   Artimissa 292,293,294,295,299
   Lizzie 214
   Sallie 197,199
   Sally 194,195
LIGHTFOOT, L J 127
LINTZ, John M 73,75,86
LLOYD
   Burnnie Lee 301,302
   Ida 301,302
   J W 301,302
   John M 301,302
LOFTIS, H L 34
LONG
   Leroy 324,326,327
   Leroy, MD 326
LYNCH
   Charles S 320,323
   Charles S, MD 323
   Chas 319
   Chas S 321
   Chas, MD 322
MCBRIDE
   J B 24,27
   M B, MD 24,27
MCCAIN, C E 312,313
MCCASLIN, Lillie 167,168,172,180
MCCCUSHIN, Lillie 169
MCCLARD, C C 256
MCCLISH, Rena 273,274
MCCURTAIN
   Green 217
   Mitchell 194
   Moll 266
   Mollie 262,263,264,265
   Thomas 80,196,197

Index

MCCUSLIN, Lillie 177
MCINTOSH
   Catharine 73,74,75,76
   Catherine 73
   J W 139,140
   John 136,137
   Joseph 73,74,75,76
   Melinda 73
   Sarah 72
   Sarrah 73,74,75,76
MCKEE
   John D 100,101,102,103,104,105
   Mary A 100,101,102,103,105
   Willie D 100,101,102,103,104,105
MCKENZIE
   Goodman 280
   Mack 280,281
MCKIBBEN, G W 308
MCKINNEY
   Cistin 36,37,38,39
   Jackson 36,37,38
   Silas B 220,224
   Sinsie 36,37,38
MCLAUGHLIN, Laura 135
MCLISH, Rena 270,271,272
MCMURTRY
   John W 238,239,240
   Lucy 238,239,240
   W J 239
   Wallace H 238,239,240
MCRAE, C M 16,20
MADDOX
   B F 59
   Hatie 129
   Katie 126
MAHAR
   C H 203
   C H, MD 203
   Charles H 205
   Charles H, MD 204
   Chas H 204
MANNING, F 43,161,162
MANSFIELD, MCMURRAY &
   CORNISH 4,65,71,177
MARTIN, Wm L 63,69
MARTIN & GIDNEY 224
MASHENTUBY, Mary 157,158

MASSEY, Edmon 165
MATTHEWS
   J H 157,158,159
   Sarah 159
   Tracy 158,159
MEASHENTUBBEE, Mary 159
MEASHINTUBEE, Mary 160
MELTON
   W J 43,46,47,89,90,91
   W J, MD 43,89
MERRICK, Edward 175,289
MILLER, H C 17,276
MONK, L 87
MOORE
   E A 9,202,203
   E W 258,259,260
   Joe 293,294,295,299
   John W 287
   Mary Harriet 220,221
   Mrs E A 9
   Nancy 220,221
   Nannie 220,221
MORAN
   Arthor C 311
   Author C 310,311
   D S 119,120
   Daisy Lily 120
   Emma 310,311
   John W 310,311
MORGAN
   Dick 39,40,41
   H Y 121
   Lorena M 39,40,41
   Sallie Puryear 39,40,41
   Thos M 120,121,122,123
   Thos M, MD 120,122
MORRIS, Rhoda F 57
NAYLOR
   Ida 257,258,259,260
   Lester 257,258,259,260
   Newton 257,258,259,260
   Sarah 258,259,260
NEEDLES, T B 223
NELSON
   Eden 82,83
   J B 225,226
   Joseph E 89

Index

Laura 83
Lura 82
O N 293
NEWMAN
   John 159
   M W 5,6
NEWTON
   Katie 284,286
   Lucinda 283,284
NICHOLAS, Wilson 113,116
NIVENS, Floyd 308
NOAH
   Emma 157,158,159,160
   John 157,158,159,160
   Newman 158,159,160,309
   Numan 157,158
NOBLE
   Pricilla A 229,230,231
   Priscilla A 229,231
NOWLIN, N R 244
OAKES
   L E 13,14
   Thos E 201
OUTAHYUBBE, Stephen 118
OVERSTREET
   Addie A 119,120,121,122,123
   Adie A 120
   Daily Lillie 120
   Daisy Lillie 119,121,122,123,124
   Daisy Lily 119,124
   Daisy Litty 121,124
   Newt 120
   William Newton 123,124
   Wm Newton 119,120,121,122
PARISH
   Elias 212,213,214
   Eliza 212,213,214
   Elza 213
   Lizzie 212,213,214
PARKE, Frank E 308
PARRISH, Lizzie 212
PATTERSON, W R 315,316
PERKINS
   S L 2,3
   S L, MD 2
PERRY
   Guy A 87

Isham 295
Ishem 293
PHILLIPS
   A Denton 60,61,62,66,67,68,209,
   210,230,231
   W I 240
   W I, MD 239
PITCHLYNN
   E P 51,52,53,54
   Ellington P 53
POE, J 211
PRITCHARD
   Beulah 250,251
   J R 92
   James 91
   James R 90,91
   James Robert 88,89
   Jane 88,89,90,91
   Jesse R 88,90,91,92
   Jesse Robert 88,89
   Lizzie 250,251
   William E 250,251
PUCKETT, William 226
PUTMAN
   Fannie 302,303,304
   S G 303,304
   Susan 303,304
QUINTON
   Elizabeth 86
   James 86,87,88
   James M 85,86
   Kate 86
   Katie 86
   Narciss 85,86,87,88
   Sallie 85,86,87,88
RABON, J W 215,216
RAINEY, Mrs J L 151,152,153
RALLS, J G 151,153
RAPPOLEE
   H E 162,163,164
   H E, MD 162
   J L 46,163,164,324,327
RATTERREE
   John Henry 9,10,11
   Rina J 9,10,11
   William E 9,10,11
RAULSTON

Index

Arabella M 142
Robert M 142,143
REEDER, J G 122,123
REXROAT, U T 268,269
RIDDLE, Coleman 293
ROBBINS
   Jack 35
   L J 34
   Rebeca 34,35
ROBENSON, Siney 72
ROBERTS
   G W 31
   Geo W 31
   Geo W, MD 31,32
   Sam T 52,54
   Sam T, Jr 305,306
ROBINSON
   Frank C 31,32
   Jane 313,314,315,316,317,318,319
   John W .. 313,314,315,316,317,318,319
   Lourena L 323,324,326
   Rena 325
   Siney 61,62
   Theodore R .. 313,315,316,317,318,319
   Theodore Roosevelt ... 313,314,315,318
   Wallace 61
ROEBUCK
   Abbie 276,277
   Carrie 81,82,83,84
   David E 81,82,83,84
   Georgia May 81,82,83
   Georgie May 84
   Isabella 276,277
   William 276,277
ROSE
   Vester 117,134,135,140,148,
   149,154
   Vester W 149,201,213,214,234,
   277,278
ROUTH, J M 225,226,227
RUNTON
   C 109,262
   Carnolie 107,260
RUSHING
   G M 40
   G M, MD 41
RUSSELL

Elum M 241,243
J C 33,35
RUSSEY, D A 125,129
RUTHERFORD
   B C 301,302
   B C, MD 302
RYBURN, W F 108
SAMMONS, Fred 121
SAMPLE, Fannie 234
SANDERS, Newt 73
SAVAGE
   C C 314,315,317,318,319
   C C, MD 317
   Christopher C 317
   Christopher C, MD 315
SAWYERS
   Malinda 73,74
   Malindie 76
   Melindie 74
SCOTT
   Chaplain 33,34
   Chapling 35
   Elizabeth 33,34,35
   Elizebeth 33,34
   Phebe Ethel 34,35
   Pheby Ethel 33,34
SEMPLE
   Frank P 56,57,58,59
   Helen Mae 57,58,59
   Hellen Mae 56,57,58
   Maud K 57
   Maud Kathryn 58
   Maude K 56
   Maude Kathryn 56,59,58
SEXTON, Henry J 254
SHARKEY 63,69
   Fabie 59,60,61,62,63,64,65
   Israel 62,63,64,68,70,71
   Isreal 60,61,65,66,67
   Lettie 63,69
   Louiza 61,63,64,66,67,69,70
   Louiza 66
   Lueza 60
   Luiza 60,61,67
   Thomas 59,66,67,68,69,70,71
SHAW, R W 290
SHERRED

Index

Josephus M 281
Wesley 280
SHIEW, Mary 87,88
SHOCKEY
  Isreal 72
  Louisa 72
  Tabie 72
SHONEY, W A 191,325
SHORES
  Callina 7
  Cellena 7
  Salena 5,8
SHULL, Chas G 142,145
SHWINOGEE, Sam 254
SILMON, Lee 272,273
SIMPSON
  Henry 283,284,285,286
  Lucinda 283,284,285,286
  Robert 283,284
  Robt C 285,286
SISK
  Dr A R 254
  A R, MD 254
SMALLWOOD, Narcissa 101,102, 103,105
SMITH
  John R 168
  S E 211
  S G 288
  Seymour G 298
  W T 43
SNOWTON, Annie 154
SOCKEY
  Billie 252,255
  Billy 253,254
  Homer 251,252,253,254,255
  Josephine 252,253,254,255
  Ned 48,49
SPENCE, M J 256
SPRING
  Earl 155,156
  Eli 155,156
  Mollie 155,156
SPRINKEL, T V 197
STANDLEY
  Mabel 136
  Mable 136

STEPHEN
  Lamus 118
  Lemus 117,118
  Lena 117,118
  Linas 117,118
STEPHENS
  J L 30
  Paul 309
STEWART, A V 292,293
STONE, W B 44,45
STOVERS, Amanda 9
STRANGE
  A B 225
  A B, MD 225,226,268,269
  Dr A B 268,269
STUDDORD, Angelina 206
SULLIVAN, T M 125,126,127
SWINK, William 204
SWISHER, O P 165
SWITZER, Martin 2,7
TANN, Albert 2,3,6
TANNER, R E 15,18,19
TEHUMBA, Eastman 61,67
THOMAS
  D 52
  Jno J 55,56
  John J 55
  Louisa 213,214
TILLEY
  Cornelius 136
  Jim 136
  Mabel 136
TILLY
  Cornelius 135,136,137,138
  Jim 135,136,137,138
  Mabel 137,138
  Mable 136
  Mable Standley 135
TIMS
  Emeline 77,79
  Mildred 76,77
  Mishel 77
  Mitchell 76,77
  Vincenta W 76,77
TOLBERT, N J 208,229,230
TONEHKA, Ardaline 37,38
TONIHKA, Ardalin 39

Index

TOWNLEY, W E 127
TRAHERN, Martha 218
TRASK, F W 24,27
TRIPLETT
   Hariett 249
   Harriet 245,246,247,248
   Harriett 249
   Thomas 245,246,247,248,249
   Thomas, Jr 244,246,247,248,249
TUEY, L C 216
TURLEY
   J D 319,320,321,322,323
   J T 320
   Nalia 320,321
   Nalio 319,320,322,323
   Nolia 319
   Sissie 319,320,321
   Sissie B 320,321,322,323
TURNER, Jesse 33,34,35
UNDERWOOD, I T 45
UPTON
   Floyd 218
   Floyd Emanuel 215,216
   Floyd Manuel 215,216,217,218
   James 215,216,217,218
   Martha 215,216,217,218
VURNOR, T T 167,168,169
WADE
   Dennis 195
   Sarah 283
WALACE, W M 185
WALCOTT
   Arthur 275,276
   Daniel Hailey 275,276
   Lutie Mary 275,276
WALL, Sam 222
WALLACE
   Dr 303
   W M 187,188,304
   W M, MD 185,186,303
   William 183
   William M 186
   Wm, MD 183
WALLS
   Jess 95
   T J 85,86,95
   Thomas J, Jr 75

WARD
   J P 13
   Mykey 201
WATSON
   Andrew 105,106
   Andrew C 110
   A C 107,108,109,111
   James Samuel 110
   Mary 105,106,107,108,109,111
   Nannie 206
   Samuel J 109
   Samuel James 105,106,107,108,
   109,110,111
WEBSTER
   Chas E 9
   Cornelia 233
   Daniel 233
   Samuel 232,233
WESLEY, Lenas 38,39
WEST, Rhoda 106,107
WESTBROOK
   Andrew J 97,98,99
   Andy J 96,97,98
   Edgar 94
   Edger 95
   Edker 94,96,97,98,99
   A J 94,95
   Maite 99
   Mattie 94,95,96,97,98,99
WHITE
   C J 108
   Deliah 53
   J M 74,290,291,293,295,298
   Myron 171
WILLIAMS
   Henry 100,101
   J E 25,28
   Joel 234
   Lucy 308,309
   Mattie 308,309
   Nora 132
   Phoebe 235,236,237
   Sarah 165
   Thomas 308,309
WILLIS
   Abner W 225,226,227
   Benjamin 55

Fannie May 224,225,226,227
Francis 225,226,227
A W 228
WILSON
    Arthur 78
    Auther 78,79
    James 78,79
    Mary 67,68,72
    Rosanna 78,79
    Thomas 72
    W A 287
    W P 36,37,38
WINLOCH, Wally 194
WINSHIP
    John 282,283
    Sampson 282,283
    Seyan 282,283
WOLFE, E S 234
WOOD, Ruby Grace 306
WOODS
    B J 55,56
    Columbus L 10
    Nancy A 305,306
    Ruby Grace 305
    Simon H 305,306
WOODSON
    Ben D 10,11
    D, MD 10
WOOLEY, Samuel L 285,286
WRIGHT
    John 286,287,288
    John W 288
    Reno Acie 288
    Reno Cecil 286,287
    Sarah Ann Margaret 286,287,288
WYERS
    Irene 307,308
    John 307
    John W 307,308
    Wyneter 306,307,308
YOTA
    Adam 193,194,195,196,197,198,199
    Jincy 193,194,195,196,197,199
    Joshua 136
    Zira 193,194,195,196,197,198, 199,200
YOUNG, J M 106,261,262